Place Pedagogy Change

TRANSGRESSIONS: CULTURAL STUDIES AND EDUCATION

Cultural studies provides an analytical toolbox for both making sense of educational practice and extending the insights of educational professionals into their labors. In this context *Transgressions: Cultural Studies and Education* provides a collection of books in the domain that specify this assertion. Crafted for an audience of teachers, teacher educators, scholars and students of cultural studies and others interested in cultural studies and pedagogy, the series documents both the possibilities of and the controversies surrounding the intersection of cultural studies and education. The editors and the authors of this series do not assume that the interaction of cultural studies and education devalues other types of knowledge and analytical forms. Rather the intersection of these knowledge disciplines offers a rejuvenating, optimistic, and positive perspective on education and educational institutions. Some might describe its contribution as democratic, emancipatory, and transformative. The editors and authors maintain that cultural studies helps free educators from sterile, monolithic analyses that have for too long undermined efforts to think of educational practices by providing other words, new languages, and fresh metaphors. Operating in an interdisciplinary cosmos, Transgressions: Cultural Studies and Education is dedicated to exploring the ways cultural studies enhances the study and practice of education. With this in mind the series focuses in a non-exclusive way on popular culture as well as other dimensions of cultural studies including social theory, social justice and positionality, cultural dimensions of technological innovation, new media and media literacy, new forms of oppression emerging in an electronic hyperreality, and postcolonial global concerns. With these concerns in mind cultural studies scholars often argue that the realm of popular culture is the most powerful educational force in contemporary culture. Indeed, in the twenty-first century this pedagogical dynamic is sweeping through the entire world. Educators, they believe, must understand these emerging realities in order to gain an important voice in the pedagogical conversation.

Without an understanding of cultural pedagogy's (education that takes place outside of formal schooling) role in the shaping of individual identity–youth identity in particular–the role educators play in the lives of their students will continue to fade. Why do so many of our students feel that life is incomprehensible and devoid of meaning? What does it mean, teachers wonder, when young people are unable to describe their moods, their affective affiliation to the society around them. Meanings provided young people by mainstream institutions often do little to help them deal with their affective complexity, their difficulty negotiating the rift between meaning and affect. School knowledge and educational expectations seem as anachronistic as a ditto machine, not that learning ways of rational thought and making sense of the world are unimportant.

But school knowledge and educational expectations often have little to offer students about making sense of the way they feel, the way their affective lives are shaped. In no way do we argue that analysis of the production of youth in an electronic mediated world demands some "touchy-feely" educational superficiality. What is needed in this context is a rigorous analysis of the interrelationship between pedagogy, popular culture, meaning making, and youth subjectivity. In an era marked by youth depression, violence, and suicide such insights become extremely important, even life saving. Pessimism about the future is the common sense of many contemporary youth with its concomitant feeling that no one can make a difference.

If affective production can be shaped to reflect these perspectives, then it can be reshaped to lay the groundwork for optimism, passionate commitment, and transformative educational and political activity. In these ways cultural studies adds a dimension to the work of education unfilled by any other sub-discipline. This is what Transgressions: Cultural Studies and Education seeks to produce—literature on these issues that makes a difference. It seeks to publish studies that help those who work with young people, those individuals involved in the disciplines that study children and youth, and young people themselves improve their lives in these bizarre times.

Place Pedagogy Change

Margaret Somerville
Monash University, Churchill, Australia

Bronwyn Davies
Melbourne University, Australia

Kerith Power
Monash University, Peninsula, Australia

Susanne Gannon
University of Western Sydney, Australia

and

Phoenix de Carteret
Monash University, Churchill, Australia

SENSE PUBLISHERS
ROTTERDAM/BOSTON/TAIPEI

A C.I.P. record for this book is available from the Library of Congress.

ISBN: 978-94-6091-613-7 (paperback)
ISBN: 978-94-6091-614-4 (hardback)
ISBN: 978-94-6091-615-1 (e-book)

Published by: Sense Publishers,
P.O. Box 21858,
3001 AW Rotterdam,
The Netherlands
www.sensepublishers.com

Printed on acid-free paper

TABLE OF CONTENTS

LIST OF AUTHORS

Margaret Somerville is newly appointed as a Professor of Education at the University of Western Sydney, previously at Monash University's Gippsland campus and the University of New England. A leading researcher in pedagogies of place, she has published six books in the area, including her latest, *Singing the Coast* (2010), and an edited collection, *Landscapes and Learning* (2009). She is interested in alternative methodologies and modes of representation in educational research, and the ways that these can be relevant and engaging for a wide general audience.

Bronwyn Davies is an independent scholar based in Sydney, Australia, and a Professorial Fellow at the University of Melbourne. The distinctive features of her work are, on the one hand, her development of innovative social science research methodologies incorporating elements of the visual, literary and performative arts, and, on the other, its strong base in the conceptual work of poststructuralist philosophers such as Deleuze, Foucault and Nancy. Her research explores the discursive practices and relations of power through which particular social worlds are constituted. She is best known for her work on gender, for her development of the methodology of collective biography, and for her writing on feminism and poststructuralist theory.

Kerith Power is a Senior Lecturer in Early Childhood Education at Monash University. She became an academic after a career as an early childhood teacher and advocate. She has contributed to the field on responsive research methodologies that cross cultural boundaries. Her interest in place arises from collaborative research into local literacies with rural, Indigenous and marginalised suburban communities. She is a member of the Space, Place and Body research group.

Susanne Gannon is an Associate Professor in the School of Education at the University of Western Sydney, Australia. She was a high school English teacher in north Queensland for many years prior to taking up an academic position in Sydney and now teaches in the Master of Education and Master of Teaching (Secondary) programs. As well as her interest in place pedagogies, her areas of research interest include writing and poetics, English curriculum, feminist and poststructural theories, Information and Communication Technologies (ICTs) and equity in education. She has published widely and is the current editor of the journal *English in Australia.*

Phoenix de Carteret is a research academic and feminist working across diverse disciplines including public health, communication studies and education. Both her academic and community work are grounded in the premise that the personal is political. Phoenix designs and runs biographical storytelling workshops for community groups, motivated by her interest in arts/health practices for community education.

ACKNOWLEDGEMENTS

Like all books, especially those produced in academic institutions in the twenty first century, *Place pedagogy change* could not have come into being without the assistance of the many people who are the invisible supporters of our work. We would like to acknowledge the many colleagues and friends, both professional support staff and academics, who worked with us during this time. We also gratefully acknowledge the many co-researchers, teacher educators, community educators, teachers and teacher education students who participated in the research and gave generously of their time and their passionate engagement.

The project on which this book was based was funded by the Australian Research Council (DP0663798) and hosted by all of the universities in which the researchers worked during the development and implementation of the project and the writing. These include the University of New England, Griffith University, the University of Western Sydney, the University of Melbourne and Monash University. Professor Shirley Steinberg enabled the publication of the manuscript through her Transgressions Series, a critically important aspect of scholarship in the current neoliberal climate. The Faculty of Education at Monash University provided a Dissemination Grant to support a writing retreat in order for the five authors to come together to workshop the chapters to make the book into a coherent whole. The University of Western Sydney provided funds to employ a copy editor. Elena Knox, Sue Collins and Miriam Potts provided excellent feedback and copy editing support in the final stages of production.

Finally we would like to acknowledge the many places and communities within which we worked and which gave us so much. Especially, Laura Brearley's hospitality in the beach house studios handsomely provided us, during times of intense work, with walks on the beach by the Great Southern Ocean to stretch out our limbs in its wild beauty.

The authors

INTRODUCTION

Place pedagogy change

Place pedagogy change is a book that explores new ways of learning and teaching about place. We are not interested in passing on a fixed body of knowledge about place, but in developing ways of knowing that are emergent in, and responsive to, particular places. We are interested in ways of knowing that change the knower— that generate a critique of existing knowledges and practices in such a way that they open up the possibility of transformation and change. We explore how one might come to know oneself differently by focussing not on one's individualised self whose identity is constructed in its separation from others and from place, but on oneself in relation to those others, including human, non-human and earth others, who make up the places we live in.

Few would dispute that we are living in times of global ecological and financial trouble, and that we do not have the answers we need for dealing with those troubles. The divisions between the wealthy and the poor are rapidly increasing. We are collectively uncertain about what changes we need to make to avert the multiple crises that loom on our horizons. In order to move beyond these discourses of crisis, we, as teacher educators in rural and urban universities in Australia, have explored how we might educate current and future generations for engaging in life in ways that are both responsible and creative—life-giving rather than diminishing. It is in the intersections among place, pedagogy and change that we have sought some strategies that could make a difference. This requires new research methodologies, new modes of learning and new modes of teaching.

Place Studies has recently emerged as a significant transdisciplinary field in which the gap between the social and the ecological is addressed (Somerville et al., 2009). Emerging place research reconceptualises the work of early place theorists by mobilising 'the recently reinvigorated and transdisciplinary interest and emphasis on all aspects of what can be described as the *spatiality of human life*' (Soja, 2000, p. 6, italics in original). Human life is constituted in taken-for-granted discourses, as occurring *in* specific places including, more recently, global space. Place Studies begins to unpick the separation implicit in the preposition *in*—and finds rather that we are *of* the landscape, indeed that we *are* the landscape. The new thinking draws on feminist, environmental, poststructuralist and postcolonial thought, and is emerging as a site where knowledges of selves-in-relation to the other, including the non-human, earth others can be, and are being, (re)formed.

The particular focus that we take up here, drawing on the work in this emergent field, is the development of a trans disciplinary pedagogy of place. The pedagogical spaces that we explore, and experiment with, in this book take up both critical and enabling perspectives. Critical perspectives recognise power; critical research 'seeks in its analyses to plumb the archaeology of taken-for-granted perspectives to understand how unjust and oppressive social conditions come to be reified as

M. Somerville, B. Davies, K. Power, S. Gannon and *P. de Carteret,*
Place Pedagogy Change, 1–12.

historical "givens"' (Canella & Lincoln, 2009, p. 54). Enabling pedagogies seek the movement from critique to transformation. These two forces, critique and transformation, are vital elements in the development of new pedagogies of place. Foucault argued that:

> ...the task of a critical analysis of our world is something that is more and more important. Maybe the most certain of all philosophical problems is the problem of the present time, and of what we are, in this very moment.
>
> Maybe the target nowadays is not to discover what we are but to refuse what we are. We have to imagine and build up what we could be to get rid of... the simultaneous individualization and totalization of modern power structures. (2000, p. 336)

This book is just such a work of refusal, of imagining and of building, resisting the intensification of neoliberal control that goes hand in hand with extreme individualisation and the (dis)illusions of freedom.

Place is productive as a framework because it occupies the space between grounded materiality and the discursive space of representation. It generates conversations across disciplinary boundaries, conversations that have become imperative when addressing questions about the relationship between social and ecological systems. According to Gruenewald, place itself is also profoundly pedagogical. He points out that 'as centres of experience, places teach us about how the world works, and how our lives fit into the spaces we occupy. Further, places make us: As occupants of particular places with particular attributes, our identity and our possibilities are shaped' (Gruenewald, 2003, p. 621).

Our own approach takes up this double interest in place—of, on the one hand, furthering knowledge, taking responsibility and having care, and on the other, finding ways to recognise our co-implication in place and our co-extension with others, human and not-human, organic and inorganic. We are earth, air, water and fire (Suzuki, 2010). What we do to the planet we do to ourselves. Care for oneself and for the other, the other including one's place of being, cannot any longer be understood as separate responsibilities or separate processes.

Our approach is quite different from the discourse of globalism and global identities. It is a world-making rather than a globe-making approach (Nancy, 2007). Globalisation, or globe-making, produces over-regulated practices focussed on the production of generic, predictable individuals responsive to the forces of government. It is geared to forging docile bodies, bodies 'that may be subjected, used, transformed and improved' (Foucault, 1977, p. 136). Globe-making dismantles the social in favour of the economic.

World-making begins with self-in-relation to the other. It requires openness to new directions and possibilities not mandated by governmental imperatives, but emergent from the specificity of particular places in the world. It focuses on engagement with the other, where the other includes human and non-human, earth others. It focuses on anticipating the eruption of the new. It has an unpredictable appearance, maintaining a crucial reference to the world as a space of relationality and as a space for the construction and negotiation of meaning. Against the disembodied and dislocated 'everywhere and anywhere' of the global, Nancy (2007) emphasises the specificity of subjects in their particular time and space of 'this place, here'. World-making is not focussed on controlling the future. Its question is, rather: How can we give ourselves, open ourselves, in order to look ahead of ourselves, where nothing is yet visible?

Our question then is: What kinds of teaching and learning experiences will enable such world-making? It is through the pivotal work of pedagogy, as it sits between place and change in our title, that we make the connection between our ideas about place and processes of change. Pedagogy can be understood as a concept that 'draws attention to the process through which knowledge is produced' (Lusted, 1986, p. 2). This process involves 'the transformation of consciousness that takes place in the interaction of three agencies—the teacher, the learner and the knowledge they together produce' (Lusted, 1986, p. 3). In this sense pedagogy is framed as a fundamentally relational process; it takes shape as it unfolds. It is only through retrospective narration that it takes a determinate form in the consciousness of participants. Pedagogy must be understood as an 'inherently relational, emergent, and non-linear process that is unpredictable and therefore unknowable in advance' (Sellar, 2009, p. 351). Sellar suggests that an ethically responsible pedagogy connects the lives of children and communities, disrupting those habits and judgments that might close down the possibilities of connection. He suggests we engage in the 'responsible uncertainty of pedagogy' (Sellar, 2009, p. 347).

In adding the element of place to the relational dynamic between teacher, learner, and knowledge, we further extend this concept to name a pedagogy of ethical uncertainty, where ethical refers to our mutual responsibilities to others and to the more-than-human world, and uncertainty to the unpredictability inherent in our relationship with this world. Such a pedagogy cannot be known in advance. In *Place pedagogy change,* we explore the nature of such pedagogies in retrospective practice. In this sense the book is a work of creative experimentation in which we tentatively explore the ways in which pedagogies of place might enable the dynamic relational learning of connections between people, places and communities.

To this end each of the researchers have engaged both individually and collectively in creative experimentation, bringing different bodies of theory together with our engagement in different places and processes of learning and teaching. The languages of methodology and method, representation and writing, are troubled in our experimentation. We have not tried to homogenise our approaches but instead to create conversations among them, to extend ourselves to the very edges of our thinking, and to create spaces for our readers to enter into those conversations. In this way, our work can also be understood as creating openings towards as yet unimaginable futures.

We have set this book in a time of unprecedented and unpredictable change in the nature of our worlds and our relationships within them. These changes demand attention to the intertwining of humans and the more-than-human world. Change engenders creative possibilities and responses. To energise the concept of change we briefly touch on Grosz's concepts of chaos and the frame (2008). These concepts enable us to both draw on the chaos, the life force of the dynamic of inevitable processes of change, and also to render our engagement with them possible and intelligible.

In *Chaos, territory, art,* Grosz proposes that chaos is the condition of the universe:

> "In the beginning" is chaos, the whirling, unpredictable movement of forces, vibratory oscillations that constitute the universe. Chaos here may be understood not as absolute disorder but rather as a plethora of orders, forms, wills—forces that cannot be distinguished or differentiated from each other, both matter and its conditions for being otherwise, both the actual and the virtual indistinguishably. (2008, p. 5)

Human activities expressed in the disciplinary constellations of art and science understand, and draw from, this chaos in different ways. The first and primary step in this process is the imperative to establish the frame: 'the first gesture of art, its metaphysical condition and universal expression, is the construction or fabrication of the frame' (Grosz, 2008, p.10). It is the frame that allows us to draw from the life force of chaos. The frame enables a part of chaos, as the unknowable real, to enter into the realm of representation, to become intelligible. Pedagogy, we suggest, participates in the nature of both art and of science, drawing from chaos through the frame of the teaching and learning activities that mediate place and change. The frame that we offer in this book is a set of understandings about enabling pedagogies of place.

ENABLING PEDAGOGIES OF PLACE

We began with three principles for an enabling pedagogy of place evolved from earlier poststructural and postcolonial theorising of place-based education (Somerville, 2010). These principles focus on the elements of *body, story,* and *contact zone.* In this book we are interested in the possibilities these principles offer for generating place pedagogies for change.

Our relationship to place is constituted in stories and other representations

Story and storytelling are central to place pedagogies for change. A story is a fundamental unit of meaning-making through which we know the world. A first strategy is to extend the concept of story to include creative representations of place in visual, aural, and performance modes as well as recognising that statistical, scientific, and popular representations of place are all versions of place stories. Australian Indigenous place stories, for example, incorporate song, music, dance, body painting, and performance, intersecting powerfully in particular places (Somerville, 2010). Extending the concept of story in this way enables the possibility of different ways of knowing places to come into conversation with each other.

The analytical strategy of storylines informs our approach to identifying dominant storylines of place and facilitating the emergence of alternative stories. A storyline is the plotline of collective stories about place. Storylines shape our modes of thinking about ourselves and others, and our place in the world. 'Stories we observe, hear, read, both lived and imaginary, form a stock of imaginary storylines through which life choices can be made' (Davies, 2000, p. 81). Australian Indigenous songlines map the actions of the creation ancestors onto the physical landscape, connecting story places to each other like beads on a string across the landscape. Each of these places is a site of meaning and song.

Changing our relationship to places involves changing the stories we tell about place. The task of generating (or making visible) alternative storylines that have the power to displace the old is extraordinarily complex and difficult. The work of *Place pedagogy change* is to articulate the nature of pedagogical processes for achieving this change.

Place learning begins with the body

Focussing on the body is the most radical, controversial and transformative of the three principles. Despite considerable recent attention to the body as a category of thought and analysis, the body remains elusive in place theory and research. Feminist philosophers such as Grosz (1994, p. 5) propose that 'putting the body at the centre of our notion of subjectivity transforms the way we think about knowledge, about power, about desire'. For us, this element of our frame is related to a necessary focus on the mutual constitution of bodies and places, and on the materialities, the 'flesh of the world' (Merleau-Ponty, 1962). Our bodies as researchers and the bodies of teachers and learners are key sites in place pedagogies for change.

Perhaps the furthest extension of this idea is an understanding of the landscape as subject, which we draw from Rose's research with Australian Indigenous communities. For Rose, the context of ecological humanities is 'rapid social and environmental change' which brings with it an ethical imperative in settler societies 'to be responsive to Indigenous peoples' knowledges and aspirations for justice' (Rose, 2004, n.p.). Rather than appropriating Indigenous knowledges, Rose proposes that we need to learn from them. She regards her Indigenous collaborators as her teachers. In *Nourishing Terrains*, Rose describes Indigenous concepts of country which inspire our own thinking about place, pedagogy and change:

> Country is a place that gives and receives life. Not just imagined or represented, it is lived in and lived with...People talk about country in the same way they would talk about a person: they speak to country, sing to country, visit country, worry about country, feel for country, and long for country. Country is not a generalised or undifferentiated type of place... country is a living entity with a yesterday, today and tomorrow with a consciousness, and a will toward life. (1996, p. 7)

According to this understanding of place, 'country' is a subject in its own right that people engage with in a reciprocal relationship. An important aspect of this understanding is that country needs care, which is expressed in speaking, singing, visiting, worrying, and longing, as an everyday enacting of that care, as well as being ritualised in ceremony. Place, in this concept, is multi-dimensional and includes human beings in relationship with both non-human others and the material terrain of an enlarged concept of landscape. Knowledge of country, and responsibilities to country, are deeply folded into the bodies, memories and imaginations of the human subjects who belong to country. An enabling pedagogy of place recognises that the condition of country is integral to human subjectivity.

Deep place learning occurs in a cultural contact zone of contestation

Indigenous knowledges of place, as identified above, are a fundamental force for change for Australian place researchers. But settler engagement with Indigenous place knowledges is fraught political terrain. The concept of the contact zone (Pratt, 1992) refers to the characteristic of specific local places as spaces for the intersection of culturally different and often contested stories of place. We understand the space of the contact zone to include the place stories of differently classed and ethnic communities, and of different religious, gendered, and sexually oriented collectivities. The in-between space of the 'contact zone' has been described as a space of transformative potential and is a highly significant consideration in *Place pedagogy change*.

Researching, teaching and learning about place means participating in a contact zone of difference. This requires continuing engagement with difficult questions, moving beyond a personal comfort zone to refuse easy answers and often to dwell in a space of unknowing. The 'borderwork' critical to negotiating difference in the contact zone (Somerville & Perkins, 2003) involves precarious, risky and emotionally difficult work (Anzaldua, 1987; hooks, 1990) and it means moving within, between, and across boundaries. Yet it is in the in-between space of energy and struggle in the contact zone where new possibilities lie.

Contemporary cultural contact zones inevitably carry with them the distinct individual, familial and collective histories that each person brings with them into the present. They have trajectories into pasts and they open towards futures. The risky borderwork that we advocate in the contact zones where human subjects collide does not elide differences, nor does it reify them. It does not seek to flatten out or homogenise our specificities. Rather, through reflexivity and careful listening, and through a willingness to suspend meaning, it opens possibilities for deep engagement across difference and for transformation into the future. This is a pedagogy of ethical uncertainty entailing mutual responsibilities and unpredictability within pedagogical relationships.

DEVELOPING NEW FORMS OF RELATIONALITY

At the heart of the enabling place pedagogies that we develop through *Place pedagogy change* is relationality. In pedagogical encounters, no less than in any other domain of human existence, relationality as an ongoing process of becoming is crucial. Education can invite the opening up of new questions, new ways of asking questions and of answering them, in an ongoing, dynamic, relational framework. New forms of relationality become possible. Cixous asks:

> Why do we live? I think: to become more human: more capable of reading the world, more capable of playing it in all ways. This does not mean nicer or more humanistic. I would say: more faithful to what we are made from and to what we can create... (Cixous & Calle-Gruber, 1997, p. 30)

We came to this project with an interest in how power works, not by shaping us against our will, but by governing the soul, generating desire that persuades us to take up dominant discourses as our own or, alternatively, to work against the grain of those discourses. We understand language as a powerful constitutive force, shaping what we understand as possible, and shaping what we desire within those (limiting) possibilities. We are also fascinated by the power of language and of art to enable us to open up the not-yet-known. Throughout this book we seek those pedagogical moments and possibilities that enable learning that shakes thought up in such ways.

In order to rethink the habituated modes of thought through which we constitute ourselves as human, and as separate from others, both human and not-human, we have sought to unsettle the sedimented practices of categorical thought. Difference has, for a long time, been understood as categorical difference; the other is discrete and distinct from the self, with difference lying in the other, whose identity is constructed through a string of binaries in which their sameness as, or difference from, oneself is made real. Deleuze (2004) offers a radically different approach to difference in which difference comes about through a continuous process of becoming different, of differenciation. In the first approach, difference is being 'divided up, a dimension of separation', while in the second, Deleuzian approach, difference is evolutionary, 'a continuum, a multiplicity of fusion...What is at issue is an insistence on the genuine openness of history, of the future' (Massey, 2005, p. 21).

In this openness to creative change there is important work to be done towards generating a new understanding of relationality, of what it means to be in relation to, and known through the other—the human other and earth other (Bergson, 1998). Cixous speaks of a complex balance between knowing and not knowing oneself in relation to the other. She develops the term *positive incomprehension* to capture something of the movement and openness of differenciation, once differenciation is no longer individualised and separated off from the other, where we are no longer fixated on capturing the essence of self and other in their difference but on being open to the unknown, to the impossibility of knowing and, simultaneously, to the beauty of moments of insight into the being of the other (Cixous & Calle-Gruber, 1997).

In order to open up the creative forces that enable us to evolve beyond the fixities and limitations of the present moment we need to both turn our attention to what we are made of, our material continuity and "ontological co-implication" with others, including non-human others, and to open ourselves to multiple points of view, while deconstructing the sacralisation and ascendance of humanity. Wilson argues that we limit our evolutionary capacity if we accept human as the dominant term, separated from and superior to other ontological systems: 'Each mode of materiality is built through its complicitous relations to others' (Wilson, 2004, p. 69). Human existence in this understanding is not an existence that is separate from other forms of existence. Human, animal, earth and other matter all exist, and exist in networks of relationality, dependence and influence. In pedagogical contexts these networks can be cherished and nurtured through creative practices that include new ways of looking, being and becoming in place that open generative spaces in which change might happen.

THE STRUCTURE OF THE BOOK

Introduction

In the introduction the authors map the central ideas of place, pedagogy and change that inform the book. We set the book in times of global ecological and economic crises but we ask, in moving beyond discourses of crisis, what might be a generative and future looking educational response. To this end we begin with the framework of place in order to explore and articulate enabling place pedagogies of ethical uncertainty that we propose as opening possibilities for change.

Section 1: Researching

We begin the story of enabling place pedagogies with the self, with the experience of our learning and researching bodies in particular locations. The first four chapters of *Place pedagogy change* explore different ways of locating the self in place, as a basis for the chapters that follow about learning and teaching across the educational curriculum.

Chapter 1: Body/place journal writing This chapter explores the process of coming to know a new place through body/place writing, and writing the sensing body-in-place. Margaret Somerville investigates the idea of liminality as a place of no words and then of the gradual unfolding of a fragmented but embodied narrative of place. Many of the ideas that emerged from this body/place journal writing directly inform her later chapters about learning place and forming community in primary schools and in adult and community education.

Chapter 2: An experiment in writing place This chapter introduces writing as a mode of inquiry into place. Drawing inspiration from a Deleuzian approach to writing, Bronwyn Davies writes a play about the street she lives in and reflects on the nature of such experimental writing. She elaborates three principles that inform her writing of her own place. Unlike ethnographic writing, which seeks objective knowledge on the basis of which the researcher can make an account of a place, this chapter argues instead for the use of imagination, for the decentring of the author's self, and for generating openness to the other and the not-yet-known.

Chapter 3: Walking my way back home Susanne Gannon works memories of place through a poem of a morning walk that maps the suburb she used to call her home, and explores her ambivalent love for this particular place. Poetry slows language to a walking pace, and creates rhythm and space and attention to the details of place and of subjectivity in place. Through the poem, home and neighbourhood are reconfigured as assemblages where soils, vegetation, birds, animals, light, landscape, people and their habitats coexist on the same plane of being.

Chapter 4: Getting lost in Logan In this chapter Kerith Power takes up Lather's (2007) question of 'what it might mean to claim getting lost as a methodology' in times of 'the loss of absolute knowledge' (p. 3). It narrates an embodied process of getting to know a suburb by driving, walking and hanging out, mapping the intersecting "natural", built and social ecologies of a particular place—Logan, a satellite city of Brisbane, the capital of Queensland on the east coast of Australia. The chapter frames the experiences through place pedagogy categories of storylines, bodies and cultural contact zones (Somerville, 2005). It problematises binary cartographies of advantage and disadvantage and explores what it means to walk to get to know a place.

Section 2: Learning

In this section we ask the question: how do learners across the curriculum learn about their places and form community? The four chapters explore innovative ways of learning place from the perspective of the learner in relation to early childhood, primary, secondary, adult and community education.

Chapter 5: Becoming-frog: learning place in primary school In Becoming-frog Margaret Somerville analyses the productions of primary school children who have participated in an integrated educational program involving local wetlands. In one of these productions the children performed frogs to music made entirely of frog calls in a perfect example of Deleuze and Guattari's 'becoming-animal' (1987, p. 274). In taking up this idea she explores the post-industrial origins of the wetlands, the integrated educational curricula associated with the wetlands, and the children's representations.

Chapter 6: Transforming self-place relations in the project approach In this chapter Kerith Power moves beyond the modernist framework of the "project approach" to read from a postmodernist perspective how foregrounding place in an early childhood teacher education context generates learning about the mutual constitution and representation of places, bodies, subjectivities and collectivities. Examples drawn from students' work during the three project phases of topic selection, field work and display will illustrate how the project approach acted as an enabling place pedagogy to facilitate students' learning about place and building community.

Chapter 7: Learning place through art and stories Susanne Gannon and Bronwyn Davies document the learning that secondary teacher education students engaged in as they took up elements of an enabling place pedagogy in an alternative model of the professional practicum. Working in the areas of Visual Arts and English, the student teachers developed place-specific projects for working with school students in their communities. These demonstrate that learning is not simply the acquisition of a fixed body of knowledge, but also openness to and experimentation with the not-yet-known.

Chapter 8: Peripheral vision: collaborative place-storytelling in community Phoenix de Carteret discusses collaborative place-storytelling workshops she designed to research women's connections to place in Gippsland, Victoria. The workshops were developed from memory work, collective biography and the place pedagogies framework to unsettle storylines of gender and the dominant economic and colonial narratives in this place. The workshop method demonstrates the enabling pedagogical potential of place to facilitate informal learning, moving adult participants towards the place-consciousness considered necessary for sustainable futures.

Section 3: Teaching

In this section we focus on enabling place pedagogies through the breadth of practice that can be considered to be teaching. The three chapters explore enabling pedagogies of place in collective biography, community place-making, and a critical approach to place-writing in secondary English to open up new ways of thinking about and practising teaching.

Chapter 9: Collective biography as pedagogical practice: being and becoming in relation to place Bronwyn Davies and Susanne Gannon detail how they worked with a small group of student teachers in a collective biography workshop about place, inviting them to examine their own experiences of being in place. This chapter outlines the methodology of collective biography as a teaching practice, and shows how it might be done in a tertiary education setting. The links between the philosophy and practice of collective biography and the principles of place pedagogy are explored. The place stories written by the pre-service teachers are used in this chapter to explore the links and to open up new ways of thinking about teaching place pedagogy in tertiary settings.

Chapter 10: Rewriting place in English Susanne Gannon explores a range of strategies for writing and reading place in English that she has developed in contexts of secondary schools and teacher education. In each of these sites, close attention to the discursive constitution and textual representations of the local becomes a springboard for creative work. The interweaving of critical and creative responses to texts, and the careful design of student learning experiences, resources and assessment, open possibilities for complex and engaging responses to particular places.

Chapter 11: The place-makers   Margaret Somerville draws on conversations and stories from a number of extraordinary community educators whom she characterises as "the placemakers". She traces the origins of their practices in their own embodied place learning, and in the places and communities which shaped them and which they in turn have shaped. Their teaching practice, which parallels their ongoing place learning, is analysed to identify the qualities that might contribute to formal educational curricula and pedagogies towards a sustainable future.

REFERENCES

Anzaldua, G. (1987). *Borderlands/La Frontera: The new mestiza*. San Francisco: Spinsters/Aunt Lute.

Bachelard, G. (1994). *The poetics of space* (M.Julas, Trans.). Boston: Beacon Press (Original 1958).

Bergson, H. (1998). *Creative evolution*. Mineola: Dover Publications.

Canella, G. S., & Lincoln, Y. (2009). Deploying qualitative methods for critical social purposes. In N. Denzin & M. D. Giardina (Eds.), *Qualitative inquiry and social justice. Toward a politics of hope*. (pp. 53–72) Walnut Creek, CA: Left Coast Press.

Cixous, H., & Calle-Gruber, M. (1997). *Rootprints. Memory and life writing*. London: Routledge.

Davies, B. (2000). *A body of writing*. Walnut Creek, CA: Altamira Press.

Deleuze, G. (2004). *Difference and repetition* (P. Patton, Trans.). London: Continuum.

Deleuze, G., & Guattari, F. (1987). *A thousand plateaus: Capitalism and schizophrenia*. (B. Massumi, Trans.) London: Athlone.

Foucault, M. (1977). *Discipline and punish: The birth of the prison*. Harmondsworth: Penguin Books.

Foucault, M. (2000). The subject and power. In J. D. Faubion (Ed.),*Michel Foucault. Power* (pp. 326–348). New York: The New Press.

Grosz, E. (1994). *Volatile bodies: Toward a corporeal feminism*. Bloomington: Indiana University Press.

Grosz, E. (2008). *Chaos, territory, art: Deleuze and the framing of the earth*. New York: Columbia University Press.

Gruenewald, D. A. (2003). Foundations of place: a multidisciplinary framework for place-conscious education. *American Educational Research Journal,40*(3), 619–654.

hooks, b. (1990). *Yearning: Race, gender and cultural politics*. Boston: South End Press.

Lusted, D. (1986). Why pedagogy? *Screen, 27*(5), 2–15.

Massey, D. (2005). *For space*. London: Sage.

Merleau-Ponty, M. (1962). *Phenomenology of perception*. New York: Humanities Press.

Nancy, J-L. (2007). *The creation of the world or globalization* (F. Raffoul & D. Pettigrew, Trans.). Albany: State University of New York Press.

Pratt, M. L. (1992). *Imperial writing and trans culturalism*. London & New York: Routledge.

Rose, D. B. (1996). *Nourishing terrains: Australian Aboriginal views of landscape and wilderness*. Canberra: Australian Heritage Commission.

Rose, D. B. (2004). The ecological humanities in action: an invitation. *The Australian Humanities Review*. Retrieved January 4, 2011 from http://www.australianhumanitiesreview.org/archive/Issue-April-2004/rose.html

Sellar, S. (2009). The responsible uncertainty of pedagogy. *Discourse: Studies in the Cultural Politics of Education, 30*(3), 347–360.

Sinclair, P. (2001). *The Murray: A river and its people*. Melbourne: Melbourne University Press.

Soja, E. W. (2000). *Postmetropolis: Critical studies of cities and regions*. Oxford: Blackwell.

Somerville, M. (2005). Working culture: expanding notions of workplace cultures and learning at work. *Pedagogy, Culture and Society, 13*(1), 5–27.

Somerville, M. (2010). A place pedagogy for global contemporaneity. *Educational Philosophy and Theory, 42*(3), 326–344.

Somerville, M., & Perkins, T. (2003). Border work in the contact zone: Thinking Indigenous/non-Indigenous collaboration spatially. *International Journal of Intercultural Studies, 24*(3), 253–266.

Somerville, M., Power, K., & de Carteret, P. (Eds.) (2009). *Landscapes and learning: Place studies for a global world*. Netherlands: Sense Publishers.

Søndergaard, D. M. (2002). Poststructural approaches to empirical analysis. *Qualitative Studies in Education, 15*(2), 187–204.

Suzuki, D. (2010, October 24). *David Suzuki—The Legacy*. Speech presented at the Sydney Opera House.

Wilson, E. A. (2004). *Psychosomatic. Feminism and the neurological body*. Durham: Duke University Press.

SECTION 1

Researching Place

This first section of *Place pedagogy change* is about new research approaches for coming to know place differently. We take as our theme the task of coming to know our own places in new and unexpected ways. Our strategies include the writing of radio drama, body/place journals and poetry, walking and getting lost. We begin with the idea that all place learning starts with the embodied self in relation to others, including non-human earth others. In the chapters in this section we look at ourselves as researchers embedded in complex contact zones that are simultaneously environmental, geological, social and cultural.

In researching place, we give space to what our senses tell us about the places in which we find ourselves. We ask ourselves what we can see, hear, feel, sense and touch in each of our places. At the same time the research requires the hard work of finding new ways to conceptualise place that enable us to break with those preconceptions that have separated us off from place and divested us of responsibility toward place.

Belonging and longing to belong are themes that arise in each of the chapters in this section. Each of the authors has moved their home at least once, or several times, whilst we have worked on *Place pedagogy change*. We have moved thousands of kilometres away from the places we have known as our homes and from our familiar landscapes, terrains and communities. The intricate work of finding our ways into new places, and working out how our old places are carried within us and as part of us, contributes to the multi-layered mapping of place we undertake in this section.

Walking and writing, writing and walking are intertwined research practices that emerge through these chapters. In different ways we each slow down our sensing through walking, enabling us to pay closer attention to where we are and who we can be in those places. The modes of writing that we develop also open up new ways of thinking about place and our immersion in place, and new ways of thinking about research and representation. We write bodies—in all the complexities of the fleshy, desirous, curious creatures that we are—back into the research texts from which they are more often elided.

We recognise, through the chapters in this section, the permeability of bodies and the places in which they are located, and the relations and responsibilities that must ethically follow such recognition. We move beyond the individual towards a collective sense of individuals as located within complex networks of interdependence with human, non-human and earth others. The personal, interpersonal and conceptual work we do here is a necessary precursor to our explorations of teaching and learning in ways that make a re-formed relation to place both imaginable and possible.

MARGARET SOMERVILLE

BODY/PLACE JOURNAL WRITING

Liminality has no words.

Only a body sense of where I lie in bed at night in my bedroom—my body in relation to the sound of frogs in the pond below the house, and further down the hill the creek, how it winds from Mount Duval towards the spot where I walk every day, each shape and curve.

Leaving is another failure of belonging.

Within six months of beginning this research project I moved from my home of twenty years on the northern tablelands of New South Wales to the Gippsland region of south-eastern Victoria in the southernmost part of the Australian continent. In that six months I prepared to leave the place where I had lived and worked happily for twenty years. I completed academic commitments, bought and sold houses, dealt with the unexpected illness and death of my estranged husband, and my own and my children's grieving. During that time I began to keep a journal about moving to Gippsland, spasmodically at first, but more regularly once I moved to my new place. This chapter explores the process of coming to know that place through body/place journal writing as a method of inquiry, and the creative evolution of a practice of body/place journal writing.

I started the process of what I came to call body/place journal writing at a hiatus in my own research trajectory. Significantly for this chapter, it emerged from my response to text I had produced from Indigenous oral place stories, and to a poststructural feminist practice of massage. I re-map this emergence here to recall the body traces of this writing practice[i]. At the time I was writing a paper about relationship to place and was aware of another dimension I wanted to write about but couldn't articulate. While searching for this new connection I kept hearing echoes of old Bill Lovelock's story of the grasses blowing up against the fence in autumn before the cold weather comes:

I've seen 'em too go and get that
you might see a lot of grass
up against a tree or a fence
very soft grass
and it would blow like the wind
they'd go and get this
stuff it into bags
and make bed ticks out of them

M. Somerville, B. Davies, K. Power, S. Gannon and P. de Carteret,
Place Pedagogy Change, 15–28.

they used this a lot
dry grass that catches up
on netting fences
soft as a bed to sleep on
very warm in winter
warms up and keeps the heat.
That's what a lot of them done,
this is about what I know.

Bill clearly articulated his story as a form of body knowledge expressed in language. I sensed the body/place connection always already there in such stories but I didn't know how to do it for myself. I thought and thought about how to articulate this missing dimension and the more I thought the more distressed I became. I felt weak and exhausted, my heart pounded, even to walk up the stairs was an effort. I had strange and frightening dreams about a fragmented body, one in which my body was sliced into fine layers of flesh which were cooked and spread with Vegemite. I was trying to think through complex theoretical problems and I could think no longer. I felt I had fallen into an abyss of dualistic thinking predicated on the separation of the body, not only from thought, but from the site of writing.

After a very hard walk in the local gorges which brought me back to my body, I began a series of massages with Cathy Carmont who was investigating the experience of massage through feminist poststructural theory. In this massage Cathy provided a space of trust where I could speak images that surfaced from tissue, organs, joints and bone, without the need to make sense. There was no system, no order, no expectations, just pleasure in the touch of skin on skin, release from pain and tension, and permission-giving in verbalising and in silences:

Margaret: It makes me think about what I said before—about moving mountains by tunnelling through or lying down rather than trying to shift whole mountains with your shoulder.

Cathy: What you said before? Being in the landscape?

Margaret: Yeah, because I think of that connection, that's like I feel now, that I can lie down real low beside the ledge of the mountain and shift it.

In the next phase of this process I began to remember these images that surfaced in the massage, and to write them down afterwards:

A tight place in my tummy, a hard black rock about fist size, round and flat. As Cathy massages the rock is washed with water that wells up into throat and eyes. A deep sadness. It belongs to the women from Coonabarabran, the undoing knots of connection made when two souls bump into each other and then the sadness of always having to leave.

I want to go to the water-splashing place where the water washes over hard smooth rocks. Rock inside and rock outside; place in body and body in place.

Committing the images to memory during the massage, however, was too disruptive to the experience itself, so I began to write down images that came to me:

Picnic with kids; little rocks in the shade inviting but kids want to play on big flat rock in the sun. Warm and sleepy, I lie in shallow dip on lichen-dimpled surface of big flat rock, face into brightness. Circles of green light form and reform behind closed eyes. My skin becomes flecked with grey and light apple-green lichen-lace. I am a lizard, grey scales and flecks, lying on a rock in the sun. I become so flat I am the rock, body blends into surface, tufts of soft green moss shape line of body and voices of children play over me. I am the surface of the earth and they are playing on my edges.

The emergence of body/place journal writing from the space between my Indigenous collaborative research and feminist poststructural theory is significant. Both of these positions are underpinned by deep theoretical work and personal experiences that are important in relation to this chapter. With Australian Indigenous people and communities I have continued to learn and write about place and country through many years of listening to stories and being in place. Feminist poststructural theory gave me a speaking position as a woman and as a mother, and theoretical ideas with which to think through the body. It was not until I began my Gippsland journal, however, that I used body/place writing as an intentional method of inquiry. In the following excerpts, selected mainly from the journal of the first six months, I ask our research question of how I learned place and community when I moved to this new place.

MY (IM)POSSIBLE GIPPSLAND

Tuesday morning, top of hill Princes Highway shock as Latrobe Valley opens out to huge power lines, power stations, coal mines. I recall puzzle of bright orange spreading like a fungus across the landscape on whereisit.com, then the recognition that they are the open cuts. Here it is the real thing. On road to Churchill sense of confrontation intensifies, massive power lines criss-cross in every direction, small and large chimneys pour out smoke (water vapour they tell me), electricity transformers, massive power lines marching across paddocks. As final visual assault, monoculture forest of blue gum or pines, planted in rows, close to each other, for the paper mill. Real estate agent says 'which ever way you travel between Morwell and Churchill you are skirting around a mine or a power station'. I decide not to drive between Morwell and Churchill to face this every day.

In Churchill we leave behind visual assault of power stations but there is the blight of shabby 1970s commission houses with unmown lawns, no gardens, torn curtains, old car bodies, and angry looking young men: male, chunky bodies walking stiffly with arms out, scowling or tailgating us. On top of the

17

hill three old weatherboard houses stand out in this desert of uniformity and on the other side, trees and hills. Churchill is saved by the hills. But even in their bright and shining air, one whole slope has been clear felled of its pine trees for the paper mill, leaving a few ugly bare timber stumps standing like amputated limbs on the hillside.

I have done bits and pieces of writing but nothing that represents my normal journal. The experience reminds me of Phoenix's *entre deux*—when the world before and the world after are completely different—there is a failure of words. I remember reading this idea in Kay Ferres' article about colonial women's writing. How much more so for them than me, moving from one side of the world to the other? Perhaps it is simply the quintessential experience of migration repeated from the psyches of grandparents over the generations.

Yesterday I woke up in the night with the strongest clearest image of the Gwydir River near where I used to live. I could identify exactly which bit of the Gwydir it was. I could visit in my body's senses, all the places where we had picnics, boiled billies, lazed in shallow water in summer, camped. But in my dream it was the shallow winding strands of gold weaving in and out on the wide sandy river bed through soft dark green casuarinas where it joins Booralong Creek. We often sat at that place and boiled a billy. There were always the marks of other fires, others sitting there. Sometimes we took food for a barbecue but often just a billy to have a cup of tea. I remember tracking the small changes in the river at that corner when heavy rains had remoulded the shape of the meandering golden water.

Body memory comes as a painful longing, a physical longing that I feel in my heart space, as I realise what I have done, how far I have come from the place that has been always there for me, for more than twenty years now, on the New England tablelands.

It is yet another (dis)placement, having grown up in Sydney and lived in many places. I was thinking about that yesterday, what is this learning place and forming community?

In the space between body/place and language there is always the liminal. Dreams and images emerge in this space where there can be no smooth and continuous narrative, to tell a story. In this early time of place learning I am suspended in this liminal space, in between here and there. Moving to a place like the Latrobe Valley, with the stories of socio-economic disadvantage that always precede it, was a strange experience. People told me about the Jaidyn Leskie story. In Moe, they said, a child was murdered and a dead pig's head was thrown into the front garden. There was the shock of moving from a pleasant rural landscape to a place that was both intensely rural and intensely industrial. (Dis)placement was a common theme in my journal at this time and I recorded the haunting sound of the little birds that sing every day before dawn. I had only heard them in the hedgerows in Scotland, the land of my old people. David Malouf says that until we have our own ghosts in this country we can never belong. I live with the ghosts of the spirits of the Old People from my Indigenous work but there are no ghosts of my ancestors here. In opening myself to this new place I become other-to-myself. It is an ontology of the in-between where I am like the ghosts that hover between two places, between dreaming and waking, between my old self and new, a pre-condition for learning and change.

I write of the undoing of self; of waiting in the chaotic space of unknowing; of the absences, silences and disjunctures of the liminal space with no narrative; of the relational nature of any coming into being; and of the messy, unfolding, open-ended and irrational nature of becoming-other-to-oneself through research engagement.

At home in the afternoon I lie on the couch with gas heater on in front room, the only room where I can see out. I still see fences, houses and roofs but a tiny view of a hilltop, or from the corner where I have placed Miss O'Donnell's chair, a larger view of a hill with the biggest house in Churchill in the foreground. I long for a fire, real flames, for something organic, for some disorder. On waking I see little wiry haired dog snuffling along the street and rain has briefly stopped so I decide to do what little dog is doing and snuffle around the streets. Starting with streets to south and west of me. There are only a few streets to the edge of town. Where the town finishes there are houses on one side of the road and none on the other, trees, grass, bit of a gully. I walk down towards this road and look at gardens, learning different plants, different seasonal responses. Bright oranges and lemons dropping off trees look like they are never picked.

Last weekend was moist gloomy grey all day both days. Each day in late afternoon just before dark I drag myself out of a dull lethargy and walk a few streets. It is a lethargy born of loss and greyness, so the little light that seeps through the moisture is necessary for survival. But this is a good strategy, tuning into the particularities of this place. On Sunday I walk the streets to the east of my house towards a main road that produces the cartographies of advantage and disadvantage. On one side the "private" area and on the other the "commission" area where the real estate agent said he would not let me live. To the west of my street the houses become more substantial. Right at the top of the south west boundary, with a backdrop of hills and bright green paddocks where cows graze is a huge new house typical of neo-colonial McMansions now spawning in prosperous outer suburbs everywhere. Just one, with double sided palatial grandiosity. But as I walk east towards the commission area the houses become more modest, a quiet suburban sort of feeling. The gardens to the east, like the houses, are less luxurious and sprinkled with the neglect that marks rental properties as different from the others. Further on are the streets where I don't go but on the road in between an abandoned plant nursery where the owner, they tell me, was murdered by a kid one Saturday morning for a bit of change.

Weather remains mainly cloudy and grey with occasional sun but walking out I see the hills, sky, feel the air, smell the freshness, feel my body warm with movement. Monday Tuesday Wednesday I walk to work and every day the same feeling of aliveness, exhilaration. Thursday and Friday driving, leaves me feeling unsatisfied. Yesterday after the fog was sunny and clear, the first sunny clear day since I arrived two weeks ago. People speak about the feeling of happiness from seeing the sun. I think it is a literal biochemical phenomenon. But because I drive to Clayton [the city] and sit in an entirely internal seminar room with no outside windows at all, I experience the sunlight as strange when I come out. It's like when I have been in the movies as a child and come out into the brightness, time has somehow warped and my sense of light and dark is disturbed at some primitive level.

Walking back up again I look at the blue sky streaked now with clouds. They come from the direction of Loy Yang Power Station and I think of reveries about clouds. But clouds here have a different provenance. The clouds that stretch out from Loy Yang's chimney stacks are formed by vapour released as part of the production of electricity from burning coal. Who knows what else is in the clouds apart from water vapour. I don't want to think about it too much but in both directions I can now see power stations and I think of the abject, the abjection of the Latrobe Valley and its de-industrialisation. With the loss of jobs due to increasing automation of the power and mining industries, we are left with a society in transition. There is no longer the heroic story of masculine hard work and sacrifice, because there are few jobs and much unemployment. And yet, we still have the incredible presence of these industrial giants, pumping out electricity, the energy furnace that keeps the city of Melbourne humming. Gippsland is what allows Melbourne to be a clean and cultured city of the arts; we are Melbourne's abject.

Through walking the streets around my house I learn the suburbs and the orderings of the suburbs according to privilege and poverty. I have only once lived in the suburbs and that was long ago, when I was a child. I chose to live tightly nestled amongst other houses in Churchill because of moving to a new state as a woman alone, but I can hear the man next door cough and clear his throat. I learn the impact of light and weather by walking, the intimate relationship between the sunlight that strikes my pineal gland and my sense of wellbeing. Walking, I also learn the power stations as an insider, becoming part of my identity in place. The Latrobe Valley chimney stacks appear every night on the television in relation to the scourge of carbon emissions, but one morning a momentary lick of pink on a power station cloud defies all logical orderings. There is no sequential process of transition that fits neatly into any schema but rather I seem to spiral through the same processes of learning place. Over this time, however, my work identity and place writing change forever, deeply influenced by living in this place of abjection and over-representation; by knowing place through movement; through walking suburban streets; through weather, greyness, and clouds.

I write of an ontology that includes our participation as bodies in the 'flesh of the world' (Merleau-Ponty, 1962), a reciprocal relationship with objects and landscapes, weather, rocks and trees, sand, mud and water, animals and plants, an ontology founded in the bodies of things. In this ontology, bodies of things are dynamic, existing in relation to each other, and it is in the dynamic of this relationship that subjectivities are formed and transformed.

The seeping moisture of this climate is so different.

My *ensuite* is dark and enclosed, like the main bedroom and house really. At night it feels womblike and I chose the house for these qualities, a safe place to land alone, start new work, make a new identity. But the *en suite* always felt a bit unsavoury. Then the other day I noticed what I thought was a piece of wet crumpled paper on the floor where the vanity meets the wall. I bent down to pick it up and realised it was alive, felt like cool moist skin, sweaty almost. Looking closer, it had two petals, curled at the edges, a delicate pale fawn colour and it was firmly rooted to the crevice between floor and wall. It smelt a bit like mushrooms, or toadstools. I cut the fungus out with a knife, and examined it closely, no ribs, just smooth pale moist flesh. The rainforest ever immanent.

In my garden rainforest trees pop up everywhere, tiny seedling trees that want to grow into rainforest giants. I was planning to go to Morwell National Park to look at these giants this afternoon but when I got into housework and garden, I put it off. Then, as evening came, the more I was in the garden, the more compelled I felt to go and walk and see what native plants grow around here.

Tall tall trees, huge girth, at the bottom of the valley, quiet, birds, air of trees, smell of moist cool tree air. I breathe the green of trees.

Movement, the feel of walking, sand underfoot, surprise of sand, I thought it would be sticky volcanic soil.

At the bottom of the valley lots of logs covered with green moss and soft green light, shaded. A huge tree with a hollow at the base, big enough to walk into, through layers of openings like dark curtains, blackened by fire.

At the bottom of the valley I startle a dark brown wallaby who hops a little into a clearing and then stops to eat again.

Ferns in the gully, I want to see more—tree ferns, ground ferns, I want to learn ferns.

Halfway up the hill as I round a corner there is a rustle and I stop still and quiet. A male lyre bird, flicking long ornate tail, moves a little way off, slowly, protected from view by ferns, and then begins to feed again, pecking into the leaf litter, busy. Further up the track another, a female this time with a tiny bird that at first I think is a chick, but is just company, hopping around her on the ferns and logs.

Walking at Morwell National Park this Sunday morning, a grey and moist day that intensifies the green of moss and light, not the same walking with company, but we pass a woman on the way back and she asks 'is it a lyre bird day?' and I say 'no, I saw them last week but none today'. She says 'that is the joy of it, you never know what you are going to see, you cannot predict'. No you cannot predict the natural world, I think, it is its own curriculum and that is the pleasure, the unpredictable, the new learning every day, every time every day a little bit different but you only get this little bit different by repetition, by the same walk in the same place over and over again. Over days weeks years, generations even.

In the gloomy light of a moist grey day it is the sound of birds that stands out. Lots of different kinds of tiny birds flitting, trilling, chattering in the undergrowth in this little valley. Then I notice a brilliant red parrot sitting on a boll on a huge old tree, head turning side to side looking at me, somehow engaged with my presence. I wonder if it is waiting for food, sitting above the car park and picnic area, or just curious. I take out my camera to photograph this beautiful bird. It feels a bit objectifying after our exchange but I want to remember that moment. The bird, of course, flies away, resisting my attempt to capture it. Then, as I put my camera into the bag, it flies back again and lands on another boll, this time a hollow one and begins chatting to noisy babies inside, poking its head in and out of the hollow, looking from me to whoever is inside. I photograph this charming display, but think that any photograph will not contain, could never capture, the brilliance of this bright moment, the bird, me, the bush, the sounds all round of birds chattering.

The sense of body, weather, climate, house, and garden is enlarged into a wider circle of being-in-place through the rainforest in the national park. Finding my way to, and then within, Morwell National Park became something of a symbol for finding myself in Gippsland. I asked: How do I find my way in(to) this place? I tracked my steps from the Tourist Information Centre where I got an information pack with local maps, to the interpretive sign in the parking area, to the pamphlet that had a mud map with numbered sites. I prefer my own responsiveness not to be mediated by maps but they gave me a safe beginning point. I also learned about Lyndon's clearing named after Mrs Ellen Lyndon of Leongatha, 'who previously lived on a farm near here. Her studies of the plant and animal life of this forest established its significance, and together with the Latrobe Valley Field Naturalists Club was instrumental in having the park proclaimed in 1967'. I felt connected to a potential network of women as in my work for *Wildflowering*. Paper knowledge and body knowledge. I think about maps as curriculum and curriculum as maps. What do they make possible? What stories do they open up and what do they hide? I think that they can only be guides to opening the self to the unpredictability of body-in-place learning.

I write about an epistemology that requires a new theory of representation. Each representation, the parrot looking at me looking at her, the brilliance of this bright moment, the bird, me, the bush, the sounds all round of birds chattering, that I cannot capture by camera but I attempt to capture in writing. It is what I call a naïve representation. It is naïve because it knows that it can never capture the moment but it tries to do it anyway. There are multiple attempts that together make an assemblage: the image of the parrot from the eye of the camera, and the black marks on the page that both mirror and do not mirror the image of the camera, but assemble the two into another image made from the reflections on the first. Each is a pause in an iterative process of representation and reflection. I become more and more interested in the (im)possibility of representation.

The Churchill Leisure Centre where I do my gym is transformed today. The quilting ladies have taken over with their first quilting exhibition. The northern end has rooms stretching endlessly, hung with quilts, embroidery and textile work, knitting, folk painting on old objects, stalls with plants, homemade candles, preserves and jams, soft toys, all the sorts of arts that women do. There are lots and lots of women here, maybe a hundred or so, looking at the quilts, laughing, exchanging words, ideas, sharing. An older woman, bent over, with sun spotted skin, says to another, 'I'm in seventh heaven'. Women laugh about how they make quilts and give them away as fast as they make them, hundreds of hours of work, they just love doing it, they say.

On one wall a large, draped, creamy-white quilt, a light delicate lacy object, catches my eye. The sign says 'Made in 1915 by Mrs Tess Mills, by hand, and by candlelight'. When I return to buy another quilt I ask if I can talk with the owner and take a photograph. The woman running the office passes me to another woman who says it belongs to Marg Whitehall and calls her. She hands me the phone and Marg talks to me, wants me to come out today.

I buy a quilt called "Roses in Spring", beige, pinks and maroons, double size to put on my bed. In the afternoon I pick up my quilt, more beautiful than I remember.

In Marg's front room the old quilt made by Mrs Tess Mills is unfurled, more light and air than fabric. It is made of small flower circles of creamy white lightly joined on four points by tendrils of fine stitching. Each small circle of cloth has been gathered to the centre so that the back looks like a flat circle and the front like a gathered flower. It is called a Sussex Puff. Marg picks out individual "puffs" where the fabric is softer and more pliable, and says these ones are probably made of muslin, the others are calico. We examine the different textures, some of the fabric would have been bought new at the shop in nearby Yinnar where Marg bought the material for her wedding dress, some would have been reused. She tells me that she got the quilt about six months ago, 'in a bad fashion, I suppose. A chappie passed away, Jeff's second cousin. I was there taking a cake, and everything had been sold up, they had a big garage sale. They only kept an old iron bed and the quilt, because no-one wanted it'. The quilt had been on the same bed in a sleepout on a farm in south Gippsland since Mrs Tess Mills made it in 1915.

I now remember the conversation with Cynthia before I left Armidale about the quilts the miners' wives made. She stroked the texture of the woollen quilt gently as she told its story: of her dad coming to work at Yallourn Power Station as an engineer, her mum buying the patchwork quilts made by miners' wives from the men's old woollen overcoats. The men needed the woollen overcoats against the cold Gippsland winters and the wool mills in England supplied superior quality woven cloth, each with their distinctive weaves. The coats were expensive and when parts of them were too worn to work as coats, they became *waggas*, homemade patchwork blankets for bedding. The quilt made of all these different woven patches is a myriad of tiny birds, delicate shades of browns and greys, feathers flecked and mottled like the different weaves and textures of the British wool mills.

Shirley came yesterday morning, her usual Friday morning to do the cleaning. I was pleased to see her, one important local connection. I was still at home, not yet ready for work, eating breakfast so I explained I had got home at one thirty that morning from a conference in Adelaide and was tired, running late. Shirley said that she was tired too, worked till after midnight. Surprised, I asked her what work she had been doing. 'Making cushions', she said, 'for the family for Christmas'. She told me she has thirty relatives, starting with three sisters, their husbands and children and every year she makes each of them a present for Christmas. This year's project is cushions. 'I couldn't just make them one cushion', she said, 'that seemed a bit strange, so I had to make them two, that made sixty cushions for the lot'. She began in April when she saw a friend knitting the diamond shaped sides with a leaf design. It took her three days to learn the pattern from her friend and then she started knitting. She explained to me that every year her presents are in the colours of their favourite football teams, counting out on her fingers the football teams that each member of her family follows—'Richmond, Collingwood, St Kilda…I did the black and gold first, and it looked stunning'. She has been working to a tight timeline to get all this done, has to stay up working till one o'clock in the morning, after long days of cleaning houses, to get the knitting finished. 'I can't wait', she said, 'to see their faces when they open their presents this Christmas'.

There have been so many threads from this entirely serendipitous quilting experience of learning place and community. The quilts tell the stories of women's lives, the constitution of the feminine in Gippsland, such an invisible story compared to the dominant masculine storyline of heroic work and subsequent loss. The quilts were a way to access these alternative stories as transitional objects, occupying a space both inside and outside the self, of the body and of the (m)other. The spring roses quilt is still on my bed, now soft and moulding to my body with five years of use. They connected me to another thread through possum skin cloaks of Aboriginal Victoria and to Treahna Hamm, a Yorta Yorta artist who was part of the revitalisation of possum skin cloak-making with Victorian Aboriginal communities.

Possum skin cloaks were practical, wrapped around the body for warmth, but equally symbolic, as they were inscribed with the maps of identity in country. In ceremony people would open the quilt to introduce themselves and their places. Treahna stitches the soft furry possum pelts together and burns her stories of the Murray River on the soft inner skin. We did a project together about the river and she made a baby cloak: 'imagine the river without a map…this is my country where I come from, you could wear it as a cloak, use it as a map, together'. She made a baby cloak for my granddaughter, when Eva was very fragile as a newborn. I am not allowed to exhibit it, except by carrying it with me, because it is needed for Eva and her new baby sister's protection.

Shirley's story of her work jolted me into a new recognition. Her work, paid and unpaid, participates in an alternative economy. She works for cash, small dollars per hour but it is all her own, or for her family in rigorous leisure pursuits that are about the same reciprocity and exchange. She manages, monitors and worries about the quality of her unpaid work, its aesthetics, whether it will please her family, and about meeting her deadlines. But also, and perhaps more importantly, it is about love. It is about labour that produces relationships, those complex webs of feeling and connection that sustain, make meaning and identity, a sense of purpose in the world. The stories of the women's quilts are about an entirely different economy that already exists for a world of "prosperity without growth", an economy of bodily care, of gift giving, and of love.

Yesterday was Armageddon day. Hot, with strong northerly winds. Went to Powerworks to do tour of power stations. Huge car park on top of a hill between Churchill and Morwell, hot dry bare and windy with power stations visible in every direction. Inside Powerworks building is cool and air-conditioned with wall displays about the history of power stations in Gippsland. Wall posters tell us, among other things, that 'the greenhouse effect is natural'. The first section of the tour is an eight minute film about production of electricity from brown coal. Brown coal is younger than black coal—from fifteen to fifty million years old, laid down in layers of petrified soft woods, rainforest trees, such as Kauri. There is a twenty kilometre seam that stretches from Morwell to Sale, virtually the whole floor of the Latrobe Valley, which is surrounded by mountains. Once a huge forest of softwood trees. As we leave the building the guide points out clouds of brown dust blowing up from the open cut coal mine. She says we might not be able to get out of the bus because of the dust. We drive through a morass of big and small power stations, electricity lines and transformer stations, and learn the many other power stations of various sizes in Latrobe Valley that are connected to Melbourne by the electricity grid.

At the brown coal mine right next to Hazelwood Power Station big clouds of brown dust rise up on the wind from the giant cavernous hole. Tiny garden sized water sprays do nothing to settle it. A couple of fires have already broken out on the northern wall, and the tour leader tells us we cannot stay because of the fires. The massive hole in the ground is like an inverted pyramid, a negative image of the huge Egyptian structures we were taught to marvel at as kids. A kind of negative tomb of our civilisation. Its walls are similarly constructed in layered steps out of those fifteen million year old rainforest trees. It takes twenty five thousand tonnes of these petrified trees to power this one power station for half a day and this one supplies about a third of the state's electricity needs. It is like a giant pot belly stove, must be the most inefficient method of producing energy in the world. By the time we leave, a fire engine is arriving and thick brown smoke billows from the mine.

Inside the huge belly of the power station it is even hotter and a walkway is lined with interpretive signs that tell us about the generation of electricity. The tour leader reads them to us, despite the fact that we have to have ear plugs against the roar of engines and that we can read anyway. The workers who operate the power station are sitting at computers behind a glassed wall in a cool air-conditioned office where they can monitor everything that the station is doing, humming its connection to electricity users in Melbourne. We move through the various processes from the massive turbines to the huge fires that seem to be only just contained inside giant furnaces where you can see the red flames flickering through triangle shaped vents.

As we drive back to Churchill the air is filled with gritty brown and I remember the day I saw this before and wondered what it was, this time I know it is brown coal dust and smoke. The next night walking home it is still hot at six in the evening, the air filled with the pungent smell of brown coal smoke. I wonder what it does to my lungs, to my body. It makes me angry that people have to put up with this desecration that no-one can speak in this university that owes its origins to the power stations. At night the fires in the mine are on the news. I am hot and tired and gritty; eyes, lungs and, even more so, psyche feel assaulted.

I know that I will not stay forever in the Latrobe Valley.

I make a veggie garden. Not directly in response to the fires in the coal mine and power station tour, but to feeling of impending doom (drought, water shortage, climate change, bird flu epidemic, nuclear war), a longer more enduring response to Churchill. I buy a compost bin. On Saturday I go to Bunnings and buy vegetable seedlings—mostly leaves—lettuce, coriander, Italian parsley, rocket, silver beet, two tomato plants and marigolds. I sit in the dirt next to the shed in overalls, mattock and fork the tough dry ground, sitting in the earth, lost totally in physical sensations, getting to know this ground. Then that evening, just before dark, I plant the little seedlings, careful of their tiny roots, and water them in. I feel the clay-ey texture of the fine silty soil, earth on hands, smell the wet soil like smell of rain on hot dry ground. The little plants look bedraggled, broken and messy, but the next morning early, they are springing up with that amazing life, reaching towards the sun.

Walking on the rail trail feels safe and healing too. It is shaded by tall gums and one early morning we discover feral plums. We eat from the first tree, picking the small just-ripe plums and eating them at the tree. Then we discover five feral plum trees, each at different stages of ripeness. Because they are seedling plums each tree has its own characteristic plum colours, flavours, and smell. Some are ripe when they are golden, others bright red and some dark maroon. We fill our hats with plums and walk back in the dappled sunlight through tall trees. All week I make my breakfast with oats and seeds and cut up plums. The plums are quite small so cutting them seems arduous and a waste of time but this kind of domestic repetitive task also opens to meditation and contemplation.

To cut these small ripe plums the knife has to be super sharp and I can feel the quality of the ripe flesh of each plum with my fingers as I select them by colour and feel for ripeness. Only the really ripe ones are fully flavoured. Each plum has a line, the line of the fold. The fold is the line of the outside folding in, where the plum blossom has been fertilised. The fold also tells me how to cut the plum. If I place the knife directly into the line of the fold, the seed lies flat to the cut. In such a small plum as seedling plums are, this is important because otherwise most of the flesh gets left on the seed. It also helps the soft juicy flesh of the plum to come away more cleanly from the seed. The seeds go into the compost and the flesh with its dark skin into my breakfast and I eat of the shady rail trail walk.

A couple of weekends ago, just into autumn, I walk along the trail and come again to the aroma of the first seedling plum tree. A strong smell of overripe plums, mostly on the ground or pecked by birds, reminds me of the smell of grapes left hanging on the vine when the season is over. They are fermented tiny globules of red wine and the bees pierce the soft thin ripe skin, getting intoxicated on the heady wine. I say goodbye to plums for the season but further down the walk the bright red colour of not-quite-ripe plums on another tree. Another gift. I pick a hatful of mixed colours from yellow-green-tinged-with-red to bright dark red. I put them in a bowl on the kitchen bench, enjoying their bright colours. Each day the miracle of plum colours unfolds. The plums change from red-tinged-green to bright red to maroon to almost black-maroon, the deepest dark maroon I have ever seen. How is it, I wonder, that colour is produced and changes so day by day? What does it mean to eat colour?

All of these stories are important place learning that gives me a deeper sense of the complex dynamics of space/time in my new location. I recall Massey's 'event of place'. Place, for Massey is defined by a quality of "thrown togetherness", which propels the need to negotiate in the here and now:

> …what is special about place is not some romance of a pre-given collective identity or of the eternity of the hills. Rather what is special about place is precisely that thrown togetherness, the unavoidable challenge of negotiating a here-and-now (itself drawing on a history and a geography of then and theres); and a negotiation which must take place within and between both human and nonhuman. (Massey, 2005, p. 140)

Massey refers to this moment of space/time conjunction in the global flows of culture and nature as the 'event of place':

> This is the event of place. It is not just that old industries will die, that new ones take their place. Not just that the hill farmers round here may one day abandon their long struggle, nor that the lovely old greengrocers is now all turned into a boutique selling tourist bric-à-brac...It is also that the hills are rising, the landscape is being eroded and deposited; the climate is shifting; the very rocks themselves continue to move on. The elements of this 'place' will be, at different times and speeds, again dispersed. (Massey, 2005, pp. 140–141)

My place research becomes all the more nuanced and complex, deeper and more extensive in its reach, but these insights do not account for the intense desire to belong somewhere. The fact that I can choose to leave Gippsland makes me feel forever an outsider here. With no place to return to this is a precarious and risky proposition. Yet, in another way this is the position that I occupy as writer and researcher of place, always both inside and outside and simultaneously neither.

Body/place journal writing as a method of inquiry has opened up many threads for me, threads that both unravel and stitch together in loose kinds of ways the story of a space/time intersection in a particular place. It is a process of coming to know. Through this writing I have come to know place as multiple; there is not one place that is Gippsland or Latrobe Valley, or even my house or my garden. They are all many places that change constantly. Place is multiple, shifting, dynamic, and always becoming, just as I am always becoming-in-place. These understandings and some of the threads that I have drawn from my body/place journal have deeply informed my ongoing research, including that reported in the other chapters in this book.

NOTES

[i] This material is taken from *Body/landscape journals* (1999, Spinifex Press, pp. 11–14), a publication which came out of my doctoral thesis, which charted the insertion of the body into my place research and writing practice.

REFERENCES

Massey, D. (2005). *For space.* London: Sage.

Merleau-Ponty, M. (1962). *Phenomenology of perception* (C. Smith, Trans.). New York: Humanities Press.

Somerville, M. (1999). *Body/landscape journals.* Melbourne: Spinifex Press.

Somerville, M. (2004). *Wildflowering: the life and places of Kathleen McArthur.* Brisbane: University of Queensland Press.

Margaret Somerville
Monash University

BRONWYN DAVIES

AN EXPERIMENT IN WRITING PLACE

In this chapter I make a space to think about the underlying principles that inform my own transgressive, emergent, experimental writing—in particular, a radio play about the place in which I live. In order to help me do this thinking I draw on poststructuralist writers, such as Barthes, Cixous and Deleuze, who suggest that it is in literary and artistic texts that new ways of thinking are most readily opened up. Integral to my thinking about experimental writing are what Butler (1997) calls the ethical necessity of disruptions to everyday ways of speaking and writing, and what she identifies as the problems generated by the ongoing repeated citations that make up the everyday world. Those repeated citations, through which the everyday, common-sense world is generated, offer some a viable life and both implicitly and explicitly deny a viable life to others. How does one disrupt those repeated citations in one's own thinking and writing? How does one launch oneself into the risky space of thinking against the grain of that which "everyone knows"?

In order to disrupt my own repeated citational practices about the new place that I had come to live in, and to open up ways of being in that place, I experimented with a form of writing that would enable me to know my new place differently, against the grain of the already known. I embarked on two closely linked writing projects. One was the play *Life in Kings Cross: a play of voices* (Davies, 2009). The other was this chapter, in which I explore the principles that informed that experimental play-writing.

Cixous asks: 'Why do we live?' And she answers: 'I think: to become more human: more capable of reading the world, more capable of playing it in all ways. This does not mean nicer or more humanistic. I would say: more faithful to what we are made from and to what we can create' (Cixous & Calle-Gruber, 1997, p. 30). Language is a powerful constitutive force, shaping what we understand as possible, and shaping what we desire within those possibilities. With Cixous I am fascinated by the intoxicating power of language that enables us to open up the not-yet-known while at the same time work out of the materiality of our bodies and of the places around them.

Cixous speaks of a complex balance between knowing and not knowing oneself in relation to the other. She develops the term *positive incomprehension* to capture something of the movement and openness of Deleuzian differenciation (2005), of the process of becoming different. Once difference is no longer about being individualised and categorised and separated off from the other, differenciation becomes instead a process of creative evolution in which we might become 'more faithful to what we are made from and to what we can create' (Cixous & Calle-Gruber, 1997, p. 30). Once we

M. Somerville, B. Davies, K. Power, S. Gannon and P. de Carteret,
Place Pedagogy Change, 29–44.

are no longer fixed on capturing the essence of self and other in their isolation, but open to the unknown, to the impossibility of knowing, to the delight of knowing differently, we are opened up to the beauty of moments of insight into the being of the other (Cixous & Calle-Gruber, 1997).

In order to open up the creative forces that enable us to evolve beyond the fixities and limitations of the present moment we need to both turn our attention to what we are made of, our material continuity and ontological co-implication with others, including non-human others, and also open ourselves to multiple points of view.Human existence in this understanding is not an existence that is separate from others or from other forms of existence. Human, animal, earth and other matter—all exist, and exist in networks of relationality, dependence and influence.

WRITING THE CROSS

Voice 1

It is late-summer, early on a Saturday morning in Springfield Plaza. The night revelers are finally gone, leaving behind them the sad detritus of the night: a splatter of blood, broken bottles, vomit, bins and gutters overflowing with wrappers from McDonalds, Sushi Hero, Garlo's Pies, The Best Kebabs, Indian Food... The revelers are unconscious in the lock-up, or at home in their suburban beds, oblivious to the day, and to whoever they might find curled up in their sweaty, rumpled, dream-filled beds. One lies safe, for the moment, snoring softly in the comforting arms of a lady of the night, who drifts softly on the enveloping waves of her latest hit.

Over by the freeway, old Professor Jones snorts and turns over, restless in his bed of rags beneath the footbridge. He dreams his complex six-legged formulae as the early morning traffic rushes past him, humming into his dreams.

[SFX Sound of seven lanes of traffic rushing past, mostly cars with an occasional truck, continuing as background to the Professor's dreams]

Professor Jones

When I walk, you see, my back and front legs on one side move in phase with the middle leg, like this, on the other side. The other side... The suction cups on my feet hold fast to the wall, to the roof. Then, watch carefully, the other three legs move together, with a relative phase of half a cycle compared with the first set...

Voice 1

He drifts again into a dreamless early morning sleep.

Voice 2

A body lies on the pavement curled up in a patterned blue doona, oblivious to the passers by.

Voice 1

Wrapped up in his doona, Harald dreams of Vikings, sailing over the wild, cold sea. Steering through the narrow waters, with sheer cliffs on either side, his ship rolls over the grey, pregnant waves. He stares out the ship window straight into the heavy deep waters, and when the ship turns on its side, as it slides down the wave, he stares at the ice cold silver sky. He is wearing his Viking helmet with two cow horns and plays on his mouth organ a sweet nostalgic tune.

[SFX Music of the mouth organ and the creaking and groaning of the ship as it rolls on the waves]

Harald

I'm Harald the Great. I write poems that make the dead rise up from the deep, and I play music to rival the Sirens. I play for my Dadda who is lost at sea. I will play so sweet he cannot resist me. Why did you leave me Dadda? I'm stretching my hand down so deep into the roiling ice-cold water. Can't you take hold of it now? Take hold of it Dadda and I'll pull you up. Can you hear me Dadda? I can see your eyes, your two soft grey eyes. Can you hear my music Dadda? Just reach for my hand Dadda.

Dadda

Those are pearls that were my eyes. You cannot see me son, my bones are all disjoint and spread about on the floor of the wide, wide sea, and my eyes picked out by wee fish long long ago. Go home Harald, go home.

Harald

Where is home Dadda? Don't leave me Dadda! I'll play you sweet music Dadda...

Voice 2

An ancient landlord, bent over his brass filigreed walking stick, walks, slowly, along Darlinghurst Road, past Andersen's Danish Ice Cream and on towards Llankelly Place. He takes one step at a time, along the new black granite pavement with its black blobs of chewing gum and its brass inlaid histories of people he remembers only too well (drunken Christopher Brennan, crazy Bea Miles, the mad witch Rosaleen Norton). Elegantly dressed in his ancient black suit, spotless starched white shirt and silk tie, he pauses to lean on his cane and catch his breath.

Landlord (traces of a Polish accent)

I am ninety eight years old, but there is life in the old dog yet. Not like my buildings.

Voice 2

He jabs his cane in the air, pointing to the buildings in Llankelly Place. He rests his cane down and leans both hands on it. He gazes for a long time along the lane, thinking…

Landlord

There are termites in my floorboards and the cockroaches swarm up my walls. The cockroaches seek the warm damp places. They lurk in the makeshift shelters put up each night by the dross that rises to the surface in the gaudy drug-filled nightlife of this rapidly decaying place. It is filled with the stench of the drunken youths who piss against my walls, and the derelicts who no longer know the difference between a latrine and the walls of my buildings. The termites come in on the roots of the plane trees. They follow the roots that travel along the surface of the sandstone in search of the sweet cool spring in the once-upon-a-time gardens of Springfield House.

Voice 2

He walks slowly step by step toward the Plaza. He stops and jabs his stick at the brass inlaid plaque in the pavement, reading:

Landlord

"Springfield House. Demolished in 1934".

Such a beautiful house with its laughter and its music—those were the days of splendour and romance—the parties that went on all weekend, with artists, playwrights, actors, beautiful women… (sighs)

[SFX A dance band strikes up a waltz]

I was eighteen years old when I first danced with her. 1926. I remember as if it were yesterday…

Voice 2

He holds his cane to his chest as if it were a beautiful woman, and sways to the music, dancing once again on the wide moonlit verandah of Springfield House, with Lily Littmann, magnificent dark-eyed beauty.

Landlord

Ah Lily, Lily, my love.

Voice 1

Back along Darlinghurst Road, Gloria da Silva leans toward the mirror inside the doorway to inspect her lipstick. Carefully and precisely she tidies her face with the tip of her elegant long nailed little finger. Long shiny black boots, black bag over her shoulder, she is ready and waiting. Fresh as a dew-dropped daisy in the early morning light.

Gloria da Silva

Ya want a lady darlin'?

Voice 1

...she says to a bleary, blond haired youth heading for his lonely, bug-ridden backpacker bed.

Voice 2

At the end of Darlinghurst Road, the El Alamein Fountain glitters in the early morning light, like a huge round dandelion, ready to blow a wish on. Next to the fountain is a sign that makes another sphere, locating this watery birth of wishes at the magnetic centre of desire: telling how far and which way to Athens, Berlin, London, Moscow, Tokyo, Seoul, New York, Rio, Auckland.

Up toward the fountain runs Georgie Delaney, dressed in a tight pink t-shirt and very short shorts, looking drop dead gorgeous, nods hello at Gloria. As she runs past the Plaza she sees a body wrapped up in its doona, dead to the world. She stops, and taking ten dollars from the pocket of her shorts, she gently tucks it into the shirt pocket of the slumbering man.

I began my own place writing for this project with the complex and sometimes deeply confronting place in which I had come to live in 2004 not long before this project began. Kings Cross is well-known as the drug, prostitution, and nightclub heart of Sydney. In the conceptual and interactive space of this group project I began to explore the possibility of writing a radio play set in that place. Although I had previously written about the places of my childhood, and my place in the tropics, it seemed in the context of this new project that I needed to begin again, to write about my new place in Sydney, in order to imagine my way into the project of teaching our own students at the University of Western Sydney to write about their places and to take up in their own teaching the practices and emergent possibilities of place pedagogy[i].

Inspired by Deleuze (2005), I wanted to engage in writing that would open me up to difference, to seeing differently, to being different, in my newly familiar place of living. I decided, therefore, neither to tell an autobiographical story of place, nor to interview others about their stories of this place. While such stories may have produced new and different insights, they were also at risk of repeating and propagating the already known stories through which "the Cross" might be said to be colonised. I chose, instead, to develop a form of writing that would draw on a different imagination, mobilising transgressive/experimental strategies for the writing of place.

As I began work on the play (its form inspired by Dylan Thomas's *Under Milk Wood* (1954)), I also began work on this theoretical analysis, inviting the play-writing to inform my theorising and the theorising to inform my play-writing. The three principles that I elaborate below became my key to the transgressive writing that I was seeking, through which I might disrupt my own repeated citations of the known order. At the same time, the writing of the play allowed me to understand in practice what the principles that I was mapping out here meant. I thus moved constantly back and forth between the two writing projects: one transgressive within usual social science practices, and the other primarily philosophical, yet each dependent on the other. In this writing of the double project I planned to work with the familiar everyday world that I lived in, and at the same time, with the help of Deleuze and others, to propel myself beyond my already-lived experience: 'Writing is a question of becoming, always incomplete, always in the midst of being formed, and goes beyond the matter of any livable or lived experience. It is a process, that is, a passage of Life that traverses both the livable and the lived' (Deleuze, 1997, p. 1).

The play was not envisaged as a realist report of a place that might be said to pre-exist the writing, or to exist independent of my experience of and experiment with it. It was thus not tied to a belief about "the real" place, even though it is named after and inspired by a place with that name. To this extent, the writing was free to move toward the not-yet-known, and I could let it unfold in an as yet unimaginable way. The way this *felt*, retrospectively, was that I could be more "intelligent" in the writing, drawing on every sense, every awareness, every memory, every experience, every thought, and every available document. I could allow my minds, conscious and unconscious, free reign among these possibilities. I was not guided by how it *should* be written but by the sense of open exploration.

The writing that I sought for the play did not, thus, begin with a place that was extrinsic to the act of writing, but with the image, the sound, the idea that was forming itself on the deep surfaces of my body. My desire was to open myself to a movement in which something as yet unknown could become visible, become thinkable. I wanted to immerse myself in the Cross in such a way that I opened myself to inhabiting it differently, and I wanted to write the play in such a way that I invited the reader to listen, not only to new possible meanings, but also to the sounds of the words, their rhythms, their poetry—to take pleasure in it, and also feel its pain. I wanted readers to feel their flesh prick, or their eyes water, as they entered the place called the Cross. I wanted them to encounter the multiple tangle of subjectivities that make up the Cross, to recognise the place as both intensely familiar and simultaneously providing an opening on non-habituated ways of seeing/feeling/hearing "the Cross".

The principles developed in what follows suggest a reconfiguration of the relations between the author, the subject/object of writing, the text, and the reader. Transgressive, experimental writing, as I am envisaging it here, invites us to discard the self-conscious "I", to abandon representation, and to experience/experiment with language and with ourselves, each in order to enable us to think beyond what is already thinkable—what is already there to be thought.

DISCARDING THE SELF-CONSCIOUS "I"

Immersed in writing the play, I walk out of my apartment and into the Cross. I have grown eyes and ears all over all my body. I no longer walk with ears closed and eyes cast down, lost in my own thoughts, speaking only to those I know. I have eyes and ears about me everywhere, seeing who is there, how they walk, how they talk, how they gesture, how they each create their own fold in the social and physical world. I notice for the first time the smallest, most precious details, the lipstick tidied in the mirror, the Viking helmet put out as a begging bowl, the cellphones glued to the ears of the young and beautiful, the man in the elegant suit pacing back and forth in the small hours of the night, the call of the currawongs in the evening. I discover that I am invisible to the drug dealers who act as if I am not there, and as if I cannot see them and do not see them. "I" have become a place where thought happens, where the Cross can write itself, opening up the fold within my monadic soul to encompass other, nomadic folds, each shining its light on this place, the Cross. In bed at night I immerse myself in texts based on this place by other writers, reading their poems and novels and short stories late into the night. I read autobiographies and histories and heated debates with developers who want to take over and "destroy" the Cross, with their cheap towers and nightclubs pandering to the tourists. Whenever I can, I participate. I talk. I listen. I walk through. I sit. I observe. I find the words to bring these folds to life in my body/my writing. I dwell in the times I have been in the Cross in the past; memories stretching back fifty years; intense passionate memories; my own search for lost time. I reread Proust, and am deeply moved by his evocation of places I have never been. (Journal)

Barthes suggests that we take as our primary research focus the text that is written, rather than the author who writes. He enjoins us to *give birth to ourselves* in our writing, that is, to know ourselves as *coincidental* with our writing. This is not in order to reveal a pre-existing, known or knowable self who can be represented, or pinned down, with the words that are fixed on the page. It is not a self in the past (prior to writing), that can be brought into the present and fixed in an imagined future. The writing is a process of bringing-to-life the process/present moment of writing and, in doing so, *unsettling* the already known. In that act of writing of, and in, the present moment, we open the possibility of going beyond the pleasurable repetition of that which is already known and already judged, and of opening up the possibility of puncturing the familiar, pleasurable surface of that which is known. Barthes calls that punctured text a text of bliss. It is the text that 'imposes a state of loss, the text that discomforts (perhaps to the state of a certain boredom), unsettles the reader's historical, cultural, psychological assumptions, the consistency of his tastes, values, memories, brings to crisis his relation with language' (1989b, p. 14). The writer of such texts is 'born *at the same time* as his text; he is not furnished with a being which precedes or exceeds his writing, he is not the subject of which his book would be the predicate; there is no time other than that of the speech-act, and every text is written eternally *here* and *now*' (Barthes, 1989a, p. 52, italics in original).

Those pleasurable repetitions that Barthes enjoins us to puncture create the habitual patterns through which we act, through which we usually engage in writing, and through which we establish the recognisable and predictable objects that "have identity". Those objects (and subjects) are already determined, even over-determined. They are the same, or opposite, or analogous to that which is already known. In each case, they are made out of the same recognisable, predictable elements. The object/subject produced in those repetitions has an essence; it may individuate or evolve but remain the same; it can be pinned down in all its possible futures as this object, 'just as white includes various intensities, while remaining essentially the same white' (Deleuze, 2005, p. 45).

The repetitions create a baggage of habits and memory, which potentially lock the individual, in this case, the author, into an undesirable stasis (a fixed identity) that is continually obliged to repeat itself—or at least to attempt to do so. Williams, in his analysis of Deleuze's *Difference and Repetition*, says: 'We come to recognise an actual thing and assign a fixed identity to it because habitual repetitions, recorded in memory, lead us to have a fixed representation of things' (Williams, 2003, p. 12). While such identities are taken for granted in liberal humanist cultures, they are made problematic by philosophers whose focus is on the emergence of difference and the process of differenciation (as when cells of the body differentiate). Deleuze sees difference and differenciation as the elements of life. Life is not static; it is movement. At the same time life requires the capacity to be immersed in the present moment. While the immersion in the *moment of being* involves connectedness to past and future, the differenciation of the emergent subject requires *at the same time* a capacity to forget, to let go of those repeated citations that hold the world in place. Williams (2003, p. 13) captures this Deleuzian point in this way: '...the abstractions of habit and memory militate against the emergence of new sensations and hence against the expression of virtual intensities and ideas...So do not make your variation depend on representation, habit and memory. *Leave all actual things behind (forget everything)*' (italics in original).

In such a conceptual framework, the individual subject, whether they be the author or a character in a play, is interesting insofar as each moment of their being reflects some aspect of the whole of reality: 'an individual is a perspective on the whole of reality, something that is connected in a singular way to the whole of reality' (Williams, 2003, p. 5). In conceptualising the human subject, Deleuze is not interested in the familiar self-conscious "I", the one that is constituted as an isolated object that struggles to know itself and be known as one who *has* a fixed identity. He conceptualises the subject as a series of processes and, most importantly, as *a place where thoughts can emerge*: 'The individual is a take on the whole of reality, where reality is not restricted to actual things that we can show or identify in the world. The individual is, rather, a series of processes that connect actual things, thoughts and sensations to the pure intensities and ideas implied by them...An individual is not a self-conscious "I", it is a location where thoughts may take place' (Williams, 2003, p. 6). For the purposes of writing my play I wanted to become that location, the location where thought could emerge and differentiate itself, where I became one of the folds of the Cross, and was open to other folds.

Deleuze draws on Leibniz's monad in spelling out the relation between the individual subject and the whole:

> Leibniz's most famous proposition is that every soul or subject (monad) is completely closed, windowless and doorless, and contains the whole world in its darkest depths, while also illuminating some little portion of the world,

each monad a differing portion. So the world is enfolded in each soul, but differently, because each illuminates only one little aspect of the overall folding…A people is always a new wave, a new fold in the social fabric; any creative work is a new way of folding adapted to new materials. (Deleuze, 1990, pp. 157–178)

As writer, I experiment with and dive down into that place, my body, searching the folds in its deep surfaces, seeking to read what I might find written there. I register my own mo(ve)ments through and within the place I am writing. My task is to see/hear/think the folds in the social fabric, as I find them in myself as a singular manifestation of it, and in others who are also manifestations of it. I must open myself to the ongoing experience of finding within myself a fold of the social fabric, and at the same time open myself to other foldings, each 'illuminating some little portion' of that place, 'each illuminat[ing] only one little aspect of the overall folding' (Deleuze, 1990, p. 157). In this sense I am co-terminous with the others I find in this place, the Cross—each of us a fold, each of us a manifestation of the whole.

As writer, then, I myself must be *emergent* in the act of writing and not separable from it. I will be not so much *represented* in the text as emerging co-extensive with the text and with the place I am writing. The author and the text will be simulacra for which there is no identifiable original. To engage in the act of writing, I must be fully present and connected and, *at the same time*, leave behind what went before—the origin, the cause, the subject "I" which was imagined to pre-exist the writing. My self-conscious "I", with all its pleasures, its preciousness and its predictability, must be abandoned in favour of an emergent subject in process, a subject that is a reflection of some aspect of the whole, a singular perspective of the whole, a place where thoughts can happen.

ABANDONING REPRESENTATION: THE LABYRINTH WITHOUT THE THREAD

Voice 1

Round the corner, Corinne the crow wakes. She's been sleeping in the warm alcove of the auto teller. She sits up, blankets still around her, her wild black hair all over the place. Her shimmy slipping down over her smooth brown round shoulder. She croaks at each passer-by.

Corinne

Spare any change for a cuppa tea? Spare any change? Got any money for a cuppa tea? Got a coupla dollars for a cuppa tea?

Voice 1

She needs a drink badly. The morning pedestrians barely notice her. Their worlds and hers run parallel and rarely meet. But now she needs money. She levers herself up to standing, using the wall of the abandoned bank to lean on, get herself steady. She needs a piss. Needs a change of clothes. Needs some grog. She grabs the bottle in its brown paper wrapper and tips it upside down. Empty. She is distracted by the vision of a young Aboriginal woman wheeling a stroller towards her. Sitting in the stroller is a gorgeous child with a black tumble of curly locks, holding tight to a knitted elephant. She stares at the child, and moves out onto the footpath, out of her warm alcove, with steps remarkably like a big cat, despite her creaking bones. She holds out both her arms to stop the stroller. Danielle, on her way to the train, stops to watch, concerned. The baby hugs its knitted elephant and looks up at Corinne with interest. Corinne bends over toward the baby and croaks:

Corinne

You're a little beauty. Aren't you? Eh? What a beauty!

Voice 1

The child stares unafraid, and Corinne reaches down gently and takes hold of the baby's toes and waggles her foot.

Corinne

I could kiss the earth you walk on.

Voice 1

The mother smiles, and Corinne lets the foot go, and turns away to gather her gear and find some food and drink. But first a piss. Her bladder is busting. Easy for the blokes who just piss in the potted plants. Just the right height. Or against the wall. She has to go all the way down to the toilets. The mother and child move on, and Danielle stands there amazed at the love that Corinne has expressed for the baby girl. Corinne is oblivious to her. She changes her top to start the day fresh, choosing a bright red one she got from the Wayside Chapel, and a blue and green striped beanie that she pulls out of an old plastic bag.

Just as the author who might be said to pre-exist the text is left behind, in writing from the imagination, so is the "real world" that exists independent of the text. Whereas *representation* might find and present again the habitual, repetitive patterns that hold the world in place, transgressive, emergent writing dissolves its dependence on the habitual perspective from which that "real" is observed. Deleuze suggests that instead of representation, or re-presentation of an imagined original, we endeavour to make observations of the world *in the process of differing in each attempt to tell what it is.*

Representation has only a single centre, a unique and receding perspective, and in consequence a false depth. It mediates everything, but mobilises and moves nothing. Movement, for its part, implies a plurality of centres, a superposition of perspectives, a tangle of points of view, a coexistence of moments which essentially distort representation: paintings or sculptures are already such 'distorters', forcing us to create movement—that is, to combine a superficial and a penetrating view, or to ascend and descend within the space as we move through it. Is it enough to multiply representations in order to obtain such effects?…Difference must become the element, the ultimate unity; it must therefore refer to other differences which never identify it but rather differentiate it…Difference must be shown *differing*…it becomes a veritable *theatre* of metamorphoses and permutations. A theatre where nothing is fixed, a labyrinth without a thread (Ariadne has hung herself). The work of art leaves the domain of representation in order to become 'experience[ii]', transcendental empiricism or science of the sensible. (Deleuze, 2005, pp. 67–68, italics in original)

Neuroscientists confirm what Deleuze is writing about here. In *Proust was a Neuroscientist*, Lehrer shows how great writers and artists worked out how the brain works long before the neuroscientists, understanding the active work the brain does in making sense of what it sees—what it imagines to be real:

Neuroscientists now know that what we end up seeing is highly influenced by something called top-down processing, a term that describes the way the cortical brain layers project down and influence (corrupt, some might say) our actual sensations. After the inputs of the eye enter the brain, they are immediately sent along two separate pathways, one of which is fast and one of which is slow. The fast pathway quickly transmits a coarse and blurry picture to our prefrontal cortex, a brain region involved in conscious thought. Meanwhile the slow pathway takes a meandering route through the visual cortex, which begins meticulously analysing and refining the lines of light. The slow image arrives in the prefrontal cortex about fifty milliseconds after the fast image.

Why does the mind see everything twice? Because our visual cortex needs help. [The mode of processing means that] the outside world is forced to conform to our expectations. If these interpretations are removed, our reality becomes unrecognizable. The light just isn't enough…It is because Cezanne knew that the impression was not enough – that the mind must *complete* the impression – that he created a style both more abstract and more truthful than the impressionists…[He] realized that everything we see is an abstraction. Before we can make sense of our sensations we have to impress our illusions upon them. (2007, pp. 107–109, italics in original)

Deleuze turns to artists who reveal in their work what it is that he is after in the written text. The linear possibilities, represented by Ariadne's thread, are gone; what we thought we knew is abandoned in favour of a certain chaos. The solution, however, does not lie in a simple multiplication of perspectives from isolated self-conscious "I"s. Each small perspective must hold the world. And in this there is the clue as to why *Under Milk Wood* was such an inspirational model for my play. It was originally conceived by Thomas as a story about a group of mad people, that is, people not reined in by the dominant perspectives of the world. As he wrote and rewrote it, it became instead an imaginary place, full of those who might have been seen as monsters, but who can be encountered as the multiple voices that make up the life of that beloved Welsh village nestling under the Milk Wood. One is drawn into a movement of understanding, of being, in that village, with its 'plurality of centres' with one perspective superimposed and disappearing into another, with its 'tangle of points of view, [and its] coexistence of moments which essentially distort representation' (Deleuze, 2005, p. 67).

The Cross is already, even before I begin, a place of such a plurality, of such tangles, such a coexistence of moments, each encompassing the whole, yet none the whole in itself. In attempting to imagine my way into that tangle, I was guided by the search for difference, for the moment of opening up to that which emerges, the movement which becomes, itself, 'the element, the ultimate unity' of the place.

In writing the play, then, I did not set out to represent individuals who "I" observed to be there each day, as if my singular perspective could re-present that place, as it really was, again and again. I did not set out to accomplish "the truth" of it, as if I had found *the* perspective from which all could be told. Instead I began from minute, observed details that might then expand into one of the multiple folds of the social reality of that place. Like Thomas I thought of many of my characters as quite mad to begin with. But as they emerged onto my imagined stage, they seemed "more human", and by this, and echoing Cixous's words, I do not mean "nicer or more humanistic". Rather they seemed 'more faithful to what we are made from and to what we can create' within the multiple folds of the places we inhabit (Cixous, in Cixous & Calle-Gruber, 1997, p. 30).

EXPERIENCING/EXPERIMENTING WITH LANGUAGE, WITH ONESELF: WRITING ON AN IMMANENT PLANE OF COMPOSITION

She lifts her face to the morning sun, startled, as she is each morning, at the quality of the golden morning light. The soft breeze that finds its way up from the boat-bobbing bay caresses her bare skin still warm from sleep. Hair rumpled every which way, she is on her way to Bondi, to swim in the salt water and early morning light. Turning into Darlinghurst Road she sees the last of the revelers huddled in the street waiting for taxis—anxious taxis crowding the curb and vying to receive them—beautiful young people with bleary waxen faces and damaged livers, not quite ready to abandon the night. She walks past the door of the Massage King, now shut, the masseurs at home in their weary beds. The dying thumps of stale music escape with a whoosh of warm air from the opening door of the Empire Hotel. An old man hunched over his cane walks along the pavement, one step at a time...

She loves this old man, the man asleep on the pavement, the small bird-like woman she helped down the stairs the day before, the mad man under the bridge... Each throws some light on this place, each folded in a cocoon, each one is this place, repelling the world, shining light on the world from within its folded space...

Writing beyond what is already known involves intense immersion in the known, an intimate knowledge of the known, gained through an intense experience of oneself and of others, and gained through endless repetitions, through habituated immurement in the known. It involves an intimate and intense immersion in the already available schemas of knowing and being. Smith writes, in his introduction to Deleuze's *Essays Critical and Cultural*:

> The writer, like each of us, begins with the multiplicities that have invented him or her as a formed subject, in an actualised world, with an organic body, in a given political order, having learned a certain language. But at its highest point, writing, as an activity, follows the abstract movement of a line of flight that extracts or produces differential elements from these multiplicities of lived experience and makes them function as variables on an immanent 'plane of composition'. (1997, p. lii)

This line of flight from the multiplicity of the known to the as yet unknown depends on the capacity for letting go, for forgetting, for allowing the known to die. These two contradictory elements work together: the principles combined invite an immersion in the intensity of being and a willingness to experience painful loss of the familiar terms that made that being possible. It is the movement from pleasure to bliss that Barthes sets out in *The Pleasure of the Text* (1989b). It is movement where immersion in the moment and movement beyond the specificity of one's own identity become possible. It is the decolonisation of identity, of place, of the other. The writer is intensely connected and, at the same time, s/he lets go and moves onto the not yet known, to which s/he will also be intensely connected: '...reality is ever changing and the challenge is how best to live with that change...This constant alteration means it is a mistake to want to hold onto everything. Individuals must find a way of connecting well but the only way of doing this is by forgetting. To connect and discard are joint actions' (Williams, 2003, p. 5). Immersion in the moment, and openness to the movement that emerges—the captured moment in which we may previously have imagined we had pinned reality down, is already movement. The task of the writer is to participate fully in that movement, understanding it as movement.

Such writing must be accomplished against the formidable weight of familiar language uses and patterns, the language whose task it is to hold everything the same. Both Deleuze and Cixous see that familiar language as full of lies, of distortions of a particular truth or sets of truths that we might otherwise struggle to express:

> It is not only that words lie; they are so burdened with calculations and significations, with intentions and personal memories, with old habits that cement them together, that one can scarcely bore into the surface before it closes up again. It sticks together. It imprisons and suffocates us...Is there then no salvation for words, like a new style in which words would at last open up by themselves, where language would become poetry, in such a way as to actually produce the visions and sounds that remained imperceptible behind the old language ("the old style")? (Deleuze, 1997, p. 173)

This is where the experimentation with language itself becomes necessary, since the burden of old habits, and the sticky surface of familiar language, must have their power displaced. It is in experimentation with language that one can learn to unlie. In learning to unlie one comes to know oneself as human, as a reflection, an instance of the human, and in moving beyond the known and the readily knowable, the individual glimpses the condition of humanity.

The attempts to describe what the experimentation with language might entail push the boundaries of what is understandable, and rely on poetic and sometimes deeply paradoxical images. Cixous quotes Kafka who says a 'book must be the axe for the frozen sea inside us' (Cixous, 1993, p. 17). She continues: 'The book strikes a blow, but you, with your book, strike the outside world with an equal blow. We cannot write in any other way—without slamming the door, without cutting ties' (Cixous, 1993, p. 20).

> What do we do with the body of the other when we are in a state of creation—and with our own bodies too? We annihilate (ourselves) (Thomas Bernhard would say), we pine (ourselves) away (Edgar Allen Poe would say), we erase (ourselves) (Henry James would say). In short, we institute immurement. It all begins with walls. Those of the tower. (Cixous, 1993, p. 27)

This blow with an axe, this dissolving, pining, erasing, this relinquishing of the familiar may take us to painful edges akin to death. 'Those I love go in the direction of what they call the last hour—what Clarice Lispector calls 'the hour of the star,' the hour of relinquishing all the lies that have helped us live' (Cixous, 1993, p. 37).

In opening ourselves to what emerges in the moment of creation, we allow what lies behind the usual practices of language to emerge, to come to the surface of writing, of consciousness. Writing is a place where we are blind and do not know what we will discover, and it is also the place where blindness and light meet, where self and other meet, and attempt to know each other, to go beyond repulsion toward love:

> The thing that is both known and unknown, the most unknown and the best unknown, this is what we are looking for when we write. We go towards the best known unknown thing, where knowing and not knowing touch, where we hope we will know what is unknown. Where we hope we will not be afraid of understanding the incomprehensible, facing the invisible, hearing the inaudible, thinking the unthinkable, which is of course: thinking. Thinking is trying to think the unthinkable: thinking the thinkable is not worth the effort. Painting is trying to paint what you cannot paint and writing is writing what you cannot know before you have written: it is preknowing and not knowing, blindly, with words. It occurs at the point where blindness and light meet. (Cixous, 1993, p. 38)

Harald dreams yet again of his lost Dadda and whimpers in his sleep. The second Professor dreams of her Uncle Llewellyn throwing back his head and laughing his huge belly laugh, in the days before he was sent from home in disgrace. Danielle dreams of a small girl whose feet she kisses. Georgie Delaney dreams of Judgement Day, and discovers to her amazement that God is Chinese. Janni writes in his journal of his new-found libido, and Jen dreams of her husband, who loved her so much, and died at sea when she was only thirty. Mollie dreams of a magnificent hat with sweeping feathers and a dress that shows off her magnificent cleavage. Corinne dreams of walking, walking endlessly, her weary feet taking one step after another, the silver mirage of her destination slipping out of sight each time she thinks she is home. The backpacker scratches himself and dreams of Queenie's breasts and sobs with pleasure as he buries his face in them.

And so the dreams weave their way in and out of the flow of traffic in the Cross, in and out of intersecting lives that do and do not touch each other.

The song of a currawong [SFX Sound of currawong] summons the faintest wash of pink into the deep night sky.

All is quiet in the Plaza.

The El Alamein Fountain flows over, and the water runs down to the sea.

In writing the play I have been guided by these three principles: letting go of the self-conscious "I" who is the centre of events, who sees only with her own "eyes"; letting go of representation (the illusion that the world can be fixed from a single perspective) in order to open up images of multiple lives, each a manifestation of the whole; and, finally, opening myself up to the experience/ experiment of writing in which the world is not reduced to what I know already, but pushes me out into other ways of knowing, into the tangled possibilities of intersecting, colliding and separate lives. I now walk differently through the Cross. I do not yet know if the play will have that effect on those who hear it. And for those who have not been to the Cross, where will this play take them in the imagining of their own places? I hope, into a possibility of disrupting their own repetitive citations in relation to their own places, opening up the ethical possibility of granting the others in that place a more viable life.

NOTES

[i]   I discuss the further work with the teacher education students that I undertook with Susanne Gannon in Chapters 7 and 9.
[ii]   Where experience incorporates the concept of experiment.

REFERENCES

Barthes, R. (1989a). *The rustle of language* (R. Howard, Trans.). Berkeley: University of California Press (Original 1986, France).
Barthes, R. (1989b). *The pleasure of the text* (R. Miller, Trans.). Oxford: Basil Blackwell (Original 1973, France).
Butler, J. (1997). *Excitable speech. A politics of the performative.* New York: Routledge.

Cixous, H. (1993). *Three steps on the ladder of writing* (S. Cornell & S. Sellers, Trans.). New York: Columbia University Press.

Cixous, H., & Calle-Gruber, M. (1997). *Hélène Cixous, rootprints: Memory and life writing* (E. Prenowitz, Trans.). London: Routledge.

Davies, B. (2009). Life in Kings Cross: a play of voices. In A. Jackson & L. Mazzei (Eds.), *Voice in qualitative inquiry: Challenging conventional, interpretive and critical conceptions in qualitative research* (pp. 197–219). New York: Routledge.

Deleuze, G. (1990). *Negotiations* (M. Joughin, Trans.). New York: Columbia University Press.

Deleuze, G. (1997). Literature and life. In G. Deleuze, *Essays critical and clinical* (D. W. Smith & M. A. Greco, Trans.) (pp. 1–6). Minneapolis: University of Minnesota Press.

Deleuze, G. (2005). *Difference and repetition* (P. Patton, Trans.). New York: Columbia University Press (Original 1968, France).

Lehrer, J. (2007). *Proust was a neuroscientist.* Boston: Houghton Mifflin Company.

Smith, D. W. (1997). "A life of pure immanence": Deleuze's "Critique et Clinique" project. In G. Deleuze, *Essays critical and clinical* (D. W. Smith & M. A. Greco, Trans.) (pp. xi-lvi). Minneapolis: University of Minnesota Press.

Thomas, D. (1954). *Under Milk Wood.* New York: New Directions Publishing Corporation.

Williams, J. (2003). *Gilles Deleuze's Difference and Repetition: A critical introduction and guide.* Edinburgh: Edinburgh University Press.

Bronwyn Davies
University of Melbourne

SUSANNE GANNON

WALKING MY WAY BACK HOME

Place-making begins with the investigation of oneself in place, and with the experience of the body—a particular enfleshed body—situated in a particular material and affective landscape. The body in this chapter is my body. It is my body in a place that I used to call home, and that I still respond to as home with a resonance in the deep folds of my body. In contrast to the writing projects in earlier chapters that focus on places of the present for their authors, on new places to which they have come to live, this chapter and the poetic text at the heart of it attends to the past as much as it does to the present. This is a poem of longing, and of the ambivalent love I continue to feel for a particular place, the small beachside suburb in the northern wet tropics of Australia, in north Queensland where I lived for more than a decade. I wrote it on a visit back there, five years after leaving, when a friend loaned me her house for a week. I lived quietly for that week in the present and the past, knowing and not knowing this place and myself within it, belonging and not belonging at the same time. Walking and writing, poetically mapping my memories of the places I passed, became my daily practice and my strategy for walking my way back home.

MAPPING MACHANS BEACH

1

Barr Creek blocks the way north except when tide fall
and sand drift open the path to the next demographic:
huge houses fringed by fallen palms, tilting
closer to the Coral Sea with each king tide

Some Sundays, I'd miss the low tide home,
carry clothes on my head, wade chest high,
thinking of young bulls floating out to sea
and crocodiles hungry and heading for home

To the south, the dark waters of Redden Creek
flooded mangroves, silence broken by tt-tt-tt-tt
of tinnies at dawn. From the bridge, cast-nets
flower and fall, rise wet and silver with fish

M. Somerville, B. Davies, K. Power, S. Gannon and *P. de Carteret,*
Place Pedagogy Change, 45–50.

Then the black slash where the Barron River
meets the sea. Across the water, tin glitters
from camps at Dungara, the new-old name
for the far shore, home for fishermen and ghosts

Here are low tide runnels and peninsulas
of toe sucking mud, a grandmother's ashes,
fragments of burnt bone, seaweed and shells
beached along the high water mark

East is water all the way to Vanuatu, drowned ridges
of reef, grief and excised borders. Granite boulders
mark land's end, mixed with concrete, stubbled
with debris, driftwood and tumbled terracotta

At low tide, crabs scuttle into shade. Locals promenade
on bitumen in sarongs and thongs, stubbies and shorts.
Morning and evening shifts for the workers, stray
fisherfolk and lost tourists looking for a beach

Westward, past streets of fibro houses, a patchwork
of cane stubble, green blades and feathered flowers
taller than a man. The creek curves by the road, flood lines
on a post: one, two, three metres above sea level

Remember post-cyclone weeks when only the post office
dinghy could get us and the beer in and out, helicopter
drops on the radar field of milk and bread and methadone.
Storm surge maps show all of it under, all of it gone

2

Half light and I rise to the *owk owk* of friarbirds. Turning
up Marshall Street, I slam the lattice gate behind me,
damp wood distended by old rain. Always looping
around the back to begin again, saving the front
for a southward tilt towards the early sun

Bitumen turns to sand and I track behind houses.
On my left a broad expanse of kikuyu, the bush beyond
where kids and kerosene collided one night in a carnival
of sirens and firetrucks and crackling spitting flames

The skirr of rainbow bee-eaters rises to meet me,
wings blurring yellow, green and black. Ragged orchards
of pink-tipped mangoes, bananas, beach almonds, Toyotas,
scruffy backsides of houses, a verandah that was almost mine

I skittered away from home then, spooked by phone calls
and a season of break and enters, slept in the bed

of a writer split between New York and the islands;
sat in her writing room, watched her long low view of the hills

The sand sweeps around to the ocean, thongs
looped in my fingers, I see again the dreadlocked man
from Fortaleza, his slow arabesque of legs and hair
spinning against a blue sky, capoeira on the beach at dawn

I step up the new metal grids, missing the old angles,
the higgledy piggledy blocks of warm stone. Once,
when the tide was high and the light low, we floated
flowers here for a neighbour who followed love too far

3

I come up by the stinger vinegar and peel-off
dog-shit bags. A gull sits on the *No Parking* sign
A Wicked Camper stirs in the morning heat, groans,
opens, unfurls blond limbs in fisherman pants

Palms along the water are bereft of coconuts.
The two old melaleucas gone from the house I shared,
and the friend who might have died any day,
who tangos with a new heart half a continent away

Hammock furled under the eaves, here is the house
of everyone's querida, now in Timor Leste
with the weaving women. Remember the telenovela Easter
when she fell through the floor and rose up laughing

The blue and orange doctor's house, long grassed,
littered with sturdy children and plastic climbing frames.
A blue pram sits by the road. There is a boom of babies
named for stars or minerals or movements of the earth

The house with red blinds like eyelids. A son-in-law
who lived one street back, beside me, night screams,
calls to cops, the wife a pale blonde wearing plaster,
their quivering child, their over-the-fence escape route

4

My ankle twitches by the paperbark roundabout where
Arnold Street hits the beach. The bitumen is smooth now,
the council wary of just-a-couple-of-glasses-after-dinner
and a-walk-around-the-block stumbles after dark

Then the louvred house of parties of tumblers
and poets, pineapple risotto and PhDs. A stranger

on an esky is the just-left-yesterday husband of
my best friend when I was seven, three states away

Losing my place, I turn back to the swollen gate.
I could go on, and do on other mornings, past houses
and people I've loved, places where waves broke
over me and showers of comets fell from the sky

WALKING, POETRY AND REMEMBERING

Though a poem can speak for itself, and by itself, and though some readers may choose to leave me here, I'd like to close this chapter with some reflections on poetic intention, poetic language and the process of walking and writing as a strategy for researching place. The works of certain theorists, including Bachelard and Deleuze and those who work with concepts generated by them, are helpful to me for thinking through these issues and broader questions about home, place, affect and subjectivity.

In writing the past into the present in the poem, I aim to multiply the narratives of this particular place as they play out on my body and in the memories evoked as I walk my old morning route. There is no dominant or singular story of me in this place. There are instead many stories, fragments of stories, sensory impressions that cross and criss-cross my path. Each step documents sights and sounds in the present alongside these memories. Spectres of the past come and go through the poem, creating a rhythm of emergence and disappearance, of remembering and of forgetting, as I move step by step along the streets and paths of my old neighbourhood. Wylie suggests that walking is always imbued with this sort of haunting, as the walker is always 'poised between the country ahead and the country behind, between one step and the next, epiphany and penumbra, he or she is, in other words, spectral; between there and not-there, perpetually caught in an apparitional process of arriving/departing' (2005, p. 237). Like Wylie's walker, I (poet-narrator-writer-walker) am both there and not-there, both here and not-here, and my stories of place-making in this walking and writing are necessarily transient, impressionistic and fragmented.

My body also has its own story of walking in this place. Its story is, like all stories, a sequence of movements through time and space. This is a walk to which my body is habituated, already deeply known in my body. My body turns in one direction rather than the other, to the left instead of to the right, when I exit the gate of my friend's house because this is how my body remembers, how it knows this story goes. My body turns this way as it calibrates for light and shadow and the direction of the sun at this time of the day and the year, and for the contours of land and the rhythms of the morning movements of the other inhabitants.

The poetic mapping in this chapter moves through multiple dimensions of place at the same time. As well as the spatial axis of my walk around the streets and pathways of the neighbourhood, the memories that rise and fade through the poem also create a temporal axis as my footsteps in the present link to moments from the past. The temporal premise of the poem suggests what Coleman describes as a

Deleuzian 'understanding of temporality not as linear but as dynamic and heterogeneous; time does not (only) progress from past to present to future but rather...time is multiple and assembling' (2008, p. 86).

Walking is crucial for the language of the poem. The pace of my walk suits the pace of this poem. They proceed step by step, syllable by syllable, phrase by phrase, line by line, stanza by stanza. In this poem I use poetic strategies of alliteration and assonance, metre, rhythm, rhyme and half rhyme to heighten the patterns of sound in the language and slow the pace of the poem for the reader. The white space in the poem on the page also slows the reader, keeps the reader following the steady pace of the walker-writer. As I wrote and rewrote the poem, I too needed to slow my thoughts and take my time. The process of writing the poem seems to be deeply entangled with the practice of walking. In writing the poem I also kept in mind that poetic language can compress meaning. Words can mean more than just one thing at a time, so it may take the reader a little longer to follow the thread of a metaphor, or to take in the surprise of a word that's not quite the most obvious one that might have been used. At the same time as poetic imagery might slow the reading, it can also be immediate in its effects, in the unpredictable and idiosyncratic ways it presses on the imagination of each reader. These were some of the ways I worked with the possibilities of poetic language in my own research and writing of place.

My writing practice resonates with Bachelard's use of poetic language for 'topoanalysis', the systematic study of the 'sites of our intimate lives' (1994, p. 8). My walk, and the poem I wrote after my walk, could be understood as topoanalysis located in the intimacy of my old neighbourhood. Bachelard suggests that poetic images provoke 'resonances and repercussions' that take the reader beyond more prosaic understandings or those that rely on causal explanations or psychological understandings (1994, p. xxiii). Poetry invokes a different sort of knowing that is at once more immediate and more subtle. For Bachelard, rather than a flat representation in language, 'the poetic image is an emergence from language, it is always a little above the language of signification' (1994, p. xxvii). Poetry weaves together real and unreal, giving 'dynamism to language' (1994, p. xxxv). In this context, poetic language can be seen as facilitating 'a vitality of the word which creates, in its flight, a reality bursting with nuances that surpass the reality signified by natural language' (Perraudin, 2008, p. 474). The objects and sensations that impress themselves on the walker draw up fragments of memory that appear and disappear instantly as they are displaced by other fragments. Poetic language provides some sense of this constant movement of thought and sensation.

This poem explores subjectivity in place as I walk (and write) through a space that is relational and dynamic, mutable and capricious. This space is created from moment to moment by complex forces, influences and practices, including the practices of encountering, remembering and forgetting. In Massey's terms, the space of the poem could be understood as a 'sphere of relations, of contemporaneous multiplicity...a change in the angle of vision...towards the entanglements and configurations of multiple trajectories, multiple histories' (2005, p. 148). In this space my body, moving through space, and through the text, is the nexus of affect, the locus of events, the point of connection of multiple lines of being and becoming. In the poem that tries to capture these entanglements, my moving body becomes a scriptural space onto which affect, memory, present and past mo(ve)ments are written in a multidimensional mapping exercise. This strategy of researching place displaces the independent researcher subject, who is disconnected and outside place, with a subject who responds to her place in a myriad of ways through her body, her memory, all her senses and all her intelligences. This project situated me as the subject as a walker, as a writer and as a researcher yet it simultaneously dissolved this subject.

This inquiry into subjectivity in place suggests a different and more complex sort of subject than that assumed by positivist research paradigms. Subjectivity in this sense is "exteriority", formed through processes that are spatial, environmental and social as well as discursive (Stratford, 2007, p. 135). Affect is of crucial importance in this project. For me as a poet writing and walking, the present and past collide in the affective domain. My body moving through this place becomes a site of affective contact with other bodies, including ethereal and atmospheric bodies as well as substantive bodies. Uhlmann describes the visceral impact of affect as what happens 'when light strikes our eyes, a sound strikes our ear drums, someone [or something] touches us, or…an image of another body occurs to us' (Uhlmann, 2009, p. 61). Affect comes from the outside, it is externally generated and it is through affective causal chains, Uhlmann argues, that the subject is constituted and becomes recognisable to herself. In this research into one of my own places, my body was moved by the movements of light and air, and of tides and time, as well as by trees, houses and birds, and the spectral figures caught in the corner of my mind's eye and conjured into the present through language. I walked and wrote myself into place, recognising myself in this place and of this place, folding myself into it through my steps and through my words.

REFERENCES

Bachelard, G. (1994). *The poetics of space* (M. Jolas, Trans.). Boston: Beacon Press (Original 1958).
Coleman, R. (2008). Things that stay: feminist theory, duration and the future. *Time and Society, 17*(1), 85–102.
Massey, D. (2005). *For space.* London: Sage.
Perraudin, J. F. (2008). A non-Bergsonian Bachelard. *Continental Philosophy Review, 41*(4), 463–479.
Stratford, H. (2007). Micro-strategies of resistance. In D. Petrescu (Ed.), *Altering practices: Feminist politics and poetics of space* (pp. 125–140). London: Routledge.
Uhlmann, A. (2009). Expression and affect in Kleist, Beckett and Deleuze. In L. Cull (Ed.), *Deleuze and performance* (pp. 54–71). Edinburgh: Edinburgh University Press.
Wylie, J. (2005). A single day's walking: narrating self and landscape on the South West Coast Path. *Transactions of the Institute of British Geographers, 30*(2), 234–247.

Susanne Gannon
University of Western Sydney

KERITH POWER

GETTING LOST IN LOGAN

One Sunday morning, as I went walking, by Brisbane waters I chanced to stray.

I heard a convict his fate bewailing, as on the sunny river bank he lay.
I am a native of Erin's island, and banished now from my native shore.
They tore me from my aged parents, and from the maiden I do adore.

For three long years I was beastly treated, and heavy irons on my legs I wore.
My back with flogging is lacerated, and often painted with my crimson gore.
And many a man from downright starvation lies mouldering now underneath the clay.
And Captain Logan he had us mangled at the triangles of Moreton Bay.

(Anon.)

Before I came to Logan the only thing I knew about it was this dark song about its name. The Governor of the former penal colony of Moreton Bay (now Brisbane, the capital city of Queensland on the north-east cost of Australia), Captain Patrick Logan, is immortalised as a brutal tyrant who was eventually killed by the spear of an Indigenous resistance warrior, to the rejoicing of the convicts. To me, on arrival in the place, it seemed no coincidence that the song refers to exile as well as to crime.

I came to Logan as a newcomer from a small country town at the beginning of 2005 to work as a teacher educator in an outer suburban campus of Griffith University. For the first two months my most consistent experience of place was getting lost in Logan. I would set out along the freeway (in itself a terrifying experience), drive rapidly for half an hour, turn off at Exit 23 and confidently follow the signs to one of many shopping centres, assuming that I could easily conduct my "settling in" business and then proceed to my new workplace. For the first few weeks I was consistently very late to work. The strip malls stretched out too far apart to walk in the thirty six degree Celsius heat and too close together for the car air conditioning to take effect. In Logan Central, Loganlea, Loganholme and Beenleigh I walked through apparently identical shopping malls, finding many people of different cultural origins, many ATM machines and consumer goods, but no bank branches or other community amenities such as a post office, library, neighbourhood centre, corner store or community information centre where I could ask my way. I could recognise nothing as a centre of Logan.

M. Somerville, B. Davies, K. Power, S. Gannon and P. de Carteret,
Place Pedagogy Change, 51–62.
© 2011 Sense Publishers. All rights reserved.

Logan is a satellite city located midway between Brisbane and the Gold Coast. It is one of the fastest growing suburban fringe cities in Australia, bisected by a major freeway and populated by one hundred and seventy thousand people from an estimated one hundred and sixty different cultural backgrounds. My experience of getting lost in Logan led me to rely more and more on a street directory. In the 2001 Australian census, thirty percent of Logan's residents reported being overseas born(Australian Bureau of Statistics, 2001). I wondered how the many newcomers from other countries, who often cannot afford cars and do not read or speak English, manage to settle in Logan, to find the services they need and to negotiate their daily lives. During my two years' stay, I collected stories from "Anglo", immigrant and Indigenous Logan "locals", from teachers in schools and colleagues on campus, from parents and children. All but a few records of these conversations were lost in a computer crash and so this account is drawn from the surviving audiotape transcripts of conversations, journal entries and memory.

Lather (2007, p. 7) describes '(post) critical ethnography' as 'what would be made possible if we were to think ethnography otherwise, as a space surprised by difference into the performance of practices of not-knowing', in which 'one situates oneself as curious and unknowing...[H]ere is where the journey of thinking differently begins'. The loss of much of my data has enabled me to think differently.

My belief that systematically collected "data" will shore up the truth and authority of the storylines I construct about Logan (see Introduction) betrays the 'positivist tail' (Davies, 2010) in my poststructuralism, what St Pierre describes as 'the belief that true knowledge is produced through the rational observation and description of a reality detached from the observer' (2000, p. 495). Freed from the anchor of data, key memories surfaced and clustered around episodes of being 'surprised by difference' (Lather, 2007, p. 7). I read the persistence of these memories of surprise as bodily signals that, at those moments, the possibility of new knowledge was enabled by my entry into a 'cultural contact zone' where presuppositions were confounded (Carter, 1992; Pratt, 1992).

Logan is portrayed on billboards, on television and on the Logan City Council website as an example of the lifestyle of Queensland's "Great South East", the fastest growing area of population in Australia. The billboards proclaim *Loving life in Logan* and portray young smiling residents doing exciting outdoor activities. The TV advertisements refer to the constant physical and social change as part of the dynamism and excitement of the area. The Council website portrays representatives of different cultures of origin, again all smiling, and has links to community festivals, activities and events. The thrust of these public stories of place is of exciting, dynamic change and an optimistic future based on getting ahead in a new country.

Community profiles on the Council website contain statistics pointing to many recent arrivals, a young population and a wide range of economic indicators. Half Logan's people have been there less than five years. While the top five languages (other than English) spoken at home at the time of my research were Samoan, Chinese, Spanish, Khmer, and Tagalog/Filipino, it was estimated that one hundred and sixty different cultures were represented in Logan (Logan City Council, 2005). In common with other marginal communities, such as the Latrobe Valley and Sydney's Kings Cross and Western Sydney (see other chapters in this book), demographic representations of Logan commonly mutate in media and community services circles into storylines of deficit, difficulty and disadvantage that erase the variety of the lived experience of many of its residents. In the public imaginary, Logan has become a pathologised place. For example, it has been identified as one of five special police districts for the purpose of dealing with substance abuse by young people (Logan Youth Legal Service, 2010) and as the site of the second highest incidence of domestic violence in Queensland (Tang, 2009). Stories based on the Indigenous, convict and settler past, others of hardship and trauma, or of leaving other places to end up in Logan, are less often told. The stories below problematise the possibility of definitively knowing Logan.

DRIVING

Getting lost in Logan began as I was daily channelled to and from the inner city in my car along freeways and main roads, separated by glass, metal and motor noise from a physical experience of place. I was disembodied, dislocated from the surroundings. This community puts priority on the car. That has implications for community cohesion, for environmental pollution, and for the ways that streets are laid out and commercial areas distributed.

Logan is bisected and bounded by freeways. From the north east, the Gateway Motorway skirts the Karawatha Forest from the airport inland to Mount Lindesay, where the Logan River rises. Making an X with the Gateway from the north west, the South East Freeway divides the flat western suburbs from the hilly, leafier east, running towards the beaches and tourist towers of "glitter city", the Gold Coast. The Logan Motorway forms the base of a triangle joining the two, roughly following a bend downstream in the lower Logan River. Kingston Road, down the middle of the triangle, surrounded by suburban housing, features a large advertising billboard picturing a forested river bend labelled *Logan: a great place for nature.* This billboard is juxtaposed against a "Boys Town" sign, a tangle of overhead powerlines, telephone wires, and a chain-link fenced and concrete-walled overpass over the suburban railway. The river portrayed in this first sign was invisible from any of the roads I travelled. Likewise, I saw the Buddhist Fo Guang Shan Chung Tian Temple pagoda only on a billboard. Labelled *Logan: a great place for culture* on the Logan Motorway, the actual temple is a place of worship, where parents can take their young children to be blessed on the Buddha's birthday.

Branching out from my initial commuting route, the freeway journey to and from the inner city, I studied the street directory to memorise the correct exits to reach students on professional placements in schools, and local organisations and residents. These patterns of movement eventually inscribed directional synapses in my brain, thicker along the major routes centred on the Meadowbrook campus, functioning more like a rhizome than a web and wisping out at the extremities like the hair roots of plants. At the destinations of these excursions I began to walk around the suburbs.

WALKING

My purpose in walking was to "learn place", to feel for myself what it might be like to live in Logan. Place, in nineteenth and twentieth century Australian early childhood educational theory and practice, has largely been delimited in discussions about "learning environments". Pedagogy expressed through architectural design can be traced in Froebel-inspired kindergarten circles symbolising "wholeness and purity", in the child-sized furniture, hand-sized learning materials and emphasis on physical order in Montessori preschools, and in the workstation/pathway designs of the British nursery school tradition. Jim Greenman (1988) brought to Australia the influence of the 1970s place-based learning movement on the design of early childhood centres. In the late twentieth century, franchised multinational childcare centres developed their own plasticised cartoon-style look and feel to create and also to cater for the demand for homogenised childhoods. Each of these design traditions, while they occurred in social, historical and spatial contexts, is characterised by a developmentalist construction of childhood. Although children have been regarded as malleable, vulnerable and nescient beings, child psychology has simultaneously constructed them as unique individuals unfolding according to a decontextualised, universal pattern that constitutes the norm. Bronfenbrenner's (1979) ecological systems theory forms a conceptual bridge to the social constructivist and postmodernist framework influencing practice in curriculum approaches, such as those practised in Reggio Emilia, Italy and more recently in the 'intra-active pedagogy' proposed by Hillevi Lenz-Taguchi (2009). While context forms the foreground of Lenz-Taguchi's recognition of the pedagogical force of physical artefacts and materials, place remains an unmarked category in early childhood education with the exception of a few examples such as the Norwegian *friluftsbarnehager*[i] and Reggio Emilia[ii]. One of the principles of the Reggio Emilia approach is that the environment is the third teacher. The spatial/aesthetic principles termed 'osmosis' and 'transparency' by Ceppi and Zini (1998) denote the pedagogical focus of Reggio Emilia schools on the space of connection between school and community.

I wanted to put place at the forefront of my own learning by placing my body physically in the streets of Logan, in the neighbourhoods surrounding schools and preschools. I chose to employ a local context observation schedule (Barnes McGuire, 1997) to systematise my observations. Originating in the discipline of community psychology, this instrument was designed to assess the amenity of neighbourhoods as places to raise young children. It was used in the United Kingdom in conjunction with other instruments to select "disadvantaged" neighbourhoods for implementing the national Sure Start program[iii]. One feature of Sure Start, distinguishing it from national programs elsewhere such as Headstart in the United States, is its focus on neighbourhoods rather than on individuals. My rationale for choosing such an instrument was the characterisation of this schedule as "place based". As a relatively non-intrusive and low risk "research method" I thought it could potentially be used by a large number of early childhood students to awaken their curiosity in learning place.

Over a period of six weeks I filled in the schedule by walking in five different areas in Logan. I selected these from the nineteen statistical local areas of Logan identified in the Australian census. In each area I walked ten residential streets and three commercial/industrial locations. I visited Shailer Park, Tanah Merah, Woodridge, Kingston and Marsden. The walk took from thirty minutes to two hours in each area. The questions in the schedule directed my attention in residential areas to the general condition of houses, the level of security employed, the volume of traffic, the prevalence and behaviour of local residents on the street and the level of personal safety and comfort I felt in each place. In commercial/industrial places I observed and recorded the street life, the physical characteristics of housing, the character of public social life and the kinds of industries, businesses and institutions.

While ethical and methodological considerations abound in making a critique of the assumptions behind a standardised instrument of this kind—how the specific wording of the questions in this particular schedule might have skewed my responses, and the potential for objectification in any act of observation—it is possible to make a rough guess at how people might live by the ways they care or do not care for their houses and surroundings. It is possible to bring a reading to some of the social life in the commercial areas from the trade taking place at a charity shop in Kingston, strip malls in Marsden, the library in the Marsden Park shopping centre, the local liquor store and betting shop in Woodridge next to a large commercial child care centre, the swimming pool factory, garden centre and funeral parlour at Tanah Merah and the palatial air conditioned Hyperdome shopping mall at Shailer Park. The absences also seem significant, such as the difficulty in finding a bank branch or post office, on foot, among the strip malls. This could be a manifestation of car culture. To document my wanderings and wonderings around Logan, I marked the places I walked on a large wall map which showed the geographical relationships between the places I walked and the areas I still had left to cover. Later I did the same with students' walking routes.

Many areas I visited fitted a stereotypical image of family accommodation in suburban Australia: detached bungalow-style houses surrounded by yards or gardens, set back from the street on separate blocks of land. In Logan, the local social status of the housing depends on whether the area is east or west of the South East Freeway leading from Brisbane to the Gold Coast. Influences on the social status of the housing are its location, whether it is owner-occupied or publicly provided, its age and condition and the size of the block of land, which impacts on the privacy of the occupants. Land located on hills with a northerly or easterly view, and which catches cool breezes, has more commercial value and social cachet than flat land. Non-tourist caravan parks and large blocks of flats house people on low incomes such as students, unemployed people and elderly/retired people. These communal types of housing are concentrated on main roads. Bus routes run along the major roads and so the people who don't own vehicles are living along the most heavily trafficked areas.

At Shailer Park, east of the freeway on a north–south ridge, house blocks were bigger, and houses were larger, newer, made of brick and set back from the street. Built-in garages and security screen doors made it possible in this suburb for the landscaped front lawns and gardens to remain unfenced. At school closing time, earlier than the end of a standard adult working day, a procession of cars picking up children led me to wonder why few children seemed to walk to and from school. In Tanah Merah, just west of the freeway, while they were varied in design, house blocks and houses were smaller, closer together, fenced off from the street and made of less expensive materials such as weatherboard, with corrugated iron roofs. They looked neat and well maintained but gave the impression of less affluence. Further west on the flat land in Woodridge, Kingston and Marsden, the bungalows were built in two or three standardised designs characteristic of public housing schemes. These houses were smaller, some constructed of fibro-cement. This dates them back to the 1950s. In Marsden, Woodridge and Tanah Merah, caravan parks and flats sat adjacent to the freeway.

My first surprise was that I was often the only person on the street. My journal records: 'the absence of people in most of my observations indicates that what I am in is a dormitory suburb: that most people are either inside or at work…or if they aren't, they're at the Logan central shopping centre'. Maybe only poor people and researchers walk in Logan. The hot summer temperatures affect people's behaviour; it is unusual to walk outdoors in the subtropical climate in summer. Air-conditioned shopping centres, a few of which also contain community amenities such as libraries and post offices, are favoured areas in which people congregate. The air conditioning alone is a huge environmental factor. Ironically, while its cooling indoors adds a degree of separation from the climate, its power consumption contributes to global warming.

Using the observation schedule was not intended to develop a representation of the reality of living in Logan. The schedule proved to be valuable in focusing my attention, through my own bodily experience of each place, on relationships between people and places. The bodily act of walking and of systematically observing places added a dimension to my emerging insights into how it might be to live, work and shop there, that would be impossible to gain in any other way. Later into my working year, I initiated a process of "hanging out" with the locals.

HANGING OUT

The local context observation survey limited my capacity to learn how people inhabit Logan. My observations of other people's bodies were the only evidence available by which to infer some aspects of their lives. Seemingly obvious "racial" markers like skin colour were not a very useful starting point, as it was not possible to determine from these alone what people's cultural or ethnic origins or current social practices might be. However, the proportion of "Anglo" to "non-Anglo" looking people indicated that particular neighbourhoods have concentrations of people from certain nationalities, cultures or ethnicities. Age, clothing, behaviour, and people's particular locations at particular times of the day seemed to tell me more, such as whether the person had access to a car, was of employable age, whether they were dressed as if for work, in school uniform or casual clothes, whether they seemed to be at leisure, buying alcohol, placing a bet, using the public phone, smoking, catching a bus or train, picking up children or taking a lunch break from work.

I have learned to read the experience of personal discomfort as a sign that I am entering a cross-cultural contact zone. Besides schools, these contact zones in Logan are found around the few public amenities, which are often commercial entities such as shopping complexes where everyone has to go to obtain food and services. In answer to the question in the local context observation schedule about how I felt administering the survey, I felt like a stranger, out of place in the poorest residential areas such as Woodridge, which seemed to have a higher proportion of Indigenous Australians and Pacific Islanders, but quite comfortable in "neutral" spaces such as the Marsden Park shopping centre, where there was a wide variety of ethnic backgrounds and some of the businesses and professional offices belonged to people from earlier waves of immigration from Greece or central Europe. My later collaborative work with Samoan colleagues eased the discomfort of unfamiliarity.

My prior teaching as a rural preschool teacher meant that hanging out in Queensland state primary schools was a shock. I was used to a single small building per site, containing up to twenty nine children and at least two adults in reasonably intimate daily communication. The sheer scale and size of Queensland schools was confronting, with eight age grades, from five to twelve, accommodated in three or four barn-like double classrooms, each holding fifty children and two teachers. The regimentation that seemed to be *de rigueur* to manage children in these numbers was different from my ideal of effective classroom practice. I consistently got lost in the schools. As I was required to show my "blue card"[iv] at each school office before finding a specific classroom, I spent the first ten or so minutes at each new school finding the office. I then cooled my heels at the reception desk, often together with a few "naughty" children. Thus demoralised, my sympathies crept towards the naughty ones. Hanging out with a second grader taking "time out" for an unknown transgression, I was delighted when I whispered that my name was Doctor Power that he whispered back, wide-eyed, 'can you fly?' It felt cruel to bring us both back to earth with the scientific truth.

English as a second language is an issue in Logan primary schools. Departmental policy is to routinely assist secondary students, but help for younger children is not guaranteed (Department of Education and Training, 2010). At the time I was "hanging out", I saw few schools dealing with language differences in the early grades. Most seemed engaged in a process of normalisation—'you will all learn English or you will drown in this community and if possible you'll paint yourself white at the same time' (Personal journal, 2005). At Griffith University some of my colleagues talked about teacher education students from different countries not being able to handle their professional placements, because they speak an accented English that Queensland children can't understand. It seemed like prejudice to me. I wondered how many teachers could accommodate, or teach the children, ways of coping with difference.

Some of the work my students did with me deepened my understanding of human issues of displacement. Kathleen, a mature age student in the specialist early childhood strand, carried out an advocacy project in her final semester with MultiLink[v]. She found that refugee children were placed in childcare while their parents attended compulsory English classes. When they were separated from their children, some recently arrived parents didn't know if they were ever going to see them again. Many of the childcare workers, monolingual in English, did not know or learn the children's names. Kathleen devised a table of "survival" phrases in twenty four different languages, like 'mum will be back soon', 'my name is...what is your name?', 'do you want to eat?', 'do you want a drink?', 'do you want to go to the toilet?', so that the child care workers could have a few words in the principal languages of the children. I knew of no system-wide strategy similar to this initiative by a teacher education student.

Last year, Woodridge State School won the 2009 Showcase Award for Excellence in Inclusive Education with a program called *We Are One In Woodridge.* The background statement of the award reads:

> At Woodridge State Primary School 75% of our students do not speak standard Australian English, however, we as educators recognize and respect the unique attributes of <u>every</u> learner...An ILC (Intensive Language Centre) is supporting all new arrival students particularly humanitarian refugees. We have 6 full-time ESL teachers who are responsible for the acceleration of the students' acquisition of the English language to enable them to participate in mainstream education with confidence as quickly as possible. (Woodridge State School, 2009)

The intensive effort put into this school's engagement with its community includes employing Community Liaison Officers from among the different immigrant groups. An Indigenous aide/liaison officer is also employed, and there are multiple links and partnerships with a brief to assist migrants and refugees directly reaching out to families and agencies. The initiatives with Samoan families, the beginnings of which I describe below, have culminated in a series of '10 illustrated bilingual texts written in Samoan and English. Each set consists of A3 Big Books and A5 readers with texts provided in both English and Samoan' (Woodridge State School, 2009).

I learned more about Logan hanging around with my final year early childhood specialist students, most of whom were Logan residents. They told me some neighbourhoods are known to have concentrations of Indigenous people: for example, Woodridge has more Aboriginal and Islander Australians and Samoan immigrants; Underwood has a concentration of Muslims. The most recent groups of refugees and immigrants in 2006 were from Sudan and Ethiopia. In 2010 the national origins of students includes Burundian, Burmese, Rwandan, Congolese, Filipino and Liberian.

In the early childhood students' final year, not wanting to single out the one Indigenous looking class member and yet wanting raise issues of Indigeneity, I initiated a discussion on "whiteness" based on work by Pettman (1992). On reading an account of how it feels to be regarded with suspicion by all around you, in contrast to the anonymity of white privilege, some non-Indigenous students were moved to tears, indignation and hopefully constructive action. A second, unexpected discursive effect of opening up this discussion occurred. An apparently "white" student presented as her final advocacy assignment a detailed project (with a side reference to Captain Logan) about the oral history, geographical boundaries, Yugambeh and Jaggera language, elders and clan groups of her Indigenous places and people in the Logan area.

The students described the freeway as a distinct social divider, recognised as such in social conversations and discourses. East (towards the Coast) is considered "posher" than west. In my second year in Logan I began a small-scale investigation called *Local Stories, Local Literacies @ Logan*. This investigation of early literacies as social practice in a group of Logan parents and children involved hanging out with the Tuesday Possums playgroup run by specialist early childhood student Annette, with her daughters Britney (four) and Alannah (two and a half) and friends, in the family backyard, one block west of the South East Freeway. With the usual set of false starts, getting lost in trying to locate the correct freeway exit, I joined these young women and their young children for one morning each week for two months.

Annette, the only person in her peer group undertaking tertiary education, would lay out a few informal activities for the children each Tuesday, such as chalk for writing on the concrete, a fabric tunnel and two or three wheeled toys. Conversations about daily lives and plans flowed around the children's play, uninterrupted by pushing toddlers on the swing, preventing accidents and supplying food, drink and comfort. My interest in these everyday conversations was in learning about how young children, in the contexts of their families and communities in Logan City, learned to communicate and make meaning. I initially learned how their parents mapped Logan. Like other aspirational parents on the west side of the freeway, Annette and her husband had carefully considered where to send Britney to her first school, and had chosen one on the eastern side because they believed it offered a higher educational quality than closer schools on their own side. Further conversations surprised me greatly, as I realised the differences between what Annette and her friends valued and my own values and playgroup experience as a parent thirty years before.

My fellow playgroup parents in the 1970s started me along the pathway to feminism. I spent much of my private and professional time in the 1980s lobbying governments to fund early childhood and women's services. I was astonished twenty five years on by these younger (Logan) women's easy acceptance of the climate of marketisation (Woodrow & Brennan, 1999) of early childhood care and education. The concept of childcare as a public good was absent from their maps.

They thought they had to buy everything. Together with the serious exchanges about educational options and how to raise children, product demonstrations and occasional adult outings (some rather *risqué*) were embedded into the playgroup routine. Britney's fifth birthday party was to be purchased at Wriggle It children's indoor play centre and café. To finance her study Annette worked at a large private childcare centre on one of Logan's major roads. To set the Bougainvillea Centre off from the other retail outlets in the strip mall, it was marked by two pairs of gigantic concrete "Greek" columns set out at right angles to each other on the street corner, with its name lettered in purple Times New Roman across the lintel and on circular cartoon-coloured billboards suspended between the columns. Was this the women's liberation I had envisaged? Did Annette experience any conflict between what she was learning at university and the commercial ambience of her workplace?

I was invited into the homes and churches of Samoan families to assist with research about the literacy of Samoan children. Concerned about cultural maintenance, parents and community leaders also wanted the best futures for their children through education (Dobrenov-Major et al., 2004). Concern about the gap between Indigenous and non-Indigenous Australians' literacy achievement in standardised tests had up to this point obscured the fact that English print literacy scores among Samoan Australian children were even lower than those among Indigenous children (Kearney, Fletcher & Dobrenov-Major, 2006). In my final close encounter with Logan locals, when I became lost in the suburbs, my guide described my landmark as 'the house with sugar cane and coconut palms growing in the front garden'. When I arrived at the house, I was surprised by the fifteen or so pairs of shoes on the front verandah, indicating that many people lived in this house. I entered a world of family and church connections, of Sundays routinely filled with deep harmony singing and group activities for every age group for the entire day. In kind consideration for me as the non-Polynesian speaking university guest, the pastor and congregation of a mega-church conducted an entire service in English.

As a respected Elder took me to visit Samoan parents at home and at work, I began to see the stores selling colourful clothing, Polynesian music and kumara.[vi] My map of Logan became enriched by traditional stories of Pacific canoe journeys, and contemporary stories of migrations, relationships and learning place in Logan. In one small house in Woodridge, the poorest suburb, I was intrigued by a pile of new electrical goods in the living room. The threads of family obligation extend from Logan families, often via New Zealand, back to Samoa. Money, consumer goods and family members frequently travel back to the home clan. In this context of rich connection, the meanings of school-based social practices are perhaps rather hard to decode or too alien to engage the children's attention.

By driving, walking and hanging out in Logan I entered into a process of learning place and building community. In this process I discovered and questioned the binary positioning of "white" and "dark" that superficially represented Logan. My bodily distress in the cultural contact zone of the streets was alleviated by meeting and getting to know some of the people to whom I had at first felt like a stranger. As I witnessed the rapid spread of housing estates into rural areas south of the Logan River, I wondered about the contradictory storylines simultaneously erasing and honouring the "natural" and "cultural" diversity of this place. The work of a minority of teacher education students and schools addresses difference and diversity by reaching out to include different language speakers in a project of inclusive education.

Somerville (2010) identifies cultural contact zones as one of the aspects of enabling place pedagogies that can generate new storylines of social and cultural identity. Public schools are the most prevalent state provided and sanctioned sites for cross cultural contact with and between children and adults. The twelve large new schools built as I left Logan were being fore grounded as potential centres for building community in South East Queensland. Place pedagogies may be an approach to accommodating the "dark" and "white" stories, the environmental effects of change, the place connections and the community-building necessities of people living in Logan's cultural contact zones.

NOTES

[i]   These are outdoor preschools where nature is the teacher.

[ii]   Reggio Emilia is a municipality in northern Italy whose school and preschools have become internationally renowned.

[iii]   Sure Start is a highly contested UK national early childhood intervention program based on providing intensive attention and resources to families with young children of preschool age, to prevent social problems later in the children's lives and encourage their parents into paid employment.

[iv]   The "blue card" in Australia certifies its holder as someone who is a suitable person to work with young children.

[v]   MultiLink is a Logan based Non Government Organisation dealing with immigrants' and refugees' multiple support needs.

[vi]   Kumara is yam or sweet potato, a staple food sometimes cooked in a hangi or earth oven.

REFERENCES

Anon. (n.d.). *Moreton Bay*.

Australian Bureau of Statistics. (2001). Census of Population and Housing. 20680 Occupation by Age by Sex - Logan City. Canberra: Author.

Barnes McGuire, J. (1997).The reliability and validity of a questionnaire describing neighborhood characteristics relevant to families and young children living in urban areas. *Journal of Community Psychology, 25*(6), 551–566.

Bronfenbrenner, U. (1979). *The ecology of human development: Experiments by nature and design.* Cambridge, MA: Harvard University Press.

Brosterman, N., & Togashi, K. (1997). *Inventing kindergarten*. New York: Harry N. Abrams.

Carter, P. (1992). *Living in a new country: History, travelling and language.* London: Faber & Faber.

Ceppi, G., & Zini, M. (Eds.) (1998). *Children, spaces, relations: Metaproject for an environment for young children.* Reggio Emilia, Italy: Reggio Children.

Chung Tian Temple. (2010). Baby blessing. Retrieved November 11, 2010 from http://www.chungtian.org.au/baby-blessing

Davies, B. (2010, November 12). Personal communication.

Department of Education and Training (DET). (2010). *ESL in Queensland.* Retrieved November 17, 2010 from http://education.qld.gov.au/studentservices/inclusive/cultural/esl/esl-qld.html

Dobrenov-Major, M., Kearney, J., Birch, G., & Cowley, T. (2004). Bridging the gap between home and school: the Samoan bilingual cultural maintenance program. In B. Bartlett, F. Bryer & D. Roebuck (Eds.), *Educating: Weaving research into practice* Vol. 2 (pp. 13–21). Nathan, QLD: Griffith University, School of Cognition, Language and Special Education. ISBN: 1921166053. Available at http://search.informit.com.au/documentSummary;dn=002999315585735;res=IELHSS

Greenman, J. (1988). *Caring spaces, learning places: Children's environments that work.* St Paul: Redleaf Press.

Hubbard, R. S., & Power, B. M. (1999). *Living the questions: A guide for teacher-researchers.* York, Maine: Stenhouse Publishers.

Kearney, J., Fletcher, M., & Dobrenov-Major, M. (2006). Improving literacy outcomes of Samoan-Australian students in Logan City. *Literacy and numeracy innovative project.* Brisbane, QLD: Department of Education, Science and Training.

Lather, P. (2007). *Getting lost: Feminist efforts toward a double(d) science.* Albany, NY: SUNY Press.

Lenz-Taguchi, H. (2009). *Going beyond the theory/practice divide in early childhood education: Introducing an intra-active pedagogy.* New York: Routledge.

Logan City Council. (2005). Homepage. Retrieved November 18, 2010 from http://www.logan.qld.gov.au/lcc/

Logan Youth Legal Service. (2010). Homepage. Retrieved November 18, 2010 from http://www.qails.org.au/01_directory/details.asp?ID=26

Pettman, J. (1992). *Living in the margins: Racism, sexism and feminism in Australia.* North Sydney, NSW: Allen & Unwin.

Pratt, M. L. (1992). *Imperial eyes: Travel writing and transculturation.* London & New York: Routledge.

Somerville, M. (2010). A place pedagogy for global contemporaneity. *Educational Philosophy and Theory, 42*(3), 326–344.

St Pierre, E. A. (2000). Poststructural feminism in education: An overview. *Qualitative Studies In Education, 13*(5), 477–515.

Tang, D. (2009, August 28). *Seasonal violence.* Albert and Logan News. Retrieved November 7, 2010 from http://albert-and-logan.whereilive.com.au/news/story/seasonal-violence/

Woodridge State School. (2009). *We are one in Woodridge.* Retrieved November 17, 2010 from http://education.qld.gov.au/apps/owa/search.AssociatedDocument?p_assoc_doc=8860471&p_keywords_exact=SHOWCASE%3B+STATE+WINNER%3B+AWARDS%3B+2009%3B

Woodrow, C., & Brennan, M. (1999). Marketised positioning of early childhood: New contexts for curriculum and professional development in Queensland, Australia. *Contemporary Issues in Early Childhood, 1*(1), 78–94.

Kerith Power
Monash University

SECTION 2

Learning Place

The chapters in this section explore the unpredictable and productive openness of learning within the enabling pedagogy of place that we develop in this book. Each finds that learning does not so much entail a fixed body of pre-conceived knowledge delivered by a teacher, but a set of possibilities taken up by learners. The pedagogical sites include a primary school wetlands program, pre-service teacher education projects that engage with communities and schools, and informal community education contexts where adult learning takes place. Arts, performance, and storytelling are taken up by learners in each of these chapters to create very different responses to place and relations to place.

Learning place need not be confined to sites that are conventionally understood as places of and for learning. Learning about place can take place in communities, among groups of people who collaborate on projects of common interest. Learning communities may begin with groups of learners situated in schools or universities, but the most powerful learning takes place when the learner takes the new concepts and experiences gathered there into other places and other modes of relationship with others.

In learning communities it can be difficult to differentiate between teachers and learners. In an enabling place pedagogy, these positions will be porous as particular skills and knowledges are shared across the learning community, with each person potentially both a learner and a teacher. In this way, place-learning becomes less subject to conventional hierarchies of domination and control that situate the institution-based teacher as the one who knows and teaches, and the learner as the one who needs to receive knowledge.

The chapters in this section suggest that learning place requires a continuous opening of the self to what is going on and to where it is going on. The learner is an embodied and mobile subject who comes into being in relation to other bodies and to bodies of knowledge and understandings that are also always changing. Rather than learning that is limited to the performance and repetition of the already known, or that takes place only in limited contexts, we advocate learning that is both deeply attuned to and aware of the present, and simultaneously open to difference, to evolution, to new formations, to new collectivities and to new sites. This is a responsive and emergent learning that draws on and extends the rich variety of experiences of which learners are capable. It recognises the particularities of people in relation to place, and extends their responsiveness and responsibility in relation to place.

MARGARET SOMERVILLE

BECOMING-FROG

Learning place in primary school

Early morning walk with dogs past the roundabout on edge of town. At roundabout world of suburban houses opens out and a wonderful big puff of cloud is licked pink from sunrise against a clear blue sky. But as the street opens on the view I see the eight chimneys of the power station, two by two by two by two, with thin trails of umbilical vapour connected to the big cloud. It's a power station cloud. I run back home to get my camera, worried that by the time I get back to this spot the blush will have gone. Dogs running, camera slung around my neck, only a few minutes—and yes, it has changed. Pink tinge gone, it is lit bright in early morning sun, more normalised, a white daytime cloud in a bright blue day. I have to take a photo so you will understand. Space, place and time, weather, climate change, culture and nature, the significance of that moment of representation.

The Commercial Road Morwell Primary School (hereafter the Primary School) is located in the heart of Latrobe Valley, in the Gippsland region of eastern Victoria. When climate change was elevated to national and global importance following the Stern Report (2006) and the Garnaut Report (2008), the iconic towers of the coal fired power stations of Latrobe Valley came to symbolise the evil of carbon emissions. The dominant storyline of climate change and identity in Latrobe Valley is one of "double exposure" which refers to:

> ...the fact that regions, sectors, ecosystems and social groups will be confronted both by the impacts of climate change and by the consequences of globalization...there are "winners" and "losers" associated with both of these global processes. Climate change and economic globalization, occurring simultaneously, will result in new or modified sets of winners and losers. (O'Brien & Leichenko, 2000, p. 222)

The sense of double exposure is well encapsulated by a storyline in the *Latrobe Valley Express* (Wragg, 2008, p. 8).

> The underpinning reason why Latrobe Valley voters turned their backs on local sitting ALP members at the last State Election is the lack of action by the Bracks-Brumby governments to ameliorate the destruction of our region's economy. Destruction that was caused by successive Labour and Liberal

M. Somerville, B. Davies, K. Power, S. Gannon and *P. de Carteret,*
Place Pedagogy Change, 65–80.

governments who sold off the SECV [State Electricity Commission of Victoria] with a direct loss of 8,000 jobs and an indirect loss of another 12,000 jobs in Gippsland...As our regional community stares down the barrel of climate change impacts, the economic and employment consequences of [the] carbon trading scheme on the energy industry, and the manoeuvring of private power companies to force and capture government compensation without regard for the welfare of the Valley families, we have yet to hear how and if the Brumby Government intends to support our community through the anticipated tough time ahead.

The processes of economic globalisation have previously had a marked effect on Latrobe Valley communities through the privatisation and automation of the power industry. Along with the loss of jobs came the loss of working class identities. A proud history of labour was replaced by intergenerational unemployment, poverty and hardship. Overlaid on the storyline of earlier experiences of victimisation, the new story repeats the victim storyline in the context of a carbon constrained future, even though this is not necessarily the outcome.

The public representations of post-industrial regions powerfully link place with identity. Dominant storylines of the Latrobe Valley are of socio-economic disadvantage alongside environmental pollution, reinforced by daily television images of Latrobe Valley smoke stacks emitting greenhouse gases. These storylines depict disaffected young people with behaviour problems, criminality and idleness. Life becomes inescapably linked with pollution, as increased attention to climate change and global warming brings a new pathology to the region. These storylines operate as public pedagogies, they not only describe, but also produce knowledge.

Young people in such regions are living in pathologised places and they too are pathologised. Of particular concern are the numbers of young people affected by the increasing prevalence of discourses about youth behaviour problems. Research by Harwood (Harwood, 2006; Harwood & Rasmussen, 2007), for example, has shown a correspondence between high levels of socio-economic disadvantage and high rates of Attention Deficit Hyperactivity Disorder (ADHD) diagnosis. Harwood's study in the Gippsland region identified how young people experience pathology in a number ways: identity of the region, youth unemployment, low educational attainment, high levels of behaviour problems and behavioural disorders.

The case study reported in this chapter seeks to understand the positive identity-shaping possibilities for children learning place in Latrobe Valley through activities arising from a partnership between the power company, the Primary School, and the Morwell River Wetlands.

THE MORWELL RIVER WETLANDS PROGRAM

Walking out of the scrub at the edge of the playing field there's a big puddle of water lying since recent rains. My heart rises the first time I see this water appear after drought. The second time there is already an amazing chorus of frogs. My son tells me they sing in unison so the females can choose a mate. But where do they come from? And where do they go? There have been no frogs singing since that first day at dawn. Why aren't they singing? Is it the time, or are they all gone again? It's Sunday morning so I wander over to the little wetland again. I think about knowing a place day in and day out, over seasons and years to really know what is going on, I think about how places teach us.

It was on a visit to a student on practicum placement that I entered the world of frogs. I had visited the crowded portable classroom earlier in the day and watched the children navigate desks, chairs, boxes, hanging artworks, and other objects that make up this decidedly working class primary school classroom. I thought about Lefebvre's contention that the whole of social space proceeds from the body (1974/1991). The social space of this classroom is produced by these movements, bodies and objects, producing, in turn, the subjectivities of the children there. My attention was especially drawn to Mary, a child with Down Syndrome, moving awkwardly in this cramped space accompanied by an integration aide. It seemed that there was just nowhere she could fit in this crowded space with her extra human attachment.

When I returned after school the teacher and the integration aide, still working in the well-worn classroom, invited me to watch a short DVD of the rehearsal for the Christmas concert. There on the interactive screen, the children came to life as frogs, dancing their frog dance to music made entirely of frog calls. The children get to know the frogs in the wetlands. They learn how frogs live and move, and the sounds of the distinctive calls of each species. The classroom, cleared of clutter becomes the space of the wetlands. Children dance to frog calls, moving frog limbs, fingers splayed, jumping, leap frogging, becoming-frog to frog music. Mary, in particular, loves the performance, moving freely in this frog collective, unaccompanied by her integration aide. In one brief sequence towards the end she smiles pure pleasure at the camera, her body liberated in her frog dance. I learn that this is just a very small part of an integrated program involving visits to the local Morwell River Wetlands.

The Morwell River itself is an interesting phenomenon. Over fifty years ago it was diverted into a pipe for the open cut coal mine. Aboriginal artefacts on display in the reception area of the power station tell a story of another time when Gunnai people sang, danced, camped and ate by the river. This year the open cut mine will be extended again. In this move, as reported in the local paper, we will have an 'improved river and an improved road'. The river will once again be diverted to expand the coal mine. This time, however, it will be liberated from its pipe and returned, according to the planning map, to a river's meandering curves. The Morwell River Wetlands are part artificial, part natural, constructed by International Power, the British Company who now own Hazelwood Power Station. The wetlands is in the original location of the overflow from the river, alternately wet and dry according to the season. Constructed by a mining rehabilitation engineer, it has pools and banks, swathes of trees, logs and dead timber, for creatures to inhabit. The school has a special relationship to the wetlands and has monitored its evolution through the frogs, native trees, shrubs and grasses, and other creatures large and small who have come to inhabit this place.

Shortly after the wetlands was developed, three local schools applied for a Science in Schools grant and received twenty thousand dollars to set up a study of the wetlands and develop a curriculum model. Regular visits to the Morwell River Wetlands are a key feature of this curriculum for the Primary School in Morwell. The Morwell River Wetlands program is integrated across all grades in the school and across all subject areas. In the early grades the children study the needs and life cycles of frogs, rearing tadpoles in the classroom. They have constructed a mini wetlands in the school grounds. The middle grades are involved in monitoring the wetlands through observation of the frogs and other animals that live there, and the upper grades conduct scientific analysis of the wetlands' health by monitoring water quality. The school draws on two key community resources to sustain this program: Waterwatch and Community Frog Census.

> Waterwatch is one of the key things that will keep this project in focus in the long term. I see Waterwatch as the hub of the wheel, things revolve around them, because they've got their macro surveys, the Waterwatch lessons they do in schools...Waterwatch gives focussed ongoing training for the skills, the bigger picture of things, what we do with the data, photopoint monitoring. (Max Sargent, 2007a, interview)

Waterwatch Victoria is a community engagement program connecting local communities with river health and sustainable water management issues. Through Waterwatch, community groups are supported and encouraged to become actively involved in local waterway monitoring and on-ground action. A network of Waterwatch Coordinators supports local communities across Victoria in monitoring, planting, communicating and caring for their local creeks, wetlands, groundwater, rivers and estuaries. They are available to work in partnership with schools and I have observed them with the children at the wetlands. They teach the children to collect samples of water from the wetlands which are poured into white plastic trays where all the small creatures of the waterways become visible. The children learn to measure the health of the water by identifying which creatures are present.

The schools also worked with the Amphibian Research Centre (ARC) to develop the Frog Census program, based on the belief that frogs are the gateway to understanding the wetlands. The ARC was established as a centre dedicated to research and conservation of Australia's unique frogs. It is self funding and provides for its valuable work through sales and sponsorships. They supply pet frogs and tadpoles bred at the ARC, as well as enclosures, food, information, materials, and resources that are needed by those wanting to keep pet frogs. They stock frog books, tapes, posters, and other frog-related items. The Centre is also involved in efforts to breed and preserve a number of Australia's most endangered frogs, and is a base for the operations of the Victorian Frog Group. Frog Watch in Victoria is a highly successful community frog conservation program that originated as a joint project between the Amphibian Research Centre and Alcoa

World Alumina Australia. Its mission is to give Victorians the opportunity to help conserve frog life in their local area. The Primary School partnered with the Amphibian Research Centre to develop family science nights.

> [An educator from the ARC] would come down for three days at a time and involve the communities and I think that's been one of the key factors in setting the scene, with each of the school communities, that wetlands are a good thing to preserve and frogs are the gateway to study the wetlands…He has his slide show and we do family science activities based on frogs and on those nights he trains the teachers, you have tea after school and he says here's the range of activities you'll be running tonight and he gives the background to each of those activities and the science behind those activities. (Sargent, 2007a)

The community education nights involved hundreds of families over the time of the grant: 'their response was so huge our multi purpose room was like a can of sardines, people outside the doors and windows'. The Primary School then established an ongoing Community Frog Census program funded by a partnership between Yallourn Energy (the owner of another power station in Latrobe Valley) and the Amphibian Research Centre. Once a month children and their parents meet at the wetlands to record frog calls: 'I think of one particular girl; in her family there's about nine kids and she's getting towards the end of all the kids, but Dad still finds time to come with her every month'. The night I visit the wetlands Kylie is there with her dad taking photographs and cavorting with twin boys who are there with their mother.

The other significant element of this program is a web-based exchange set up by primary school teachers in Latrobe Valley to interact with primary schools in Oregon, USA, who also have a program in relation to their local wetlands. The joint web-based program is called *Corroboree*:

> The word corroboree is the aboriginal word for a gathering or meeting. The meaning is complex, including not just the idea of a physical bringing together of tribes, but a meeting of minds and philosophies, of gradual growth—a gathering of momentum as the tribes arrive.

> This project will be implemented in the broadest spirit of corroboree. Initially teachers and learners from three Australian schools and three Oregon schools will be involved in the design and development of a secured web site where they will gather to exchange ideas and data on their school's science projects. (Oregon State University, n.d.)

This aspect of the wetlands program initially involved face to face exchange visits between Oregon in the USA and Morwell, Latrobe Valley, by participating teachers involved in the wetlands projects. The website is a learning place set up to facilitate ongoing exchange between teachers and learners from the USA and teachers and learners from Australia. The website is populated by both the teachers' and children's representations of the wetlands. They exchange digital photos, audio recordings of frog calls, graphs of water quality, drawings, stories and blogs.

SEEING DIFFERENCE DIFFERENTLY

I crouch down beside the water in the pose of the child, down beside this place just to see what I can see. I smell the rank smell of childhood water holes filled after rain. Peering in to the shallow pool I enter a still, tea coloured world of decaying leaves and grass, tiny creatures minutely disturbing the surface with their movements. But there are no tadpoles at the edges of this water. Why, I do not know. I walk a little further, feet squelching in the mud, looking for tell-tale signs of frogs' eggs with their tiny black dots of tadpoles coming into being, the sort of clear gelatinous globs on the smooth surface of the water. How did I learn that these were baby tadpoles?

My relationship with the Morwell River Wetlands program has been participatory and engaged. I have documented many activities and events over the time I have been in Gippsland. My interest is underpinned by place, and the elements of body, story, and contact zone as constituting an enabling pedagogy of place (Somerville, 2010). In analysing children's learning through the wetlands, it is the element of body that came into focus. I found Grosz' (1994) interpretation of Deleuzian body theory illuminating for this analysis.

I have discussed previously the power of the body in disrupting binary structures of language and thought in relation to body/place connections. In the chapter on body/place journal writing I referred to the space between body and writing as a site of transformation. In relation to the Morwell River Wetlands program, and the complex relationships between bodies, places, cyberspace, and pedagogies, Deleuze's ideas about the body had the most explanatory power. While Grosz summarises the extensive feminist criticisms of Deleuze and Guattari, she suggests that their work shares a feminist concern to overcome the binary dualisms pervasive in Western thought. She believes they offer 'an altogether different way of understanding the body in its connections with other bodies, both human and non-human, animate and inanimate, linking organs and biological processes to material objects and social practices' (Grosz, 1994, pp. 164–165).

There are two key and interrelated ideas that I want to take up in this analysis—"becomings" and "assemblages". Becomings as a concept focuses on the body-in-process, a dynamic conception of the body that includes 'the transformations and becomings it undergoes, and the machinic connections it forms with other bodies, what it can link with' (Grosz, 1994, p. 165). It is a body that is dynamically constituted as part of other bodies, as part of 'the flesh of the world' (Merleau-Ponty, 1962). I find this particularly useful when thinking of the human body's relationship with landscapes, weather, rocks and mountains, as well as with other non-human animate beings. These aspects have been disregarded in Western thought, especially in relation to place and place pedagogies. For Deleuze, the process of becoming, whereby the links between humans and animate and inanimate others are formed, is conceived as a 'production' of 'assemblages':

Subject and object are series of flows, energies, movements, strata, segments, organs, intensities—fragments capable of being linked together or severed in potentially infinite ways other than those which congeal them into identities. Production consists of those processes which create linkages between fragments, fragments of bodies and fragments of objects. Assemblages or machines are heterogeneous, disparate, discontinuous alignments or linkages brought together in conjunctions.... . (Grosz, 1994, p. 167)

Human bodies, then, as corporeal entities, are continuous with other humans and non-human others but also with artefacts such as cameras and recorders, pens, paper, paints, computers, fabric, metal and machines. They are linked together through the production of assemblages. In other words, the representations we produce are conceived as part of our bodies. Assemblages are a way of understanding both process and product. Through the processes of assemblage, linkages are created between fragments, but an assemblage can also be seen as the product of this process, a pause in a continuous and iterative process of representation (Somerville, 2007). One of the outcomes of such thinking is to disrupt the usual binaries through which we understand our identities in places— such as the binaries of nature/culture, material/spiritual, and also more recently the cyber and the real.

It is interesting to note here that these ideas have many similarities to interconnected concepts of place, subjectivity, and representation in Australian Indigenous enactments of place, which are also based on a non-binary ontology and epistemology. For example, in ritual ceremony place, human bodies, song, dance, music, performance, and animal intersect momentarily in the creation of all that is (Somerville, 1999). This understanding of 'ecological connectivity' (Rose, 2004, p. 1) permeates an Indigenous ontology and epistemology. The translations, however, from such Indigenous understandings are both intellectually and politically complex (Somerville & Perkins, 2010). It is important to ask what Western theorists offer in terms of these ideas, as Grosz (1994) does in her project to interrogate Western philosophy from the perspective of the body. For these reasons, in this chapter I take up Deleuze's playful thinking to ask: What place learning is made visible by thinking through bodies in this way?

Human bodies have typically been conceived in Western thought from an anthropocentric, Enlightenment perspective as discrete, rational, autonomous entities whose most important function is to house the soul or, more recently, consciousness. Bodily knowledge is regarded as base, to be erased, or subverted to the more important mind, or intellectual knowledge. Deleuze and Guattari's concepts of bodies, becomings and assemblages, with their focus on process and productions, promise useful insights for a pedagogical practice of place that understands place as both material and metaphysical, constructed and natural, cyber and real.

My engagement in this program is perhaps best described as participatory action research in the sense that I have been involved actively as a participant in Community Frog Census, in school visits to the wetlands, in collaborations between teacher education students and children at the wetlands, and in lecturing to primary teacher education students with Waterwatch. I have had many informal conversations with Max Sargent, the lead teacher in this initiative, and have recorded a two hour semi structured interview about his work with the wetlands. I have visited the Morwell River Wetlands and the Science in Schools websites on many occasions and analysed the material there. In this chapter I use only the material that is available in the public domain on the website. The school is identified on this site so I have not sought to make the school anonymous but children's names have been changed. I am interested in analysing the relationship between the place, the integrated program, the website, and particularly the children's representations, in order to understand children's learning in this enabling pedagogy of place.

WHAT DID I SEE?

It's just on dusk, mid Autumn when we drive into the site. A half full moon and cool wind blow over the Wetlands, the freeway humming in front of us and the Hazelwood Power Station behind. Here in the wetlands the frog chorus begins. Frogs' skin is a membrane, permeable between inside and out, so frogs are a good measure of a place. Ben and Jim, ten year old twins, run down the road to join us, followed by their mum, and then Kylie, one of nine children, with her dad. Last month, because of the drought, there was no Community Frog Watch. Snakes hide in the giant open cracks, we were warned. Tonight, after recent rains, we make our way through frog calls, along softening cracked edges of the water, under the rising moon. Kids playfully use digital camera/recorders to take photos and record frog calls. We hear a whistling tree frog and a common froglet, and on the ground we read the tell-tale signs of fox, wallaby and kangaroo.

Entering into the Morwell River Wetlands on the web is a playful learning experience, in itself reminiscent of Deleuze and Guattari's 'practical geophilosophy' and 'rhizomes' (Gough, 2006). It is a visual cartographic experience of mapping knowledge in a non-linear way. The purpose of Deleuze and Guattari's practical geophilosophy is 'to describe the relations between particular spatial configurations and locations and the philosophical formations that arise therein' (Gough, 2006, p. 265). It is from this stance that I approach the website. Gough suggests that we should become nomadic in theorising science education and, quoting from Deleuze and Guattari, that '[r]hizomes affirm what is excluded from Western thought and reintroduce reality as dynamic, heterogeneous, and non-dichotomous' (Deleuze & Guattari, in Gough, 2006, p. 628). Deleuze and Guattari offer the rhizome, a root that spreads laterally underneath the ground, as an alternative to the tree. The tree, as in the tree of knowledge, symbolises the structure of patriarchal, authoritative knowledge.

When I type Morwell River Wetlands into Google, there are three immediately relevant sites and because I do not know the precise location of the student work on the web I visit all three. I navigate my way around these linked sites, in rhizomatic ways, until I decide to systematically investigate the material for this chapter. I do this by using a combination of looking at the web, downloading some material directly onto my laptop for later analysis, and writing with pencil and paper some headings and sequences so I can understand layout and structure and the relationship between the different sites. In my head, and in my body, I have images and embodied experiences of the physical place itself through which I interpret its meanings. I move between these sensory images and memories of the physical place and the representations on the web.

In this sense the analysis is a map of learning; part of the analysis is recognising the map of linked information and sites. There is also a sense, however, that unlike navigating in geographical space, there are no recognisable landmarks and I can become irretrievably lost. I recognise this being lost, 'abandoning one's previous frameworks, getting lost, unsettling what was previously secure and clear' (Grosz, 1994, p. 166), as part of the process of rhizomatic thinking. I cannot, for example, re-locate some of the items that I have printed during my wandering on the web, nor can I re-find some places I have been. There is a conflict between the logical demands of analysis and rhizomatic thought. I respond to this by writing in layers. The first layer responds rhizomatically, making connections poetically rather than logically, to what I experience. Later layers organise the writing more systematically into the logical requirements of scientific analysis. Traces of earlier layers are maintained, however, in a process of palimpsest, so the final imaginary is a layered map where traces of earlier thinking remain visible.

There is a large amount of information about the Morwell River Wetlands. The overall storyline is the history of its construction by Hazelwood Power, now International Power, 'as a replacement for another wetland which will be dug up to access coal in the future' (Morwell Wetlands Project, 2007). Another site tells me that:

> Before European settlement, the Morwell River provided a major floodplain tributary of the Latrobe River and the Gippsland Lakes. A major wetland extended from the confluence with the Latrobe River, as far upstream as Boolarra. Over time, the wetlands associated with the river have been eaten away by land development and river diversions. (Morwell River Wetlands, 2007)

This story of a bioregion gives time depth to my imaginings. I can also view a contemporary satellite map of the area, showing the location of the current Morwell River Wetlands in relation to the freeway, the railway line, and the Morwell River whose dark curvy line disappears abruptly, I presume into the pipe in the ground. I cannot see the open cut coal mine which I know is nearby and which appears as a massive red sore on Google Earth. The open cut is usually concealed from public view. I can see photos of the development of the wetlands over time until I recognise the place of my recent visit, deeply changed by the effects of severe drought. In this place described as the carbon capital of Australia I read the deep cracks in the ground as a local sign of the global effects of carbon emissions on the Earth's climate. I remember that my first Frog Census visit to the wetlands was cancelled due to the danger of snakes hiding in these deep cracks. I am aware of the minute and material effects of the global on the local. From these websites I gain a layered understanding of the place and its relationship to landscapes that have been dramatically altered by human habitation but continue to evolve in the complex relationship between human and ecological systems.

One site tells me hopefully that the 'opportunity now exists to coordinate several projects along the Morwell River. The result could see wetlands re-established similar to those which existed prior to European habitation' (Latrobe City, 2011). A pedagogy of hope has been noted elsewhere as important in relation to climate change, but while I admire the sentiment, I am looking for a more precise articulation of the nature of hope. Here the most hopeful thing for me is the link between the power generator and an educational agenda: '[a]s part of their responsibility to the community they have included scope for educational opportunities in their plans' (Corroboree, 2011). It is this particular assemblage that has allowed the wetlands program to emerge and thus destabilise the binary of pathology that establishes the power company as evil.

I find the activities of the Primary School on Google when I type in the words 'Science in Schools', and more when I search just 'Morwell River Wetlands'. It is on these sites that I can observe how these children from Latrobe Valley have engaged with a pedagogy of place. The site contains graphs of Waterwatch activities which measure the health of the water at different times, photos taken by children of the wetlands in different seasons and stages of its development, Frog Census data as a measure of their inhabitation of the wetlands, interviews the children have recorded with local knowledge holders, information about the Corroboree Club, and teachers' resources. I navigate this populated and complex site along pathways of desire. I listen to the calls of many different frogs and match their calls with their photos and names. My greatest excitement, however, is when I find the photos and audio-recordings of the place as it was when I was there with the children that evening in the wetlands. I recognise the photos and sounds in my body memory: the dragonfly, yabby hole, kangaroo prints, kangaroo scats, brown tree frog, and common froglet. Yes, we were all there. Then there is Kylie's brief voice recording:

Quarter to seven pm
29th of March 2007
Morwell River Wetlands
a half moon
getting bigger
it's pretty dark,
about to record
some frogs.
[And the sound of frog calls.]

When I listen to the frog calls I am returned to that autumn night in the wetlands, a cool breeze, a half full moon, just on dusk as the frogs begin to sing. There are two things that strike me about the sound of these words. One is that the words are so precise, so of the moment, so spare and simple as to be poetic, a poem made of the moment in sound of voice and frog calls, a precise conjunction of time and place. The second is the significance of that moment being communicated globally on a website dispersed through time and space. The moment itself is so significant in a pedagogy of place because it is about knowing place in all its intimate detail as a place of inhabitation, a place where we dwell with other creatures. It is only knowing place in its ever changing forms through thousands of such intimate moments that we can read a place, that we can know how a place is going, how well it is. It is only through knowing a place in those thousands of intimate moments that we can learn to love a place and have the knowledge to be able to take care of it. The assemblage of voice, image, and embodied memory connected and dispersed in time and space on the web is a powerful pedagogy of place.

The other thing that struck me is that if Kylie and I had not been there together in that physical place this would mean so much less to me. However much can be learned from the web, for me it is the fact that it is referential to a material place and to physical bodies interacting with that place that gives it meaning. To the extent that the qualities of that place can be expressed and communicated through digital recordings and images the knowledge can be shared. Even then it will be in reference to some other physical place of body memory through which it can be made meaningful as embodied learning.

I also find a marked Indigenous presence on the Primary School's site, unlike in most local information in Latrobe Valley. Doris Paton, a Gunnai/Kurnai Elder, speaks to the primary school children at the wetlands about the local Indigenous relationship to wetlands. On the website I can see her photo and hear her talk. I can also travel through hyperlinks to the story of 'The Port Albert Frog':

> Once long ago there was a big frog, Tidda-lick. He was sick and got full of water. He could not get rid of this water and did not know what to do. One day he was walking where Port Albert is now, where he saw a sand eel dancing on his tail, on a mud flat by the sea. It made him laugh so much that he burst and all the water ran out. There was a great flood and all the blackfellows were drowned except two or three men and a woman, who got on a mud flat island.

> While they were there, a pelican came by in his canoe. He took off the men, one at a time, but left the woman till last, he wanted her for himself. She was frightened and so she put a log in her possum rug, like a person asleep and swam to shore. When the pelican returned, he called her to come. No answer. Then he got very angry and went off to paint himself with pipeclay to go out and look for a fight with the blackfellows.

> Before that time pelicans were all black. When he was partly painted with Marloo (clay) another pelican came by, and not liking the look of him, hit him with his beak and killed him. That is the reason that pelicans are partly black and partly white to this day.

> There was a time when the first Kurnai, who was Borun the pelican, came down from the mountains of the north west, and reached the level country. He crossed the Latrobe River near Sale, and continued his journey to Port Albert. He was alone and carrying a bark canoe on his head.

As he was walking he heard a constant tapping sound, but look as he may he could not find the source of it. At last he reached the deep water of the inlets and put his canoe down. Much to his surprise, he saw a woman sitting in it. She was Tuk. The musk duck. He was very pleased to see her and she became his wife and mother of all the Kurnai. (International Project with Oregon, 2011)

This Gunnai/Kurnai storyline traverses the wetlands and links me to its other places. It is replete with bodies and bodily events and the materiality of those places. A number of human and non-human characters, materials and artefacts come into being in this journey through country. Because of my familiarity with Indigenous place stories I can read something of the body/place codes embedded here, of human-becoming-animal re-enacted through ceremony in place. Even in such a simple account of a creation story it is possible to discern a storyline of connections between special story places across a vast geographic region where the physical shapes and contours of the landscape, the creatures that inhabit it, and the epic journeys of the ancestral beings are intertwined. These are the creatures of the wetlands, the pelican, the duck and the frog, and the interconnected story places are specific local wetland sites. The story tells of the interchangeability of pelican-human and duck-human, notably in this case beginning with pelican and duck, rather than human.

The story also creates an assemblage, linking material/geographical places, human and non-human bodies, and artefacts. The white clay used to paint bodies for ceremony, the possum skin coat, and the canoe are noteworthy in a story that is sparse in regard to the presence of cultural artefacts. The becomings and assemblages in this story illustrate my earlier point that there are close similarities between the Deleuzian theorising in this chapter and the underpinning Indigenous ontology and epistemology told through story. I have a memory image that connects this story to place as enacted in ceremony where song, dance, music, sound, place and bodies are simultaneously created and re-created in place (Somerville, 1999), and it is the echo of such a performance that I sense here.

By the end of the story I have travelled hundreds of kilometers on a journey through time and space from the Morwell River Wetlands to Sale in east Gippsland and down to Port Albert on the coast. Songlines are lines of place learning where children acquired knowledge by walking, camping, collecting and gathering food. They were initiated into higher levels of place learning through song and ceremony. While there I imagine the sand islands in the estuarine flats where the event in this story takes place. Because I have travelled through these physical places I can imagine them as now inscribed with these stories and events, a new transformed landscape. This story, in turn, is part of the Bataluk Cultural Trail, hyperlinked to six other cultural sites to which I can journey on the web to find out about different Gunnai/Kurnai story places. These include post-contact stories and place-histories such as the sites of massacres and missions. The web represents the songline, traversing the landscape and mapping the possibility of a postcolonial pedagogy of place for 'global contemporaneity' (Somerville, 2010). I connect to this storyline and make meaning of it from my intimate embodied knowledge of the Morwell River Wetlands.

Moving out of the website, and my journeying, I wonder if primary school children access this story and how they make sense of it, but this is another project. I remember that in the primary school classroom Max Sargent drew my attention to one child's book-making project. This child had recently discovered his Indigenous heritage and made a book based on an interview with his grandfather using Powerpoint software. I looked at his stories of language, loss, and discovery of places. Pedagogically it confirms the significance of the category of 'contact zone' in any place learning. The contact zone opens up alternative and invisible place stories and practices to generate a broader and more inclusive understanding of a place. These stories of the contact zone have been present for the children in their classroom and in the wetlands so maybe they will have some basis for moving out from the wetlands as home, to these more distant places and imaginations of otherness.

The enormous complexity for me of living in Latrobe Valley is mirrored in the complexity of analysing the place learning of the Morwell River Wetlands project as an integrated curriculum at the Primary School. Through applying the framework of place, and asking the question what does place do, it is possible to gain some insight into the operation of an enabling pedagogy of place in a primary school. The particular focus on web-based representations and Deleuzian concepts of becomings and assemblages served to unsettle 'what was previously secure and clear', what might have been congealed into a fixed identity in my learning. It was however, a rhizomatic process of research emergence through which the digital DVD made visible and significant the performance of becoming-frog and called forth a Deleuzian response.

The storyline of the wetlands resonates with the remarkable tension between the technologies and operations of the power stations and open cut coal mines, and the Aboriginal songline of a system of rivers and wetlands. The Morwell River Wetlands, as place, sits in the space between these two storylines. Neither entirely natural, nor entirely artificial, it can in no way be regarded as a wilderness site for a romantic notion of nature. It is a truly postmodern place of the in-between, both natural and constructed, rural and industrial, cyber and real, global and local. In answer, then, to the question: how is place pedagogical?, it illuminates the ways in which a specific site can make available such complex learnings of place.

The question of the extent to which individual children learn these levels of complexity would require further research. However, having experienced these multiple practices as a pedagogy of place, it is unlikely that these children, growing up in the heart of Latrobe Valley, will have the same understandings of place as their parents and grandparents did. The Morwell River Wetlands requires complex place learning and offers the opportunity for a postmodern engagement with the place and its multiple and contested stories. These stories 'reintroduce reality as dynamic, heterogeneous, and non-dichotomous' and confirm the power of rhizomatic thought in that place learning.

The children's engagement with the wetlands is most evident in the activities on the website that are framed in terms of science: Waterwatch and Frog Census, for example. There are other forms of engagement, however, such as children's interviews with knowledge holders, talks from Aboriginal Elders, samples of children's drawings, and stories. There are strong enough traces of the embodied experiences of place in the web-based representations of the March 2007 Community Frog Census to make some analytical comments about bodies as becomings and assemblages.

Kylie engages with the wetlands as a social experience with her father, other children and their parents and her one time teacher, and other occasional adults. She uses the digital camera/recorder with ease and simplicity as an extension of the expression of self, reproduced in photos, voice, and frog sounds on the web. These elements—her body, the place as material/geographical terrain, water, mud, plants, wind, the light of a half full moon, frog sounds and camera/recorder—are linked in that moment of becoming. To analyse her learning through Deleuzian notions of becoming and assemblage offers new iterative understandings of an enabling pedagogy of place.

I return now to the nature and meaning of the frog dance, which seems to me to be a production of a different order. When I watch the DVD I can feel in my body the extension of self-into-other required to perform frog. How does a frog move? What do its limbs do? How can your fingers be frog fingers, how does your body move to frog music? In this sense it is not mimicry that is required, but a becoming-other. And yet, this becoming is still underpinned by that intimate knowledge of place and its creatures that refers to that which is beyond the self. The frog calls, for example, enter the body in this performance in a way that is evident and undeniable. The performance itself transforms the space of the classroom. The classroom-becoming-wetlands in the production of frogs, and children's bodies, are transformed through a different body/place learning. This human-becoming-other, body/place learning is produced in relationship with the material/geographic place and its relationship to other places, both real and imaginary.

Finally I ask myself whether this complex theorising is completely divorced from the practices and meanings this activity has for the teachers and learners. I position myself as a learner/participant in this process, as a newcomer to both Latrobe Valley and the primary school classroom. I am an outsider and my task is to understand all of the activities in the Morwell River Wetlands program theoretically. In pondering this question in the writing of this chapter, I remembered an email exchange with Max Sargent, the teacher, about the April visit to the wetlands in which I was unable to participate. He told me that there were no frogs calling so the children engaged in other wetlands activities. I asked him why the frogs were not singing at the wetlands. He wrote:

> Well I can't answer it for sure but if I try to think like a frog I would not want to be about tonight as the moonlight was strong making me more visible, the ground was very dry when I need to keep my skin moist. Perhaps the males said it was no point expending energy croaking for a mate, one who wouldn't want to travel any distance in these conditions. (Sargent, 2007b, email)

Max's response is as Deleuzian as my analysis of his understanding, in his story, of the pedagogical power of becoming-frog.

REFERENCES

Deleuze G., & Guattari, F. (1987). *A thousand plateaus: Capitalism and schizophrenia* (B. Massumi, Trans.). Minneapolis: University of Minnesota Press.

Garnaut, R. (2008). *The Garnaut Climate Change Review—Final Report*. Melbourne: Cambridge University Press.

Gough, N. (2006). Shaking the tree, making a rhizome: Towards a nomadic geophilosophy of science education. *Educational Philosophy and Theory, 38*(5), 625–645.

Grosz, E. (1994).*Volatile bodies: Toward a corporeal feminism*. Bloomington: Indiana University Press.

Harwood, V. (2006). *Diagnosing disorderly children: A critique of behaviour disorder discourses*. London: Routledge.

Harwood, V., & Rasmussen, M.L. (2008). Scrutinizing sexuality and psychopathology: A Foucauldian inspired strategy for qualitative data analysis. *International Journal of Qualitative Studies in Education, 20*(1), 31–50.

International Project with Oregon. The Port Albert Frog. Retrieved January 5, 2011 from http://www.commercialps.vic.edu.au/Science/Articles/PortAlbertFrog/index.htm

Latrobe City Council. Neighbourhood environment improvement plan, 2007. Retrieved January 5, 2011 from http://www.latrobe.vic.gov.au/WebFiles/Council%20Services/Sustainability%20and%20Environment/Morwell%20River%20NEIP%20Plan%20-%20web%20version.pdf

Lefebvre, H. (1991). *The production of space* (D. Nicholson-Smith, Trans.). Oxford: Blackwell (Original 1974).

O'Brien, K., & Leichenko, R. M. (2000). Double exposure: Assessing the impacts of climate change within the context of economic globalization. *Global Environmental Change, 10*(3), 221–232.

Oregon State University. (n.d.). *Corroboree: 4-H across the seas*. Retrieved January 5, 2011 from http://www.4hcorroboree.org/project%20data/new_groupHome.asp?pid=108

Rose, D. B. (2004). *Reports from a wild country: Ethics for decolonisation*. Sydney: UNSW Press.

Merleau-Ponty, M. (1962). *Phenomenology of perception* (C. Smith, Trans.). New York: Humanities Press.

Sargent, M. (2007a). Interview with Margaret Somerville.

Sargent, M. (2007b). Email to Margaret Somerville.

Science in Schools. Homepage. Retrieved January 5, 2011 from http://www.commercialps.vic.edu.au/Science/index.htm

Somerville, M. (1999). *Body/landscape journals*. Melbourne: Spinifex Press.

Somerville, M. (2007). Postmodern emergence. *Qualitative Studies in Education, 20*(2), 225–243.

Somerville, M. (2010). A place pedagogy for 'global contemporaneity'. *Educational Philosophy and Theory, 42*(3), 326–343.

Somerville, M., & Perkins, T. (2010). *Singing the coast*. Canberra: Aboriginal Studies Press.

Stern, N. (2006). *The economics of climate change: The Stern Review*. Cambridge: Cambridge University Press.

Wragg, C. (2008, June 30). Reader's say. *Latrobe Valley Express*.

Margaret Somerville
Monash University

KERITH POWER

TRANSFORMING SELF-PLACE RELATIONS

In the project approach

In response to the question: how do people learn place and build community?, this chapter asks how framing a teaching initiative through a lens of place for first year teacher education students opened up a cultural contact zone in which students enacted the mutual constitution of places, bodies and subjectivities in Logan, south east Queensland, Australia. The students explored local places in an embodied way by engaging in three major phases of conducting a project: topic selection, fieldwork and display. These phases are outlined in the 'project approach' (Katz & Chard, 2000)[i] as developed from the English and North American early childhood education tradition. The rationale for using this approach, re-framed as an enabling place pedagogy, was to decolonise and re-inhabit schools and the teaching profession (Gruenewald, 2003a, p. 1) by taking a new perspective on educational practice, to encourage students to see teaching and learning through a lens of place, and to shift their taken-for-granted notions of their place as teachers and of the place of schooling in education.

Traditionally, approaches to professional placement in early childhood education re-locate student teachers, many of whom have only recently left school, back into classrooms (albeit in an altered role). My assumption is that most students who succeed in entering teacher education do so by compliance with the dominant values and practices of schooling. Novice teachers are often not familiar enough with schools as workplaces, or with schools' place in the community, to take a critically reflective perspective on how schools and teachers operate (Atherton, 2010). Supervising teachers' mentorship is highly variable, dependent on individual attitudes and often at odds what universities are trying to teach (Scott & Dinham, 2008). Such a starting point does little to disrupt students' naïve perceptions from their own school days of how learning takes place.

Student teachers' concerns in their first classrooms are typically about themselves, in terms of their ability to 'cope with the workload, high personal expectations of performance, and being observed and evaluated by their supervisor' (Murray-Harvey, Silins & Saebel, 1999). By contrast, in the general community, schools and teachers are considered to be just one of many factors contributing to local area amenity (Pope & Zhang, 2010). I wanted the students to have an early opportunity to shift their perspective on self to connect with the lived experience of the children and their families in the neighbourhoods surrounding schools. In the long term, I hoped they would look back on their own project experience as an enjoyable and productive way to learn to belong, and contribute to, their local places and

M. Somerville, B. Davies, K. Power, S. Gannon and *P. de Carteret,*
Place Pedagogy Change, 81–96.

communities. They might then see their own experience as a potential model through which to engage their own pupils in place-making and community building at school.

I understood the project activities as having the potential to shift students' participation in teaching and learning towards an alternative, spatial turn in education (Gieryn, 2000; Gruenewald, 2003a; Gulson & Symes, 2007; Holloway & Valentine, 2000; Somerville, 2005, 2007). To re-focus student teachers' attention to the potential contribution of local places to their own learning might encourage them to see its relevance to children's schooling. I planned to re-frame the project approach as an enabling place pedagogy, aimed at opening up a space, or cultural contact zone (Pratt, 1992), for the student teachers to consider alternative ways of learning place and building community. I thought that a systematic process of investigating the neighbourhoods surrounding schools before locating students in classrooms had the potential to provoke them, in becoming teachers, to think differently about the environmental and social ecologies they were entering.

Katz and Chard (2000, p. 21) claim of their original project approach that 'the major aim of education in the early years...is to strengthen children's confidence in their understanding of their own environment and experience'. My pedagogical rationale was different: I wanted to unsettle and disrupt my students' taken-for-granted understandings, to offer them opportunities to frame their teacher and learner subjectivities as changing, emergent, mutually constituted with specific places and contexts. The focus I adopted was not so much on the development of my students' individual professional skills, or on transmitting the values of a particular department of education or curriculum, but on assuming that learners, as already 'fully participating social subjects' or persons (Burman, 2008, p. 67) need to make meaning of the place they have arrived in, and learn to inhabit it in responsible ways. I hoped that our teacher education students might better learn their place in the world of teaching by carrying out a project in which they explored alternative ways to inhabit it that would sustain an expanded vision of its areas and its communities. I hoped to draw attention to the cultural contact zones that constitute schools and the communities around them by asking students to collectively make their own meanings of these places, and further, as teachers, to draw on the situated knowledges of the people they encountered as contexts and resources for their own learning.

As a researcher I was interested in how the project approach might prompt the students to enact the mutual constitution of places, bodies and subjectivities. Who we are and choose to be, shapes and is shaped by the physical, social, cultural and political locations in which we find ourselves. Conventional schooling is open to the criticism that the decontextualised knowledge it transmits can make us 'careless and ignorant of [our] own surroundings' (Gruenewald, 2003b, p. 625). This viewpoint is supported by the negative ecological and social consequences of the ways in which teachers and others, as potential place-makers and community builders, currently inhabit the world. I wanted the students to open up to becoming committed to their new surroundings by developing a conscious awareness of how to extend their prior knowledge, and to become careful, knowledgeable and constructive in relation to their new places and social positionings.

My task, in researching enabling place pedagogies, was to investigate these questions in the early childhood education sector. I carried it out in a teacher education context at Griffith University, Brisbane, Queensland, at the Logan campus. For our students, Logan represented one of the most likely places for them to be employed at the beginning of their teaching careers. Griffith University's response to the roll-out of a new Early Years Curriculum was to re-design its Bachelor of Education degree so that all primary teacher education students had an introduction to early childhood education. My role was to design and coordinate this first year core unit of study, which integrated early childhood education with disciplinary content in the visual and performing arts, early mathematics and physical education and took up half the students' study time in their first semester. The entire Bachelor of Primary Education cohort of four hundred and fifty students across three campuses attended lectures and workshops and experienced their first professional placement. For one of their two assignments, we asked students to work in groups using a project approach to investigate their local places.

Because of the large number of students in the cohort, and the institutional requirement to include disciplinary experts in the teaching process, my own direct contact and interaction with students was confined to mass lecture times, online responses to their questions about the assignments and coordinating the marking of their written work. To answer the research questions posed in this inquiry, I asked the sessional tutors to document both the processes and products of the students' learning. In this chapter I present photographs of students working on campus in the visual arts studio, of some of the artefacts they produced, of their fieldwork, performances and displays documenting their work.

To prepare for our teaching I asked four of the tutors to participate with me in *Engaging Children's Minds: The Project Approach*, a Summer Institute (Chard & Brooks, 2006) for teachers at the University of New England (UNE), Australia. Professor Sylvia Chard guided us through projects around the UNE campus, directly carrying out the cyclic phases of topic selection, fieldwork and display that make up the project approach.

PHASE 1: TOPIC SELECTION

The topic selection phase of planning a project is intended to engage students' interest, and potentially leads to the investigation of a question a group of learners have co-developed within a significant broad topic proposed by the project facilitator. The activity starts with a tutor-prompted "brainstorming" exercise. Without discussion, individual students generate as many ideas as possible, writing each one at a time on post-it notes. Secondly, they are asked in small groups to discuss and cluster their individual ideas around the topic into categories, forming a "mind map".

Figure 1 shows individual students in a topic group clustering their ideas into themes to construct a group mind map. Using the mind map as a guide, the group then comes to a consensus decision with the tutor about which aspect of the topic to investigate. I read this exercise as students starting to build community amongst themselves. Debriefing with the tutors on the semester's teaching, I asked about the students' choice of topics.

Figure 1. Topic selection: creating a group mind map.

KERITH: What topics did they choose? What I had in mind was to tie it to their teaching sites.

HAZEL (tutor 1): I think in the end we just said to them it had to be something to do with young children—something that would be interesting for young children…what we thought was that if it was something they were genuinely interested in, they'd be more involved in it. There was Pirates; there was one on dogs—they went to the most amazing lengths; there were two water ones; one group did The Wiggles[ii] and got totally excited about The Wiggles: went to Dreamworld[iii], went to Wiggles concerts…

KERITH: They became The Wiggles, didn't they, in the end?

Sharon (tutor 2) took photographs of students at work and prepared a written reflection.

SHARON: The principal factor was to keep it simple, but it needed to focus on issues in early childhood development.

Hazel and Sharon named the following topics chosen by the students: skin cancer protection, healthy eating, dental hygiene, cows on the Logan campus, dogs, child abuse, domestic violence, multiculturalism in the Logan community, the Logan water supply, destruction of wildlife habitat, pirates, and The Wiggles. When I thought about these in relation to Somerville's (2005) three necessary conditions for an enabling place pedagogy (body, story, and contact zone; see Introduction), each topic seemed potentially authentic except for the final two. Table 1 below represents my preliminary reading of how the students' learning in the first topic-setting 'discussion' phase of their projects corresponded with Somerville's (2005) three necessary conditions of an enabling place pedagogy.

Table 1. Students' Topics related to principles of embodied and local learning, place storylines and cultural contact zones

Project Topics	Principles of an Enabling Place Pedagogy		
	Embodied and Local	*Stories and Representations*	*Contact Zone of Contested Place Stories*
1. Skin cancer protection	√	People and nature	
2. Healthy eating	√	Health and welfare	
3. Dental hygiene	√	Health and welfare	
4. Cows on the Logan campus	√	Cultural contact; Health/nutrition	√
5. Child abuse	√	Conflict/welfare	
6. Domestic violence	√	Conflict/welfare	√
7. Multiculturalism in Logan	√	Cultural contact	√
8. Logan water supply	√	People and nature	√
9. Wildlife habitat	√	People and nature; Other entities	√
10. The magistrates' court	√	Conflict/law	√
11. Water	√	People and nature	√
12. Dogs	√	Other entities	√
13. Pirates		Fictionalised conflict/law	
14. The Wiggles		Childhood as a market niche	

I thought the first twelve topics of the list in table 1 were directly about bodies or showed potential for embodied learning. I was doubtful about Pirates and The Wiggles. Four topics linked storylines involving people and nature. Four raised issues about physical health and the same number addressed human welfare. Two directly confronted issues of family conflict and violence. Two adopted a "play" orientation and two mentioned other-than-human entities. While it would be possible to read cultural contestation into every topic, I ticked six topics that seemed to explicitly address this issue: cows, child abuse, domestic violence, multiculturalism, water and habitat. The outliers in this list were Pirates and The Wiggles as these fictionalised topics seemed to me to be culturally irrelevant. At the time of this research, Queensland was in the grip of a ten year drought. Several groups of students investigated Water, a key local, national and global issue.

To complete phase 1, students made artworks to document their existing knowledge of their topics, prior to the next phase of fieldwork. Students were asked to express their thoughts, feelings and learning about the content areas of the unit, communicating with each other through repeated cycles of discussion and exploration and then portraying their emerging stories using a range of media. This was an opportunity for us to introduce drawing, clay, construction and performance as modes of exploration and representation. Projects in process require repeated cycles of documentation though many different modes of representation. Relations between the students, their research topics, the art materials and artefacts, people, structured interactions and other resources are open to various readings. If we think about these students' work as little research projects, using the media enabled them to locate their starting points as researchers, exploring, using the full range of their senses, their relationships to each other, to the places of their research and to their own emerging subjectivities as researchers. In terms of a re-framed project approach, the art workshops therefore afforded opportunities for embodied learning and cultural encounter.

Figure 2. Students working with clay, a potentially grounding experience.

Working with clay, as in figure 2 above, can be read as a literally "grounding" experience wherein the students' bodies connect to country through touch. Seeing students handle clay, possibly for the first time since making mud pies as children, reminded me of traditional Indigenous place rituals such as coating a newborn baby with a slurry of ant bed or ashes to bond it to its birthplace. 'Born of woman, and by woman born of earth, the infant becomes a person with specific attachments to country' (Rose, 1992, p. 63). Reading about Indigenous leaders' stories of their early childhood experiences and working with Indigenous early childhood teachers has deeply influenced my own attachment to country and to place-oriented education.

In the original project approach, this one of several stages of the learning design involving representation is interpreted as contributing to students' cognitive development by drawing out their existing knowledge of their topic and refining the focus of their fieldwork. The questions to ask are: What is our experience of this topic up to now? What do we already know? What do we wonder and want to find out? How are we planning to learn what we want to know? From a re-framed place pedagogies perspective, the Experience, Knowledge, Wonder and Learn (EKWL) exercise opened up a space of play (a contested notion in early childhood education, here meaning a relatively self-directed and open-ended activity) that enabled students' agency, in the geographic and disciplinary location of the arts studio, to enact a mutual constitution of bodies with clay, paper, paint and construction tools. The students, through interacting with other bodies, with art materials and with each other, constructed subjectivities as place-makers, community builders and researchers that they could then take into the communities and landscapes they would investigate.

Figure 3. A launching place.

My reading of figure 3 is that the students put together their ideas to construct a place, a metaphor and an event of embarkation. In making a group construction representing their knowledge, the learners generated new knowledge, storying themselves as art-makers, place-makers, community builders and explorers.

Sharon's story about this representational phase emphasised 'the powerful impact of visual imagery in expressing knowledge, feelings and ideas'. Hazel's story focussed on community building among the students:

> The Pirates group was the most interesting because you had three mature age students, a student with not much English and [two younger, academically weaker students repeating the unit from the previous year]. One of them came to me at the beginning and said 'I think we've got a problem' and we talked about it and she said 'well, we'll just make it work'.

PHASE 2: FIELDWORK INVESTIGATIONS

My hope for the fieldwork phase of the learning design was that positioning students in relations of 'legitimate peripheral participation' (Lave & Wenger, 1991, p. 29) within the communities surrounding their placement sites might enable them to problematise received notions of the purposes and processes of teaching and learning. Rather than complying to received mandated (decontextualised) curricula, I hoped that in connecting to place the students might encounter possibilities for re-imagining and co-constructing a curriculum, alive and relevant to the interdisciplinary learning opportunities, relationships and resources of local places.

Sharon wrote: 'The majority of the groups worked tirelessly on their projects. They were beginning to see [a] broader picture...the students were now exhibiting independent learning'. Hazel told a story of the Pirates group: 'I think it was fun; the reason was it was fun, because they got all dressed up and went to a beach and the police came along and wanted to know what on Earth they were doing digging up beaches, because they had empty wine bottles and shovels'. This discussion of how the "pirates" interpreted the fieldwork requirements of their project led me to re-think my dismissal of their project as inauthentic and unlikely to lead to useful learning. Though their project bore little relation to their placement sites, it seems that through this mildly transgressive exercise they managed to visit a real beach, engage in physical activity, build some sense of community amongst themselves and simulate pirate behaviour enough to attract the attention of the real forces of the law.

To this point, students had worked in groups to decide on topics to investigate, located themselves and their prior knowledge in relation to the topics, to each other and to the research sites, and developed some methods to carry out their explorations. The third phase of the project was to collate and make meaning of the information they had gathered in ways that would represent what they had learned and how they had learned it.

PHASE 3: DOCUMENTATION AND DISPLAY

I have selected three examples of student work to portray a range of the embodied, narrative and culturally complex final displays and performances that told their stories of what they had learned from their projects.

Cows on the Logan Campus

The Cows topic literally presented itself through the tutorial room windows. The neighbouring farmer's cattle, as a reminder of Logan's existent but rapidly changing rural land use, occasionally strayed onto the lush lawns of the university. This project is an example of stories one group of students elicited and told about their local place. Their topic title, 'The Milk Cycle', told a rather conventionally "educational" storyline about health and nutrition for young children, but their representations opened up a space of cultural contact.

The student poster in figure 4 humorously re-created shared feelings amongst Logan students and staff of surprise, slight alarm and incongruity at occasionally seeing a large Friesian cow peering in through the tutorial room window. The portrayal is open to a reading of mutual curiosity, perhaps a "cultural contact zone" between humans and cows?

The student impersonating a cow in figure 5 was enacting an embodied knowledge of selves-in-relation to the other, including non-human, earth others (see Introduction) in a similar way to the child "becoming-frog" in the previous chapter.

The "invasion" of farm animals onto the campus potentially invites underlying narratives of rapid change that could arise for the students as future school teachers in Logan: for example, urban versus rural land use issues, cultures with different (non-dairy) dietary preferences, food security, animal rights and so on. This representation of learning from an immediate, everyday occurrence enacted an implicit rather than explicit awareness of the mutual constitution of places, bodies and subjectivities through a joyful, embodied, interdisciplinary and expressive engagement with the topic, in itself subversive of much contemporary classroom practice.

Domestic Violence

The students' choice of this topic, while raising 'dark funds of knowledge' (Zipin, 2009), counters a major discursive strand in early childhood education which constructs both young children and their teachers as 'innocent' (Woodrow, 1999). It may be that Logan students are more likely than other beginning teachers to encounter children who are affected by domestic violence (Tang, 2010). Directly addressing it, however, is a risky enterprise that interrupts 'usual institutional denial mechanisms that sustain boundaries between dark knowledge and school curriculum' (Zipin, 2009, p. 321). This group's choice offers a contrast to those of some of the other groups of students, who chose to learn place and build community through "lighter" projects.

Figure 4. Student poster of cows on the Logan campus.

Figure 5. Becoming-Cow?

Figure 6. Students investigating domestic violence directly confronted a difficult social problem.

This group invited their audience to engage with the issue by incorporating a comment box into their static display. This opened up a space for expressions of a range of alternative opinions; that is, the students demonstrated awareness of the discursive space around domestic violence as a contact zone of contested meanings.

Multiculturalism: The Game Show

The final project I discuss here was chosen by a large group of students who, between them, embodied a number of different countries of origin, for example Greece, Turkey, Croatia, Serbia, Samoa, New Zealand and Australia. The game show format of their final performance involved audience participation by two teams of students.

The quiz: How well do you know Logan culture? was hosted TV-style by a young Australian of Turkish origin who had arrived at the age of eight speaking no English and had subsequently achieved university entry.

Figure 7. Multiculturalism, the game show: how well do you know Logan culture?

Figure 8. Blindfold food tasting: dolmades.

Many aspects of this performance lent themselves readily to a place pedagogy analysis. Local knowledge of Logan as a meeting place of diverse global cultural and place origins was embodied, directly addressed and celebrated in the membership and topic choice of the group. Their game show format countered both the deficit constructions and media erasure of non-English cultural identity characteristic of mainstream Australian life. They coined the term "Logan culture" to set up the premise of their game. The game itself honoured place-based cultural knowledges such as bilingualism, and embodied social practices around food and language.

While multiculturalism is a highly contested intellectual and political concept, these students, as potential new teachers, took up a position of having access to valued community place knowledge that was qualitatively different from an homogenous, monocultural positioning. The invention of "Logan culture" as a storyline encompassing many different (and, in some countries such as Turkey, Greece, Croatia and Serbia, highly contested) traditions was an act of decolonisation and re-inhabitation. Like the Turkish Australian host, the students in this group refused to take up subordinate subject positions as the non-English speaking minority of "others" in an English language dominant society, or of inhabitants of Logan as constructed on a deficit model living in a pathologised place. Instead they constructed and celebrated their cultural differences as positive factors contributing to a new, positive place identity.

My initial concern about the decontextualising effects of choosing *ersatz* topics such as Pirates or The Wiggles was tempered by the active involvement demanded by projects that inevitably encouraged place learning through direct sensory engagement with physical locations and/or bodily movement. The "pirates" came into cultural contact with authentic law enforcement, while the "Wiggles" embodied their learning in their final all-singing, all-dancing performance.

Multiple storylines of place co-existed and came into discursive relationship through the medium of the project workshops. The place of the lecture theatre became a cultural contact zone as groups performed part of their learning for the semester. Modes of embodied learning in the performances included dramatic genres such as game shows, role play, songs, plays and mime. The static displays, interactive by virtue of the comment boxes, raised social concerns such as water management, environmental degradation and domestic violence.

The project approach enabled first year university students to learn place through direct physical engagement, stories and cross-cultural contact and to build community through collaborative group work.

ACKNOWLEDEGMENTS

Thanks to Helen Alley. Most photographs are the work of Sheryl Fainges. Supplementary photographs are by Kerith Power.

NOTES

[i]   Helm, Benecke and Steinheimer (1989) and Katz and Chard (2000) now acknowledge the parallel development of a project approach in Reggio Emilia early childhood schools in Italy. Whatever the

merits of this internationally renowned tradition, access to it is limited by the "branding", commercialisation and tight control of information and professional development about Reggio schooling.

[ii] "'The Wiggles" album has...achieved Gold and Platinum status and The Wiggles themselves have gone on to become one of the most popular and successful performing acts in Australia, in any age group' (http://www.thewiggles.com.au/au/about/).

[iii] Dreamworld is a theme park on Australia's Gold Coast.

REFERENCES

Atherton, J. S. (2010). *Reflection; an idea whose time is past.* UK: Doceo. Retrieved December 16, 2010 from http://www.doceo.co.uk/heterodoxy/reflection.htm

Burman, E. (2008). *Developments: child, image, nation.* London & New York: Routledge.

Chard, S., & Brooks, M. (2006). Staff profile: Dr Margaret L. Brooks. Retrieved November 27, 2010 from http://www.une.edu.au/staff/mbrooks3.php

Gieryn, T. F. (2000). A space for place in sociology. *Annual Review of Sociology, 26,* 463–496.

Gruenewald, D. (2003a). The best of both worlds: A critical pedagogy of place. *Educational Researcher, 32*(4).

Gruenewald, D. (2003b). Foundations of place: A multidisciplinary framework for place-conscious education. *American Educational Research Journal, 40*(3), 619–654.

Gulson, K., & Symes, C. (2007). Knowing one's place: educational theory, policy and the spatial turn. In K. N. Gulson, & C. Symes (Eds.), *Spatial theories of education: Policy and geography matters.* London & New York: Routledge.

Helm, J. H., Beneke, S., & Steinheimer, K. (1998). *Windows on learning: Documenting young children's work.* New York: Teachers College Press.

Holloway, S., & Valentine, G. (2000). Spatiality and the new social studies of childhood. *Sociology, 34*(4), 763–783.

Katz, L., & Chard, S. (2000). *Engaging children's minds: The project approach* (2nd ed.). New Jersey: Ablex Publishing Corporation.

Lave, J., & Wenger, E. (1991). *Situated learning: Legitimate peripheral participation.* Cambridge: Cambridge University Press.

Logan City Council. (2010). About Logan. Retrieved November 8, 2010 from http://www.logan.qld.gov.au/LCC/logan/profile

Murray-Harvey, R., Silins, H., & Saebel, J. (1999). A cross-cultural comparison of student concerns in the teaching practicum, 1(1). Retrieved December 18, 2010 from http://hdl.handle.net/2328/3000

New London Group. (1996). A pedagogy of multiliteracies: Designing social futures. *Harvard Educational Review, 66*(1).

Pope, J.,& Zhang, W. (2008). *Indicators of community strength at the local government area level in Victoria 2008.* Melbourne: Strategic Policy, Research and Forecasting, Department of Planning and Community Development.

Pratt, M. L. (1991). Arts of the contact zone. *Profession, 91,* 33–40.

Robbins, J. (2008, July 4). The mediation of young children's thinking about natural phenomena through conversation and drawing. Paper presented at the 39th Annual Conference of the Australasian Science Education Research Association, Brisbane.

Rose, D. B. (1992). Dingo makes us human: Life and land in an Aboriginal Australian culture. New York: Cambridge University Press.

Scott, C., & Dinham, S. (2008). Born not made: The nativist myth and teachers' thinking. *Teacher Development, 12*(2), 127–136.

Somerville, M. (2005, May 6). Researching place pedagogies. Paper presented at the International Congress of Qualitative Inquiry, University of Illinois, Urbana-Champaign.

Somerville, M., Davies, B., Power, K., & Gannon, S. (2006). Enabling place pedagogies in rural and urban Australia. Australian Research Council Discovery Project DP0663798. Retrieved November 7, 2010 from http://www.education.monash.edu.au/research/projects/place-pedagogies/enabling-place-pedagogies.html

Somerville, M. (2007). Place literacy. *Australian Journal of Language and Literacy, 31*(2), 149–164.

Tang, D. (2009, August 28). Seasonal violence. *Albert and Logan News.* Retrieved November 7, 2010 from http://albert-and-logan.whereilive.com.au/news/story/seasonal-violence/

The Wiggles. (n.d.). About The Wiggles. Retrieved November 11, 2010 from http://www.thewiggles.com.au/au/about/

Woodrow, C. (1999). Revisiting images of the child in early childhood education: Reflections and considerations. *Australian Journal of Early Childhood, 24*(4), 7–12.

Zipin, L. (2009). Dark funds of knowledge, deep funds of pedagogy: Exploring boundaries between lifeworlds and schools. *Discourse: Studies in the Cultural Politics of Education, 30*(3), 317–331.

Kerith Power
Monash University

SUSANNE GANNON AND BRONWYN DAVIES

LEARNING PLACE THROUGH ART AND STORIES

The place writing that we have each included in the first part of this book was integral to the place pedagogy work with our secondary teacher education students. This chapter is the story of those students learning place pedagogy through translating it into their own teaching practices. We included earlier versions of our place writing in the readings we gave them to launch their own re-thinking of place and their relation to it. We will focus in particular on the way two of our students translated their new ideas about place into work with their own school students in surprising, original and creative ways.

In Chapter 9 we elaborate our own teaching strategies with this group of students, focussing on the collective biography work we did with them. But here, we want to focus on the learning that was made possible in an enabling place pedagogy framework. The course the students were enrolled in with us was a strand within an alternative Professional Experience unit offered to secondary teacher education students at the University of Western Sydney (UWS). This dynamic alternative practicum, commonly called PE3, short for "Professional Experience Three", was subsequently given a National Australian Learning and Teaching Council Award for Excellence in the category of Programs that Enhance Learning[i].

In our strand within PE3 we set out to make visible and analysable the subjectification of people-within-place and the play of power on and through human subjects and the places they are part of. We wanted to open up ways in which the students could reflect on, and find ways to mobilise, socially just pedagogical practices based on an awareness of the embeddedness of human life in relationships and in relation to place. The practice of enabling place pedagogies begins with previously invisible place stories and, in Gruenewald's (2003a and 2003b) terms, seeks the possibility of *decolonisation* and *reinhabitation* through decomposing dominant place stories and opening up other ways of telling and inhabiting place. The practice makes space for previously silenced voices, and for previously unavailable ways of seeing and being in relation to others, including human and non-human others.

The task students in our place pedagogy strand of PE3 were given was to develop their own place pedagogy project, building on what they had learned from the workshop and their own reading and reflection on enabling place pedagogies. The challenge was to learn to think differently about place, and, as part of that learning, to develop and implement site and discipline specific projects that invited young people in schools and people in their communities to engage in their own reflective and critical investigations of subjectivities in place. Places can be

M. Somerville, B. Davies, K. Power, S. Gannon and *P. de Carteret,*
Place Pedagogy Change, 97–110.

colonised by old stories and images that serve to hold everything in static and sometimes unproductive, even destructive, patterns. We were interested in working with the students to generate possibilities of reinhabiting familiar places in ways that unlock creative evolutionary possibilities (Bergson, 1998).

The particular use that art makes of 'sensations, affects, intensities as its mode of addressing problems' (Grosz, 2008, p. 1) makes it a most suitable modality for investigations of embodied relations to place and space. Art-making, as our students took it up in their projects, was not directed at fixing or capturing some realist or recognisable representation of the world. In a Deleuzian spirit, the students mobilised artistic and literary strategies that drew on a conception of art as affect rather than representation, art as 'a system of dynamized and impacting forces rather than a system of unique images that function under the regime of signs' (Grosz, 2008, p. 3). Representation through arts practice becomes 'no longer a process of fixing but an element in a continuous production; a part of it all, and constantly becoming...Not representation but experimentation' (Massey, 2005, p. 28). The students' learning, then, was experimental, engaged, and opened up the not-yet-known.

PLACE PEDAGOGIES AND PRACTICUM ALTERNATIVES

PE3 students choose from a range of placement strands, each of which enables them to work with young people, with communities, and with each other. They may work in service learning contexts that directly address social disadvantage and equity issues, and they may be located in schools or outside them in community based programs. They may be involved in peer support programs, or in research oriented programs. They may extend their own expertise and knowledge in their discipline areas in ways that are enriching for young people. They develop their relationships with and understandings of the diverse needs and interests of young people. They are likely to work one-on-one or in small groups with learners, unlike in the large classes of their conventional block practicum placements. Their experiences of teaching and learning an enabling place pedagogy in our strand of PE3 made them highly attuned to the normalisation practices that are so pervasive in educational contexts. We encouraged them to develop projects oriented toward the creative evolution of themselves in relation to others and in relation to place. The movement we wanted to open up was from striated to smooth space (Hickey-Moody & Malins, 2007, p. 11):

> Striated spaces are those which are rigidly structured and organized, and which produce particular, limited movements and relations between bodies. ...Smooth spaces, by contrast, are those in which movement is less regulated or controlled, and where bodies can interact—and transform themselves—in endlessly different ways.

The students who enrol in PE3 have already completed at least one of their two school based practicum placements, and they have completed at least one of their two disciplinary teaching Method units. They are well on their ways to becoming teachers, and have begun to locate themselves on the more familiar territory or "striations" of the profession in terms of syllabus and reporting requirements, and of the daily practices that characterise teachers' work. At this point in their trajectory towards the profession, the alternative practicum experience can serve to interrupt processes of normalisation, creating 'a hybrid, in-between, disruptive space that can operate to disturb normative or deficit perceptions and to disrupt pre-service teacher subjectivities' (Gannon, 2010, p. 21). In Deleuze and Guattari's terms, we might consider that at this stage of their trajectory towards the profession these beginning teachers have each established the striated knowledge, the safe space, the 'small plot of land' (1987, p. 161) from which they can begin their experimentation with decolonisation and reinhabitation.

To move beyond the already known striations, to take off in ways that open up the new, is to engage in what Deleuze and Guattari call a line of flight. But as Albrecht-Crane and Slack point out, there is a creative tension between the repetitive citations of institutions and bureaucracies and the line of flight where something new emerges. Institutions need the creative life force that comes from new ideas in order to survive. At the same time their tendency is to regulate and control the new, bringing it within the province of its own regulatory or territorialising practices:

> [The line of flight] is characterized by excess; that is, by what is left or escapes the territorializing work of the molar lines. Lines of flight decode and deterritorialize, but can be—and always eventually are—recaptured or reterritorialized in molar processes such as institutionalized and bureaucratic education practices... (Albrecht-Crane & Slack, 2007, p. 104)

PE3 sits at the edge of this double movement. Enabling place pedagogies can open unpredictable, uncontained, positive and productive lines of flight to new ways of thinking about pedagogical encounters, new ways of imagining the subjectivities of learners, and new ways of constituting oneself as a beginning teacher. At the same time, it takes place within a university, a highly regulated environment; it is part of a teacher's training to take up work in the highly regulated school environment.

In our PE3 strand we invited our students to experiment and to develop original and creative engagements with place and subjectivities in place. In a Deleuzian sense, the strand aimed to open them to difference as a continuous process of differenciation, oriented to intensities and creative evolution (Bergson, 1998). This space of differenciation, which Davies elaborated in Chapter 2, is a space of 'de-individualization, an escape to some degree from the limits of the individual' that enables the 'constitution of new ways of being in the world, new ways of thinking and feeling, new ways of being a subject' (Roffe, 2007, p. 43). Integral to that de-individualising move is the recognition of oneself as a being-in-relation.

The collective biography workshop we conducted within our PE3 strand began the processes of differenciation that were crucial in shaping the projects being developed. We set out to provoke imaginative leaps through working with memory and the senses, with art and literature, generating 'imaginative leaps...in relation to memory...placing ourselves 'at once' in the past; in relation to language, of jumping into the element of sense' (Massey, 2005, p. 59). We thus encouraged the participants to work with the sensory and affective dimensions of memory and to carry this into their projects. At the same time we encouraged them to think of pedagogy as emergent, as open to place and to relationality, drawing out the 'embeddedness of each human being in relations with others and with the physical and psychic environment' (Davies & Gannon, 2009, p. 12).

Emergent pedagogies enable teachers and students to be responsive to the circumstances and the local contexts of learning, and the emergent understandings through which pedagogical communities are formed. The students in PE3 created conditions within their projects by which the others with whom they worked could experience this emergent pedagogy. Their work was creative in the sense that Rinaldi describes creativity, as 'an interactive, relational and social project' that 'requires a context that allows it to exist, to be expressed, to become visible' (2006, pp. 119–120).

Enabling place pedagogies also involved the students in developing a critical stance in relation to the more usual negative, clichéd representations of Sydney's western suburbs, including their own internalised negativities. Their reinhabitation of the westerns suburbs meant generating, through their own work, new ways of viewing and creating stories and texts of the western suburbs. They developed individually significant projects that incorporated their own emergent understandings of, and positionings in relation to, place in general, and to their place—western Sydney—in particular. The projects that we examine in this chapter take up this critical/creative capacity in different ways. An English/History student decided to focus on listening, and made an audio-documentary of her village that lies at the edge of western Sydney. Two Visual Arts students collaboratively developed a program that extended school students' collaborative skills as well as their conceptual and technical understandings of arts practice. Their project culminated in an outstanding public exhibition at the University of Western Sydney art gallery, curated by the students and accompanied by a catalogue that we used our research funds to have printed[ii].

AUDIO-DOCUMENTARY: *VOICES FROM THE VILLAGE*

Gail, an English/History student, was intrigued by the notion of "voice" in Bronwyn's analysis of her experimental writing of place (Chapter 2), and created an audio-documentary of her own village community. She wanted to work with sound to capture her sense that place is formed in embodied encounters, and in the overlapping layers of multiple voices and multiple lives. Inspired by the reading she had done within the PE3 strand, and by the work in the collective biography workshop where writing memories and then reading out loud bring voice and memory together, Gail posed herself a significant challenge in planning her project—could she bring sound to the surface of attention through recording it and so change the participants' sense of place?

[T]he idea that noises are selectively transmitted to another section of our brain and we only consciously deal with those sounds that have already been subconsciously prioritised from birth is of great interest. Do these sounds that permeate our subconscious have an effect on our sense of place? If these sounds were brought forward into consciousness would we have a different sense of place? Would we find wonder and joy in the simple everyday sounds of our surroundings? (Gail's journal)

Her initial plan was to explore the voices of students at the large secondary school where she was situated for her regular practicum placement. However the students were not interested in participating in her project, insisting that, for them, school—in contrast to the sites of their out-of-school lives—was a non-place, not worth talking about, not of sufficient interest or particularly notable. This in itself is an intriguing perspective on secondary schooling, and not altogether different from the PE3 students' own reluctance to tell stories of school in their collective biography workshop. We had found that their most potent memories of teaching and learning were as likely to be situated outside schools as in them. Although schools can provide crucial sites for 'movement, invention and the constitution of new ways of being in the world' (Ellwood, 2009, p. 35) they can also be oddly bland and repetitive—colonised, perhaps, to the point of boredom. As Lehrer observes in the context of the neuroscience of music, 'before a pattern can be desired by the brain, that pattern must play hard to get. Music only excites us when it makes the auditory cortex struggle to uncover its order. If the music is too obvious, if its patterns are always present, it is annoyingly boring' (2007, p. 131).

In the face of the lack of interest of the students in her initial project, Gail chose to shift her attention to her own small community on the precarious rural edge of the suburban sprawl of western Sydney. She created an audio-documentary of the sounds and voices of her community. It incorporated original music, commentary by young children about their lives in the village, memories of elderly residents about past times and specific locations, early morning birdsong and other local ambient sounds including highway sounds, and her own narration and musings on the meaning of place. Her fascination with voice focuses on sound and memory and the relations between them:

The memories of our childhood are so deeply embedded, and when [they are] brought forward to conscious, current thought I can hear a change in people's voices. They become animated in voice or in action. The inflection in their voice changes or the rate of speech varies as they search through emotion to choose the correct word. (Gail's journal)

Gail's acute awareness of the effects of the spoken voice—of tone, pace and other predominantly aural effects—is brought to the recording. In terms of her discipline and teaching methods of English (where spoken English is a mandatory element of the syllabus) and History (where oral history is a topic area) she has developed an excellent resource for her own future use with students. Her flexibility and willingness to change direction in relation to her students' initial inability or unwillingness to relate to her project paid off. That initial refusal heightened her awareness of the possible impact of globalisation on people's inability to think of their own place as interesting. She wrote in her journal:

> The grand idea of globalisation holds within it the notion or yearning to be elsewhere and loss of a sense of belonging to the here and now. The aim of this project is to discover how one small outer western suburbs village feels about change and globalisation and how this affects their own sense of community. (Gail's journal)

Toward the end of her recording process Gail was able to incorporate creative responses from students who lived in her own village. After recording a range of sounds, she played them to the students and invited them to write 'a poem, a song or a story' about the village. By creatively engaging with the sounds and bringing them to life in her recording, the emerging sound-scape engaged the children's interest and alertness to the multiple layers of the sounds of the village. She inspired them to generate their own audio layers and effects. The sounds were no longer the white noise of their too-familiar local place, but sounds that engaged them and inspired them to listen and to write and to make their own sounds. These texts became part of the audio collage that she edited together for her final product, a twenty minute audio documentary on CD entitled *Voices from the Village*. The engagement with school age students was thus, finally, part of the texture of the layered voices and sounds of her village.

Gail's project, focussing on the subtleties of aural responses to place, using sound rather than vision, was creative and different. Her discipline areas of History and English continue to privilege written text over spoken accounts and to poorly understand the components and nuances of sound and of spoken language. Her concern to ensure the highest quality sound-scape of the village led her to purchase her own quality sound recording equipment and software, enabling her to maximise the impact and complexity of the text she produced. Sounds like those that Gail orchestrated and arranged in layers in the audio-documentary have the immediacy that Grosz suggests is characteristic of all art in that, rather than abstractions or rationalisations or other modes of logic, art uses 'sensations, affects, intensities as its mode of addressing problems' (2008, p. 1).

Painting, architecture and music, Grosz suggests, are of the body, and it is the body's capacity for excess, for experiencing, before language, sounds and sights that are more beautiful and more appealing than we need them to be for our survival, that gives art its creative evolutionary capacity. Gail's use of voice and local sounds as the artistic media for her work enabled her to find a way to create a sense of community and place that excited the students in the school in her village. It generated a sense of community in which both children and other community members could find a sense of belonging, whilst also generating an intense and new experience of their specific place. Gail's learning process was one of differenciation for herself and the people she worked with—working with their familiar place they found a way, collectively, to turn it into a palimpsest of sounds that generated a new awareness of and involvement in their place.

This awareness and involvement are also apparent in the second project that we discuss in this chapter, where two PE3 students, Jade and Alicia, led school students through an intense and critical engagement with the places of their memories and their current place in the particular western Sydney suburb where they live and attend school. Their artistic media were paint, photos and found objects.

ART EXHIBITION: *PLACE*

Jade and Alicia devised and taught their place pedagogies project as an after-school art extension program for year 10 students at the school in western Sydney where they had once been students. At the time they enrolled in our PE3 strand, they had completed Visual Arts undergraduate degrees at UWS before enrolling in the Master of Teaching (Secondary) degree. They began work with their after-school art students by replicating the collective biography workshop that they had undertaken with us. They led them through an investigation of their own moments of being, writing and reading out loud the memories of themselves in their early childhood landscapes. These memories became part of the collaborative artworks the year 10 art students developed into a series of installations that they exhibited at the university art gallery.

Integral to the place pedagogy work that was begun with storytelling and writing was the contesting of the students' usual representations of the western suburbs. The clichéd images found in the press and in the students' own talk were countered with the teachers' and students' early childhood memories of that place. Jade and Alicia developed an elaborate teaching program called "Reading place" to guide their workshops with the year 10 students. Their teaching program was subsequently submitted by the Principal of their school to the Arts Curriculum Adviser of the New South Wales Department of Education and Training, as an exemplary program of work that creatively combined literacy and visual arts practice. Central to the program was a range of strategies for *relearning* or decolonising place. One of the first activities was an examination of the dominant discourses through which western Sydney is constituted in media and popular culture as a pathologised place. This included the students' own familiar, repeated citations.

Jade and Alicia, having grown up in western Sydney, had also taken on those pathologising discourses. The work they were doing with their school students involved working to become reflexively aware of their own discursive practices at the same time as they opened up this possibility for their students. Together, through a series of collaborative mind maps, they identified and critiqued the negative repeated citations of western Sydney, documenting and shifting the angle of their gaze from "dole bludgers, bogan, Mt Druitt trash with no shoes eating McDonalds and yelling out the window" to a multicultural place of "family and neighbours, playgrounds, parks, sports fields and bush reserves", a place that is "home". Jade and Alicia worked collaboratively with the students, using memory and art as means to move through critique to transformation. These two forces, critique and transformation, are vital elements in the development of an enabling pedagogy of place. Foucault argued that

> the task of a critical analysis of our world is something that is more and more important. Maybe the most certain of all philosophical problems is the problem of the present time, and of what we are, in this very moment.

> Maybe the target nowadays is not to discover what we are but to refuse what we are. We have to imagine and build up what we could be to get rid of...the simultaneous individualization and totalization of modern power structures. (2000, p. 336)

Both collective biography and collaborative art work are ideal means of working beyond individualisation and totalisation—the simultaneous imposition of globalised power disguised through repeated citations of individual freedom (Nancy, 2007). Using art and memory stories the students constructed a different kind of mindmap.

Together with their students, Jade and Alicia developed "at home in western Sydney" stories, each telling, writing and working visually with fragments from their own memories of childhood in western Sydney. Their students engaged in brainstorming and discussion of particular places in western Sydney, telling stories about outdoor places and their memories of being in them.

Each of the year 10 students took a series of five digital photos depicting aspects of western Sydney. The students were instructed to seek '[n]ot representation but experimentation' (Massey, 2005, p. 28), and to move away from literal and realist images, and instead to 'record signs and symbols'. They were to 'use the macro setting to amplify the subject, to create abstract images and interesting compositions'. In another photography exercise the students were required to take a further set of five photos focussing on the use of text in their environment including street signs, number plates, letter boxes etc. In combination, these instructions to students as to how they might see their worlds differently through the lenses of their cameras, enabled representation to become 'no longer a process of fixing, but an element in a continuous production; a part of it all, and constantly becoming...reject[ing] a strict separation between world and text' (Massey, 2005, p. 28).

The role of the student teachers in this art project was not merely to facilitate student discovery. Alicia and Jade, using their disciplinary expertise, tutored students in practices of looking in non-habituated ways, in decolonising and re-inhabiting their place through art. The pedagogical processes they developed for disrupting habitual ways of thinking and seeing provided the school students with direct instruction on exactly *how* they might shake things up, through the viewfinder in the first instance, and so begin to see differently. It seems that learning happens in the in-between of striated and smooth spaces (Ellwood, 2009, p. 45). The smooth spaces of discovery and invention are at least partially contingent on the striated pedagogical work. The work of a teacher might be understood, in part, as creating a 'space that oscillates between smoothness and striations, a space that is both new and replete with possibilities, and tightly controlled' (Gannon, 2009, p. 81). From this perspective, we might suggest that in classrooms 'some spatial striations are very useful' (Hickey-Moody & Malins, 2007, p. 11).

Each week Alicia and Jade included some memory writing and reading activities in their art workshops. These activities were directly informed by what they had learned in their collective biography with us. Their approach was foreshadowed in their collaborative reflective journal notes written after reading Bronwyn's play (Davies, 2008) and the paper on the principles informing that writing (Chapter 2): 'It feels like such a huge privilege to be able to see and hear so much, I hope that by reading your play and this text that I begin to notice more, to remember more'. The pedagogy of place that Jade and Alicia developed for students in the art class was a pedagogy of noticing, of attending to the close detail of what may not even have been seen without stopping, without using the lens of the camera. They created a space of learning in which they, together with their students, could move beyond the repeated citations of a pathologised place. In their journal the idea for the program is evident right at the beginning, in notes written straight after our collective biography workshop and attached to a particular section of a particular story: 'the sun is shining through the sheets, and there is a pinkish glow inside our cubby'. An arrow leads from here to the comment 'represent collective biography visually'. The notes on place record a developing personal definition:

Place → identity
Place → a frame of mind
Place → a location
A location → that links to my identity
My own place in the world
My place as a 22 year old in the world
My place as a child is different to as an adult. As a child my place was my house, my backyard
My family → was my place to be a child
As an adult → my room? my own house?

As well as for the collective biography work, the art workshops were a site for developing theoretical and conceptual knowledge of art. For example, students were introduced to the works of Jari Silomäki, a contemporary Finnish landscape photographer influenced by Constable, whose work *My weather diary* featured in the 2004 Sydney Biennale. Silomäki's photographs are overwritten with white handwritten text that reads like diary entries for each day's photo. The students responded to this work in their reflective process journals, which served not only to inform their collaborative installations, but also to prepare students for the requirements of visual arts in senior secondary school. One of the students wrote in her journal: 'I find it interesting that Silomäki's "place", the place where he takes photographs, is ultimately influenced by the things around him and other people's places [and that] the photograph itself may have a mood or a feeling that then is changed by the text'.

This strategy of inclusion of journal and story writing within the artwork emerged in the work for the collaborative installations for the exhibition. The artists also made use of electronic texts such as the Community Walk project (www.communitywalk.com), a neighbourhood storytelling project contributed to by children in schools, about which one of the year 10 students reflected: 'I like that people don't only have to write but can add photographs and sound. I think seeing and hearing adds depth to one's feelings of events. The stories are beautiful and I can really see how a place you grew up in—your home, your school—a location or space or place can become such an attachment'.

Jade and Alicia led the art students through a sequence of activities that realised their intention to "represent collective biography visually". Their students generated written stories and created a bank of digital images (including symbols and signs, textures, abstractions and environmental text). These texts became bridges into diverse arts media. Students were asked to select from their photographs, simplify them into "simple shapes and forms" and create silk-screen prints from these on a variety of fabrics and surfaces including hessian, wood and canvas. They used paint on stretched canvas and were asked to focus on creating layers and using a variety of materials and techniques to reflect the colours, shapes and textures of their environment. The mixed media materials that were used in the artworks included acrylic paint, bitumen, shellac, spray paint, enamel, watercolour, oil pastel, impasto, rust paint, varnish, hessian, wood, cardboard, wire, fabric, sandpaper, plastic, foil, sticks, and other found objects. The colour range was restricted to brown, black, red and white so that the artworks could work together as well as separately. Students were required to select from their written texts "a paragraph, key words, a sentence" to print onto their canvas and to work visually with that text by attending to elements such as size, font, layering, direction and inversion.

The art students' process of development from digital photos and collective biography stories to visual artwork can be traced in the text and images published in the catalogue for the exhibition (Ball & Vardon, 2007). Many of them include found objects such as hinges, pieces of wood and wire, and handwritten paper, so that the final works appear more like assemblages than paintings.

The students' stories of childhood evoke many of the small moments when children are connected to each other and to other people and to the possibilities that the landscape and the environment afford them in their play. The story that is included in the artwork in Figure 1 describes an afternoon of intensely engaged but unstructured summer holiday play making mud pancakes. Their stories, dense with other people, are reminders that 'to be a body is to be continuously in relation with other bodies in the world' (Springgay, 2008, p. 12). The final version of the story about mud play appears in the catalogue.

It was a hot summer day, with sprinklers surrounding us. Our faces covered in droplets of water. As the afternoon would pass by we would always resort to making pancakes. We'd start off by stealing some plastic plates and mixing dirt, sand and live worms with water. We'd use our fingers to squash everything together. We'd get into trouble for messing up our clothes. My frilly socks would be stained with mud. We'd end up having to throw away our mud drenched shoes and overalls stinking of sun and sweat. The funniest would be walking back into the house leaving a trail of dirt on the carpet, streak marks of dried mud. After we "baked" our pancake in the hot sweltering sun we would get sticks off the ground and slice it into eight pieces. One for each adult around us. Their red flushed cheeks and piercing eyes soon turned into happy smiles and laughter. Finally, the night would end with us being chased into a warm bubble bath.

Figure 1. Student artwork (untitled).

The artworks selected by the students for inclusion in the catalogue demonstrate the process of shifting the text and memory generated through collective biography into visual form. The image of the frilly socks, for example, appears in multiple locations around the exhibition, taken up into the larger collaborative installation that was created *in situ* in the gallery, demonstrating how one detail can migrate from an individual memory into a collective pool of resources for coming to know western Sydney with new eyes, eyes that are open to new ways of seeing.

The catalogue image below shows how the students also worked experimentally with a key word—golden—from one of their stories. Notably, this word does not appear in any of the final versions of the ten stories that are published in the catalogue, or that were exhibited alongside the images in the gallery. Rather, "golden" remains in the artworks as a trace of earlier drafts of stories and as a word that has a particular resonance with a memory that the students wanted to retain. In the mounted exhibition all of the works appeared as part of a collaborative installation that covered a large wall along one side of the gallery. Only the stories themselves, mounted at eye level as small text blocks along the opposite wall, were attached to the names of particular individuals.

Figure 2. Student artwork (untitled).

PLACE PEDAGOGIES AND INQUIRY

These projects, and the place pedagogies approach that we took up with our students in the place pedagogy strand of PE3, have some of the characteristics of what Springgay calls 'a/r/tography', a pedagogy that she describes as a 'rupture that is open, full of excess and uncertainty' (2008, p. 2). Springgay's pedagogy of touch, drawing from the theoretical work of Deleuze and other poststructural thinkers, aims to write the body into the teaching and learning of visual arts in secondary schools. Meaning is allowed 'to emerge more from what is absent, tacit, literalised and forgotten than from what is present, explicit, figurative and conscious' (Springgay, 2008, p. 8). It insists that 'no single meaning is intended.

Rather each time the work is viewed/read, new and individual meanings, purposes and experiences are created, materialising multifaceted interpretations while simultaneously de-centring the authorial voice' (Springgay, 2008, p. 8).

The artistic and literary practices that we have taken up in our overall place pedagogy project have included play-writing, poetics and art. In re-imagining oneself in place, in finding a new relation to place, and in finding ways to enter a place differently, these aesthetic practices have been vital. The place that one is developing a new relation to might be a place that is almost too familiar through a lifetime of habitation, or it might be a new place that is full of raw and unfamiliar images. In either place artistic and literary practices offer a line of flight that takes off from familiar habitual ways of seeing and being and opens up the possibility of differenciation, of becoming something other than one's individualised and totalised self. It opens up the possibility of decolonising place, and a creative evolution where new thought and new ways of being become possible. In these particular projects, Gail and her community, and Jade and Alicia and their year 10 students, all demonstrate that learning is not simply the acquisition of a fixed body of knowledge, but also openness to and experimentation with the not-yet-known.

NOTES

[i] The submission for the award was called Beyond Institutional Walls: Community Engagement in Secondary Teacher Education, and the award was conferred in Canberra in 2010.

[ii] The students gave us permission to use the journal writing that they engaged in throughout their enrolment in PE3, and the catalogue, for our own place pedagogy research.

REFERENCES

Albrecht-Crane, C., & Slack, J. (2007). Toward a pedagogy of affect. In A. Hickey-Moody & P. Malins (Eds.), *Deleuzian encounters. Studies in contemporary social issues* (pp. 99–110). New York: Palgrave Macmillan.

Ball, A., & Vardon, J. (2007). Place. An exhibition of students' artwork from Erskine Park High School. University of Western Sydney.

Bergson, H. (1998). *Creative evolution.* Mineola: Dover Publications.

Community Walk Project. (n.d.). Homepage. Retrieved February 10, 2010 from http://www.communitywalk.com/

Davies, B. (2008). Life in Kings Cross: A play of voices. *In A. Jackson & L. Mazzei (Eds.),Voice in qualitative inquiry: Challenging conventional, interpretive and critical conceptions in qualitative research* (pp. 197–219). New York: Routledge.

Davies, B., & Gannon, S. (Eds.) (2009). *Pedagogical encounters.* New York: Peter Lang.

Deleuze, G., & Guattari, F. (1987). *A thousand plateaus: Capitalism and schizophrenia* (B. Massumi, Trans.). Minneapolis: University of Minnesota Press.

Ellwood, C. (2009). Listening to homeless young people. In B. Davies & S. Gannon (Eds.), *Pedagogical encounters* (pp. 31–52). New York: Peter Lang.

Foucault, M. (2000). The subject and power. In J. D. Faubion (Ed.), *Michel Foucault. Power* (pp. 326–348). New York: The New Press.

Gannon, S. (2009). Difference as ethical encounter. In B. Davies & S. Gannon (Eds.), *Pedagogical encounters* (pp. 69–88). New York: Peter Lang.

Gannon, S. (2010). Service learning as a third space in pre-service teacher education. *Issues in Educational Research, 20*(1), 21–28. Online. Available at http://www.iier.org.au/iier20/gannon.pdf

Grosz, E. (2008). *Chaos, territory, art. Deleuze and the framing of the earth.* New York: Columbia University Press.

Gruenewald, D. (2003a). The best of both worlds: a critical pedagogy of place. *Educational Researcher, 32*(4), 3–12.

Gruenewald, D. (2003b). Foundations of place: A multidisciplinary framework for place-conscious education. *American Educational Research Journal, 40*(3), 619–654.

Hickey-Moody, A., & Malins, P. (2007). Introduction: Gilles Deleuze and four movements in social thought. In A. Hickey-Moody & P. Malins (Eds.), *Deleuzian encounters. Studies in contemporary social issues* (pp. 1–24). New York: Palgrave Macmillan.

Lehrer, J. (2007). *Proust was a neuroscientist.* Boston: Houghton Mifflin Company.

Massey, D. (2005). *For space.* London: Sage.

Nancy, J-L. (2007). *The creation of the world or globalization* (F. Raffoul & D. Pettigrew, Trans.). Albany: State University of New York Press.

Rinaldi, C. (2006). *In dialogue with Reggio Emilia. Listening, researching and learning.* London: Routledge.

Roffe, J. (2007). Politics beyond identity. In A. Hickey-Moody & P. Malins (Eds.), *Deleuzian encounters. Studies in contemporary social issues* (pp. 40–49). New York: Palgrave Macmillan.

Silomäki, J. (2004). My weather diary. Retrieved November 24, 2010 from http://www.etjcollection.com/Collection_Artist_ Silomaki.html

Springgay, S. (2008). *Body knowledge and curriculum: Pedagogies of touch in youth and visual culture.* New York: Peter Lang.

Bronwyn Davies
Melbourne University
Susanne Gannon
University of Western Sydney

PHOENIX DE CARTERET

PERIPHERAL VISION

Collaborative place-storytelling in community

This chapter looks to the region known as Gippsland, Victoria, in the south eastern corner of Australia, and women who call it home. In the research underpinning the chapter I was interested in women's connection to place and community, and aware that gender remains ineffectively addressed in the environmental social sciences (Banerjee & Bell, 2007). Storytelling and narrative are useful research methods but are also valuable in adult learning, particularly in exploring the constraint of socially constructed narratives (Clark, 2010; Michelson, 2010). The initial focus of the chapter is on prominent storylines about Gippsland, mindful that 'a society produces and perpetuates its history and identity through storytelling' (Carr, 2001, p. 3). Later I outline the place-storytelling workshops I developed to research women's experiences through the theme *At Home in Gippsland*. The workshop method was devised to provoke memories beyond storylines (Søndergaard, 2002) shaped by dominant discourses and public pedagogy[ii] (Giroux, 2004). The storytelling approach provided an opportunity for participants to reflect on personal experiences, while the collaborative group process was a means of learning to discuss 'social norms and power relationships...and how they are located...in larger cultural narratives' (Clark & Rossiter, 2008, p. 66). In this learning the women explored emerging themes and new stories of self and community. Their stories slip between the personal and the collective, and it was this discovery that motivated the women to create a book and later a DVD of stories.

Stretching east beyond the metropolitan sprawl of Melbourne, Gippsland is a place of contrasts. Rich soil and abundant rainfall belie the threat of wild fires in summer. Old and newer stacks pump vapours from coal fired power stations, clouding the open sky. The membrane of dominant narratives preserves pride in the achievements of settler history. The economic base of Gippsland is diverse, encompassing dairy, logging, tourism, gourmet food and wine, but most significantly the region is responsible for the generation of eighty five percent of the state's electricity and the distribution of gas. Yet, even with today's concern for the environment, there's a lingering nostalgia for the prosperous days before privatisation when the power industry first moved into the Latrobe Valley at the heart of Gippsland. Migrant workers and cash-strapped Australians flooded into the valley after World War Two. They lived in makeshift camps and settlements that blanketed the region with hope and possibility. Their rough dwellings could lay no claim of ownership to the land. The wealth below, carved up by the leases and the claims of others, still takes precedence over the settlements above. Habitation is

M. Somerville, B. Davies, K. Power, S. Gannon and *P. de Carteret,*
Place Pedagogy Change, 111–126.

skin deep, leaving no town secure. It's only in the very recent past that the newer city of Traralgon has secured its future, finally assured it wont be dug up for coal (Fletcher, 2002).

The most common stories about women in Gippsland's history and mythology typically position women in discourses that prop up colonisation and masculinity (Carr, 2001, p. 254). Women were portrayed as being at risk from the inhospitable environment, or from harm at the hands of dangerous Aboriginal men or outlaws (McLeary & Dingle, 1998; Carr, 2001; Shears, 2008). Even the valorous women botanists of Gippsland are seen as having engaged in risky business given the wildness of the land, and the strictures relating to appropriate gendered attire and activities of their time (Gitsham-Allen, 2007). Anxieties about women's identity, place and belonging (Carr, 2001, p. 2) portray relationships between women, men and place as clear-cut and conservative.

The colonial history typified by stories of heroic masculinity also leaves Gippsland disconnected from its Indigenous heritage. The original inhabitants are most often remembered as hostile warriors on account of their fierce resistance to the early settlers. There are traces of their stories in local place names, and creation stories are taken up, as in using the representation of two eels for the corporate logo of the power station Loy Yang, a name said to have derived from Aboriginal language[iii]. Indigenous connection to place is easily elided as Loy Yang, adjacent to Eel Creek, generates its own new life.

On the road between Traralgon and Morwell, an immigration memorial has been constructed. The centrepiece is the sculpture of a lone man, arriving with just one small suitcase. He stands high, flanked by an honour roll of names. The man has the trace of a larrikin and the tarnished twinkle of an adventurer. Regardless of age he's wearied, and no matter his origins, he represents an Aussie bloke come home. The imagined future was colonised with belief in the power of hard work to make a man and build a country. These and other culturally sanctioned narratives are a significant form of learning, effective from childhood (Eakin 1999, p. 112). Image, symbol, naming and monuments convey dominant storylines and narrow public histories that shape the way we understand our individual experiences and the kind of stories it is appropriate to tell. But now, in the aftermath of significant job losses on account of downsizing subsequent to the privatisation of the power industry, there's an 'overarching sense of despair' (Cameron & Gibson, 2005, p. 274) furrowed deep on the rugged masculinity of the Valley. Kenway calls it 'melancholic masculinity' (2009, p. 204).

Moving into Gippsland I was struck by the confluence of socio-economic depression and the intense loyalty often voiced for the place by local people, especially the women I came into contact with at work, in the supermarket and on other daily rounds. I wanted to research relations in this confluence, particularly women's attachment to the place they call home. Similar to Cameron and Gibson-Graham, I was seeking insight into 'the valuing and strengthening of traditionally coded *'feminine'* qualities such as nurture, cooperation, sharing, giving, concern for the other, attentiveness to nature, and so on, as well as traditionally coded *'masculine'* qualities such as independence, experimentation, leadership and adventurousness' (2003, p. 153, italics in original). These qualities give an indication of relationship to place, yet are often overlooked in economic rationalist summations and statistical accounts that paint their own images. Cameron and Gibson-Graham argue that a feminist approach to economics forces 'a recognition of the creativity, productivity, resilience and solidarity of that half of the economy that has traditionally not been seen or accounted for' (2003, p. 153). While women's loyalty to Gippsland reflects these attributes, they are generally absent from the dominant storylines of place.

Lower than average standards of living and income, poor educational attainment and generational unemployment compound the bleak outlook that this resource rich region is socially and environmentally at risk. A public pedagogy of improvement does little to assuage the sense of deficit and depression, though Government and local authorities are at pains to strengthen the social fabric of the Latrobe Valley through adult education and community engagement. Neighbourhood Houses and Learning Centres (NHLCs) dotted throughout Gippsland have assumed an important role in this process. I'd had the opportunity to visit many of these centres to interview their coordinators, and this gave me insight into the importance of the centres in the community. At the height of women's liberation in the 1970s, the first rural Neighbourhood Houses (NH) opened in Victoria. It was largely through the drive of local Gippsland woman Bette Boynton that Neighbourhood Houses were established in the region (Landon et al., 2008). Boynton was a union activist whose own sense of rural isolation motivated her to lobby for the first regional NH. Initially the centres provided childcare, learning and social activities for women isolated in the home by their domestic duties. Now they respond to broader community needs for vocational and non-vocational courses, but one Coordinator told me that in spite of welcoming both men and women, the idea persists that they are women's places. My decision to use the local NHLC as the venue for the workshops acknowledged this interrelationship between women, place and adult learning.

BACKGROUND TO THE COLLABORATIVE PLACE-STORYTELLING METHOD

The collaborative place-storytelling method was developed from memory work (Haug 1987, 2000; Onyx & Small, 2001), collective biography (Davies & Gannon, 2006), and Somerville's place pedagogies framework (2008). These approaches begin with lived experience and provide strategies by which to examine dominant storylines and narratives that emerge from embodied memory stories.Memory work was first developed as a collaborative research method in the 1980s by Frigga Haug and her colleagues, to explore female socialisation (1987, 1992). As suggested by Haug, the method has since been developed and modified. In a discussion of adaptations, Onyx and Small (2001) identify phases that broadly characterise developments of the method. The collaborative place-storytelling workshops follow a similar pattern, but while the *At Home in Gippsland* research was one strand of a collaborative project, it was not in itself collaborative research. The workshops were offered as a series in the program of courses offered by the local NHLC, and clearly identified as part of a research project. Participants self-selected on the basis of their interest in the activity and were not recruited as co-researchers.

OUTLINE OF *AT HOME IN GIPPSLAND* STORYTELLING WORKSHOPS

The first phase of the place-storytelling workshops is 'talking story' (Onyx & Small, 2001, p. 779), where each person tells the group a memory story in response to a prompt. Others can then ask questions to clarify or deepen the story, sometimes adding their own experiences. As Onyx and Small note, the initial memory stories in this phase may take the participants by surprise (2001, p. 779), but in our group surprising stories were more often unleashed by the conversations that followed the first memory telling. The sessions were digitally recorded and later professionally transcribed. The transcript then became a text the group used to further discuss the personal stories and also to cut, paste and edit collective stories crafted collaboratively from the transcribed conversation. This extended the second phase, which Onyx and Small identify as writing up the personal stories that emerge in the discussion (2001, p. 777). The stories were discussed and clarified through group conversations, looking for indicators of taken-for-granted understandings, social meanings and silences, teasing out emergent themes or embodied memories. The revised stories were reread in the third phase (Onyx & Small, 2001, p. 777), and often provoked further spirited discussions. Conversations sometimes wandered from the topic into personal reminiscences. My role as facilitator was initially pivotal in refocussing reminiscences, but the women soon took up the task of managing digressions of their own accord, with quips and questions that redirected discussion to the group purpose. The conversational ranging over topics reminded me of more traditional cultures where storytelling is often the central mode of passing information, and learning is achieved over long periods of journeying in a broad narrative landscape. The transcripts captured the breadth and depth of the discussions and proved to be generative, to the point of building creative confidence. Working collaboratively helped the women to negotiate potential barriers in the pursuit of the perfect story—fears about literacy, of not being skilled enough writers, or the question of how to begin. The fourth phase of theoretical analysis was my sole responsibility as researcher, yet the development of the book and DVD were collaborative outcomes of group discussions that paralleled the theoretical work.

THE WORKSHOP SESSIONS

I chose an image of another prominent local monument for the flyer advertising the workshops. The Big Cigar pays tribute to Sir Winston Churchill, and presides over the shopping precinct in the township of Churchill, named after him amid local controversy. It's an incongruous place marker and memorial now, in this district known for its greenhouse emissions and expanding open cut mines. The image of the Big Cigar captures paradox and framed the workshops as a contact zone (Pratt, 1991) where diverse stories were welcome.

The series began with an information session where I explained the research, outlined the program, discussed ethics and privacy issues, and suggested the production of a tangible joint outcome. My intention was to establish a material reciprocity between us as collaborative partners, where my role as facilitator was extended to participant, and the women were not construed as passive subjects. The first workshop was an introduction to collaborative storytelling and I took a collection of items to use as memory prompts. There was an armful of greenery and colourful cuttings from my garden, an old postcard of Churchill, a map, a tourist brochure and several of my own old family photographs. They made an attractive centrepiece on the tables (pulled together to create a large square workspace with chairs around the edge), dressing up the plain classroom. When all the women were settled and introductions made, I asked them to choose one item they were drawn to, and invited each to tell a memory that it provoked. As stories were told and comments made, conversation began to thread the stories together. The exercise generated interested listening and a lively sharing of experiences. Afterwards we discussed the method. The women had experienced how the images and objects provoked wonderfully rich and varied stories of lived experiences. In their pleasure and enthusiasm for talking story, the women recognised embodied memories as significant to storytelling, and the value of their conversations in deepening the stories.

The next talking story session used a single question as a prompt to the whole group: *what is your earliest memory of home in Gippsland?* Some participants were very involved in local and family history and used their family connection to locate themselves in place (Mayne, 2009, p. 177). Women are often familiar with this way of storytelling and also with keeping family albums or scrapbooks, which are individual activities and modes of authorisation (Gudmundsdottir, 2006, p. 220). These women initially told stories about their male predecessors. Some of their ancestors were Gippsland pioneers, others had come to the Valley to work in the mines or migrated in the mid twentieth century. Dee explained her heritage this way: *I'm absolutely Gippslander through and through. My ancestors on both sides have been Gippslanders. This is my home.* This intergenerational connection prompted a discussion about time in relation to belonging, and the question of belonging raised concern over the title of the project. Was it right to claim Gippsland as home when most of us lived in the Latrobe Valley? These anxieties over belonging and the right to speak were vigorously discussed. It emerged that the women know Gippsland and the Latrobe Valley as discrete yet interconnected landscapes—one primarily natural, the other industrial. Most of the participants know the overall region very well through family holidays and outings, or through families dispersing to other towns. They talked about the responsibility of the Latrobe Valley to provide natural resources for Melbourne and the rest of Victoria. The women thought the Valley is viewed from Melbourne without care, seen as a *big black hole, a dirty big black hole* (Bonnie). Kaye explained that Gippsland is *the other* to Melbourne, while Jan commented with slippery meaning that *the energy of the Valley is the energy of the whole state.* The women perceived that a negative image of the Valley is created in this juxtaposition of centre and margins, pivoting on the responsibility to supply resources for the whole state.

In the following conversation among participants, the women speak of the Latrobe Valley and demonstrate Paul Carter's (2009, p. 25) notion of place-making in 'terms of creating the conditions of meeting':

> *It's such a rich tapestry because of the coal. Such a lot of different people came here from Europe and places like that after the war, and they used to send the men that had got out of jail up to Moe and they'd send them there for work, to give them a bit of a start. They would send them in, with a suit and ordinary shoes in their cardboard cases and they had to work in the mud and in the slush, you know, totally inappropriate, and they had like singles men's quarters.*

> *Yallourn North used to be called Old Brown Coal Mine, and when I was growing up, Traralgon was the clean town, the posh town, do you know what I mean? It still is, you know what I mean, it has wider streets.*

> [All laughing and talking over each other]

> *Yeah, wider streets but that horrible odour from the paper mill.*

> *There's always been a sort of a, a richness, not just the power source but so many different people.*

> *Yeah, it's a bit of a tartan.*

Even this snippet of conversation displays complex place awareness, skimming over the environmental impact of weather and social considerations: coal as the reason for being in Gippsland, the wetness commonly underfoot on account of high rainfall and soil conditions, the social strata and the competition between towns. This interrelationship weaves the fabric of place. With enthusiasm and laughter the women played out the irony and substance of the issues they raised.

Some of the first memory stories about fathers' jobs needed only gentle nudging for the women's own experiences to unfurl. The fragments of their embodied memories became the nodes in shared stories, but the women could also gather up personal fragments into individual stories. Some women pursued those individual stories at home, writing poetry or short pieces provoked by the group work. The group conversations were the wellspring of fluid, even mercurial memories that slipped effortlessly between family, broader social questions and back to the intimate; between the personal and the collective.

One such conversation involved two fathers, one an engineer and the other a bricklayer. Discussion had developed around the demand for builders and tradesmen to construct new homes and public buildings during the surge of prosperity in Gippsland. A rambling conversation about the old Traralgon Hospital consolidated into thoughtful discussion, as the topic shifted from men's work to the women's embodied memories. Initial reminiscences about fundraising for equipment when the hospital was first built became a reflective discussion about progress and the value of women's unpaid community work, and later about mothers' work. The following snippet reveals pride built through intimate connections, tinged with a desire to keep up with change.

I can remember we used to pick mushrooms on the old Traralgon Hospital site—that was one of our out of town mushroom paddocks. We used to pick mushrooms and then it was built and all the Italian bricklayers came to town and did all the work on it.

And we had this beautiful new hospital, and then many years later it's pulled down. No one would imagine that our beautiful pride we had in our hospital, it just wouldn't exist anymore. But that's change.

Well, I've got to tell you that I had an emergency caesarean operation three months after that hospital was opened. And the sterilisation unit broke down and the doctor told me afterwards, 'we boiled everything up in a kettle for you'. That was the original hospital, near where the motel is, coming into Traralgon, on the top of the hill, where there's a little footbridge that goes over the railway line. There's a big bare patch there now. We had this great building, the biggest building in Traralgon, and now it's gone.

That was our mushroom paddock, and there it is now, a paddock full of rubble.

Well, I did a year of nursing there.

If you remember it, it's still there, it's just another room.

This tiny potted history of the hospital site skips from the mushroom paddock, to the new hospital building, its later obsolescence and demolition and its return to being a paddock, littered with rubble. Though conversations in the group traversed many rooms of memory, some stories were returned to again and again. From this first mention, Dee's caesarean section became one such story. It became an intimate connection for the women, and richer stories emerged through that intimacy. Eventually the scar from the operation became the focus, standing in for the uncertainty of taking home a fragile new baby. The scar and the uncertainty it represented became a point of connection that gave way to memories of our own mothers.

I can't think about home without thinking about my mum.

Mum was a really quiet person so a lot of the weekend [recently spent with my brothers] was about our time with Dad rather than her, because she was a really quiet person. But her essence was there in the background just as it always was.

From this background, stories emerged of women's physical and emotional survival through adversity. One mother took her children down a well to escape a bushfire. Another woman told of her mother's ongoing work to protect and care for her family, with an alcoholic husband. The father had come back from war, taking his family to the Valley so he could work in the mine. Jaye told us he was emotionally damaged but that in those days there was no support, and he started drinking. Her mother's difficult work can be pieced together from many small stories (Bamberg, 2006; Georgakopoulou, 2006). Jaye talked about life in the temporary settlement at Derhams Hill and later, when the family moved to a more permanent house at Yallourn. In one particularly poignant piece she explained that when money was short, her mother would sometimes use the tissue paper pieces of dress patterns to wrap the school lunch. Jaye had to take the pieces back home each afternoon and her mother would clean and straighten them so as not to waste the pattern.

Memory work in the storytelling workshops unfolded embodied memory stories such as this one. The heightened level of reflection revealed embodied feelings in glimpses and, while painful emotions sometimes came to awareness, the process allowed each individual to stretch into new memories, gradually finding increased suppleness and courage in the process of re-membering, like peeling through layers. The collaborative process limbers up storytelling rather than catapulting participants into suppressed memories. At all times the choice to participate in the conversation, or not, was up to each individual. Often one woman or another would listen for some time before joining in to ask a question or add a personal story. At other times the group ran with a topic raised. Conversation would shift spontaneously and with enthusiasm in the new direction, moving to unexpected stories and emotions. After the initial phase of talking story, the memories were fleshed out this way, as the experience was remembered in more detail through the group conversations.

CARE AT A DISTANCE

The women's stories reveal a sense of home created in dynamic links across generations through time, purpose and the particularities of place laced with emotion. Bonnie wrote a story that she brought in to share with the group. For her it contains the essence of living and participating in community life that is so central to her sense of home in Gippsland. Her story is about the Scottish Festival held at Glenmaggie in Northern Gippsland. Bonnie whimsically suggests that Nessie, the Loch Ness Monster, has taken up residence in the local Lake Glenmaggie. She also hunted out her friend's recipe for tattie scones, further reinscribing her connection with childhood and a distant home place. Carter calls this movement between distant places and local experiences 'doublings' (2009, p. 1). Doubling is a reflexivity that recognises different histories, complex con- nections and disconnections in local places. Carter writes that care for places is made in the to-ing and fro-ing through complexity, in actual physical journeying but also in stories, associations and artistic representations that bring the places we've come from to our sense of the places we love (2009, p. 10). Place is made in the complex layers of historical, environmental, spiritual and social interaction. Like other stories that emerged in the group, Bonnie's story about the Glenmaggie

Festival colours her daily life in an aged care unit in Morwell with memories of home in Scotland and Ireland as a child, even of opportunities missed.

In Ireland my Grandma said to me, 'there's a hundred and one cures in this garden'. I was a child, what do I know about cures or sicknesses? Her words often come back to me. I wish she'd either written them down, or verbally passed them on to my older cousins who are twenty years older than me, or [to] my mother.

The group understood "home" as made in the keeping of tangible links passed through family possessions, recipes and plant cuttings, but Bonnie's words show connection layered across gaps and intangible links. Diane Bell explains that not only are links made, but the understanding of oneself is crafted as well: 'what one generation bestows on the next gives significance to the particular events and relationships. Bonds are created, ideas and values from which to construct a sense of self, of place, of belonging, spun' (Bell, 1987, p. 256). The bonds are resilient yet opaque and crafted with the fragility of tissue paper, requiring care and attention.

Stories like Bonnie's demonstrate awareness of interrelationship between people and place. Like many of the participants' conversations they show the women as embedded in local place and culture where time and place are not immutably fixed (Atkinson & Silverman, 2006, p. 2). Some stories express the women's love of the natural environment, here tempered by the impact of humanity on the landscape:

Spending a night in the Gippsland bush is a memorable experience—no man made industrial noise, no motors, no lights, isolated but peaceful, falling asleep conscious of our human presence intruding in the natural environment while listening for a snuffling wombat, or a Boobook owl.

…or they hint towards reverence of the land's connection to the women:

I just like going to Bulga Park and being part of the bush. There's some sort of connection, there's nothing else going on, just wind blowing, and water trickling through, and the little bugs scurrying everywhere.

In this way some stories veer into a spiritual sense of belonging inseparable from everyday life. Carol wrote a poem[iv] casting herself as physically connected with Gippsland.

I'm a woman of the Gipps Lands
Traralgon native
Born and bred
Valley coal in my blood
Valley thoughts in my head
Gippsland is the place I live
The place of my birth
The place of my connection
To this very earth

So when I go away from here
I take the essence of the Valley with me
Part of the Gipps Lands
The part that I call me

The women were delighted by the nascent creativity and insight evident in the transcribed conversations. The transcripts did not identify speakers by name and individuals were often surprised to realise they had made a particular comment, and amazed at the wisdom in their words. Although establishing confidence and candour in one-on-one interviews can be difficult (Kikumura, 1998, p. 142), trust grew in the safe, supported, and self-paced environment of the workshops. The collaborative method fostered participants' confidence to speak with honesty. This opened up subjects I had not thought of exploring, for example problem gambling in Gippsland. While levels of participation varied, the memory stories and conversations raised significant storylines which, I perceived, reflected the women's embodied attitudes and experiences, providing clues to underpinning social concepts and conventions (Tonkin, 1990, p. 34). The women found pleasure in sharing stories and knowledge of Gippsland, but most importantly, in uncovering experiences from embodied memory, they learnt the value of reflection that affirmed their place in community.

THE BOOK: *PERIPHERAL VISION*

Together the group worked to produce a book of the stories, by picking themes from the memory stories and transcribed conversations. The women were surprised to see the variety of topics and the depth of their interest and engagement with local issues. Cutting and pasting together fragments of conversations kept the flow between different voices, decentring the authorial subject and maintaining diversity. As weeks passed, the women brought in more photographs, recipes, biographical writing, journal entries, poems and snippets of personal wisdom, inspired by the collaborative storytelling, to include in the book. As they were compiling the text, conversations and debates would often ensue over the meaning of particular words or a turn of phrase and what to include. The creative process stimulated the participants to individually pursue themes they were particularly interested in, or to further research issues that had come up in the group. Bonnie collected newspaper articles and found statistics about gambling, and Dee searched for the meaning of Aboriginal words. Kaye did archival research at the local history centre, looking for information about a floral display made for the Queen's visit in the 1950s. Carol interviewed a friend about the threatened closure of a sundries market still running at the local saleyards. In these pursuits, seeking information to deepen our stories, the women made new connections in the wider community.

Discussing the demolition of the hospital, alcoholism, gambling and other issues creates what Karina Eileraas refers to as 'stammers in dominant discourses'. Stammers, she explains, can disrupt or misrecognise the dominant imaginary. They create fissures and stimulate new ethical modes of exchange and alternative stories (2007, p. 159). The workshops produced many stammers and as the women explored their memories, they began to describe their stories as peripheral to dominant history, eventually naming the completed book *Peripheral Vision: A kaleidoscope of stories by women*. While peripheral vision suggests movement, sensation and detail perceived beyond the central line of sight[v], use of the metaphor of the kaleidoscope is an attempt to invoke the fluidity and diversity. We wanted to encourage readers to give flight to their own stories from the fragments, as the following extract from *Peripheral Vision* suggests.

With each turn of the hand, the individual fragments of our kaleidoscope fall for a moment into another pattern and the beginning of other stories.

Making sense from diversity is not necessarily an easy task as Dee commented, saying she *was puzzled how such a diverse group could work; however we are an interesting lot, and have become a caring group of friends* (March 12, 2008). And though contact zones are not always comfortable, I was surprised to hear Jaye later describe the work as a personal challenge for her. She had participated with humour, contributing to lively discussions and debate with enthusiasm but, as she explains in this inscription, the sessions provided her with an opportunity

to grow,
get out of your comfort zone,
gather up your courage, feel the fear,
find your hill
AND
climb it.

THE DVD: *COMMON THREADS*

Peripheral Vision was well received in the community, but the women wanted the stories to be even more accessible. To this end, we pursued the idea of recording a talking book and eventually this idea morphed into producing a DVD. Content was chosen and edited collaboratively in several more group sessions. There was also a weekend retreat where we walked and told stories, creatively stretching our voices. Carol set about learning all aspects of making a DVD and she produced *Common Threads* from digitally recorded sound and images. There is a very brief discussion about the method on the DVD because the group wanted it to be useful as a learning resource for others.

The women had sometimes spoken about bush fires during the initial series of workshops leading up to the production of *Peripheral Vision*. We didn't use those stories in the book but later when we rerecorded their stories for the DVD, the subject of bush fires came up again. Two women remembered back to the 1939 fires and to others in the 1940s. Fires were part of their stock of family stories. Initially aware of the gravity of loss of life and property in the fires of their childhoods, the first stories in the group were objective and well practised, but through opening up to the collaborative process, they came to talk about how it *felt* as children to experience bush fire. One woman remembered her fascination with the fires when she was a young girl. Seeing the glow of fires dotted far away on the hills she had imagined it was how a city would look at night with flickering bright lights.

Midway through recording the DVD, the disastrous Black Saturday bushfires swept across Victoria. One hundred and seventy three people died with hundreds more injured, and the place of fires in the women's lives loomed larger in our conversations. We were all spectators in the 2009 fire. Though some of us were forced to evacuate our homes we all watched from a distance as Gippsland was ravaged and eleven people died in the Latrobe Valley. Forced to stand back, the women spoke about experiencing the fires from a distance through the changing colour and intensity of the smoky sky. Jaye talked of her fascination with the glow, imagining this was what the end of the world or hell would look like. The women's preoccupation with the appearance of the sky was tinged with guilt in their adult minds, that as children they were observers who did not really understand the serious implications of the tragedy that unfolded around them. There were traces of this observers' guilt in our conversations after Black Saturday too—guilt at being safe, and even shame at not having an active role in protecting lives and property. Embodied memories of fires wound the years into each other, threading unpredictability through the sense of Gippsland as home.

In the '39 fire we didn't have time...we were sitting in the swamp and Dad kept putting saturated bags around our shoulders. We lived lower than the road and you couldn't see through the smoke where the fires were. Then my cousin came on a motorbike across the hill and said the road was safe and we should go because the fire was coming our way, and I remember driving away and looking back at the house and just wondering if it would still be there, but of course, it wasn't.

The women's memories of loss in the fires of their childhoods remain strong. Dee recalled the loss of Christmas gifts and a paper fairy dress made and worn for the Christmas play at school in 1938. Her photo in the dress and another telling of the story brought sombre tones to the group after Black Saturday. Again the memory was tinged with a trace of guilt, evident in uneasy laughter at the in/significance of the loss.

I thought I was a princess in that dress, and my sister had gone away and hadn't played with the little piano she'd got for Christmas. A year or so later, having just moved back to the rebuilt house, we were threatened by fire again. This time my sister and I were going to save the orchard, I was about eight. We had big cream cans of water and buckets, then the wind changed and blew the fire back towards us and we just ran. But there was only grass and the fire burnt out before it reached us.

Yet that second fire, when Dee and her sister valiantly determined to save the orchard, actually burnt down their local school at Callignee, and Dee couldn't go to school for a whole year. The Black Saturday fires of 2009 burnt through the same area and the property once owned by her family, taking the second house. She told us how she had listened to reports about the fires on the radio all that 2009 night:

And I keep going back to the '39 fire, but now the huge loss of life has been horrendous. I kept getting up all night and thinking about people who'd been through the fires before, but there we were safe, and we just felt guilty.

Sharing fire stories revealed resilience and an undercurrent of resistance to the not knowing where or when bush fire will strike next time. Women's stories suggest fire as a continuous thread, punctuated by named years when fires burn. Fire is integral to their experience of place. Their stories reveal the complexity of emotions spanning fear, guilt, survival, determination, acceptance, shame and more.

At each phase of the work the women would talk about the project to families, friends and other groups they belonged to. They gathered more stories, photos, songs and ideas in this sharing. When it came time to launch the DVD, the women wanted to invite everyone who had shown interest or made a contribution to participate in a celebratory public launch. Each woman took a role inviting people, distributing posters, planning, preparing food and bringing the evening to fruition. Other groups were invited to participate, to promote the diverse ways it is possible to tell stories. Local choral group Gippsappella and a belly dancing group performed. Others contributed to material displays that embody storytelling: patchwork, art, family albums, a wall-hanging embroidered with a wedding gown, photographs and jewellery, baby clothes, and historical magazines. A friend donated huge bunches of native flowers from their wholesale nursery to decorate the hall. The women brought lemons and herbs, pot plants and cuttings to give away in the spirit of sharing and reciprocity. There was food, and sherry was offered because it is *a genteel social drink* (Dee). The launch mapped Gippsland with women's sense of home as it was 'sung, chanted, stitched and woven, told in stories, and danced across the fire-lit skies' (Aberley, in Lippard, 1997, p. 76). As a public event it was a celebration of stories peripheral to dominant narratives and resistant to public pedagogy that foregrounds individualism (Giroux, 2004).

LEARNING SELF—BUILDING COMMUNITY

The collaborative place-storytelling workshops engaged women who are largely outside of formal educational programs. They participated in spirited and reflexive discussions that facilitated new learning and built confidence. Time and again the women spoke about their pleasure in conversations that they would not usually have. They talked about stereotypes that blanket possibility with constraint, and they staked new claims on the present and on the future too.

I had to let go of the past, to approach the future, to live here and now. It's like the rings of a tree, that's got its latest year out here and yet, the latest year encompasses everything it's been before, and it's ready to give birth to more.

Increasingly the women were aware of inhibiting storylines that pushed some emotions and experiences to the back of awareness. Talking, listening and reflecting moved their memories beyond familiar, taken-for-granted storylines, generating the curiosity to follow new ideas, to flesh out fragments of memory and emotion. Friendships grew and the workshops did the work of building community, pointing to new place-conscious ways of engaging with community in a bottom up, assets based approach (Ife & Tesoriero, 2006; Kretzmann & McKnight, 1993). This is a multi layered place-conscious approach to both community development and adult education that is joyful. Grounded in lived experience the workshop method fostered learning from each other about self and community. The work foregrounded rich human resources of resilience, care and reciprocity, and with all its diversity Gippsland remains a meaningful connection between us.

Common threads join us
Through the tartan we call life
Connected by the seam of coal
Through all the joys
And our strife[vi].

Through their place-storytelling women learnt the conjunction of body, space and time (Simonsen, 2005, p. 10). Connection and commonality did not homogenise their experiences but affirmed the interconnection of the personal, the social and the physical place through telling, listening, and hearing stories. Clark explains this type of learning as important in adult education because it is a means of making sense of self and experiences and of learning how we are positioned by narratives, and because from telling stories we learn to teach others (Clark, 2010, p. 6). The women's newly learnt appreciation of storytelling prompted their desire to teach others how to unlock personal stories from embodied memory, and this was perhaps the most surprising outcome of all.

ACKNOWLEDGEMENTS

Phoenix is grateful for two small grants from Monash University that funded the initial research project, the publication of *Peripheral Vision* and the subsequent development of the DVD.

NOTES

[i] *At Home in Gippsland* is one strand of an Arts-Education Research Project, *Gender, Body, Work, Place* funded by Monash University and undertaken in collaboration with Margaret Somerville, Meredith Fletcher and Eva Bendix-Petersen.
[ii] 'Public pedagogy in this sense refers to a powerful ensemble of ideological and institutional forces whose aim is to produce competitive, self interested individuals vying for their own material and ideological gain' (Giroux, 2004, p. 74).
[iii] Powerworks Tour commentary, 2007.
[iv] *I'm a woman of the Gipps Lands*, Carol Campbell, 2007. Three stanzas of thirteen.
[v] http://en.wikipedia.org/wiki/Peripheral_vision
[vi] *I'm a woman of the Gipps Lands*, Carol Campbell. 2007. One stanza of thirteen.

REFERENCES

Atkinson, P., & Silverman, D. (Eds.) (2006). Kundera's immortality: the interview society and the invention of the self. In P. Atkinson & S. Delamont (Eds.), *Narrative Methods* Vol. 2. London: Sage.

Bamberg, M. (2006). Stories: big or small. Why do we care? *Narrative Inquiry, 16*(1), 139–157.

Banerjee, D., & Bell, M. M. (2007). Ecogender: Locating gender in environmental social science. *Society and Natural Resources, 20*(1), 3–19.

Bell, D. (1987). *Generations: Grandmothers, mothers and daughters.* Melbourne: Penguin Books.

Cameron, J., & Gibson, K. (2005). Alternative pathways to community and economic development: The Latrobe Valley Community Partnering Project. *Geographical Research, 43*(3), 274–285.

Cameron, J., & Gibson-Graham, J. K. (2003). Feminising the economy: metaphors, strategies, politics. *Gender, Place and Culture, 10*(2), 145–157.

Campbell, C. (2007). I'm a woman of the Gipps Lands. In P. de Carteret (Ed.), *Peripheral vision: A kaleidoscope of stories by women in Gippsland* (pp. 8–9). Churchill, Victoria: Off-campus Learning Centre Printery.

Carr, J. (2001). *The captive white woman of Gipps Land: In pursuit of the legend.* Carlton South: Melbourne University Press.

Carter, P. (2009). Care at a distance: Affiliations to country in a global context. In M. Somerville, K. Power & P. de Carteret (Eds.), *Landscapes and learning: Place studies for a global world* (pp. 21–33). Rotterdam: Sense Publishers.

Clark, C., & Rossiter, M. (2008). Narrative learning in adulthood. *New Directions for Adult and Continuing Education, 2008*(119).

Clark, C. M. (2010). Narrative learning: its contours and its possibilities. *New Directions for Adult and Continuing Education, 2010*(126).

Crawford, J., Kippax, S., Onyx, S., Gault, U., & Benton, P. (1992). *Emotion and gender: Constructing meaning from memory.* London: Sage.

Davies, B., & Gannon, S. (Eds.) (2006). *Doing collective biography: Investigating the production of subjectivity.* Maidenhead: Open University Press.

Eakin, P. J. (1999). *How our lives become stories: Making selves.* Ithaca, USA: Cornell University Press.

Eileraas, K. (2007). *Between image and identity: Transnational fantasy, symbolic violence and feminist misrecognition.* Plymouth: Lexington Books.

Fletcher, M. (2002). *Digging people up for coal: A history of Yallourn.* Melbourne: Melbourne University Press.

Georgabkopoulou, A. (2006). Thinking big with small stories in narrative and identity analysis. *Narrative Inquiry, 16*(1), 122–130.

Giroux, H. A. (2004). Cultural studies and the politics of public pedagogy: Making the political more pedagogical. *Parallax, 10*(2), 73–89.

Gitsham-Allen, T. (2007). *Gippsland lady botanists.* Inverloch, Victoria: South Gippsland Conservation Society Inc.

Gudmunsdottir, S. (2006). The teller, the tale and the one being told: The narrative nature of the research interview. In P. Atkinson & S. Delamont (Eds.), *Narrative Methods* Vol. 2. London: Sage.

Haug, F. (Ed.) (1987, 1999*). Female sexualization: A collective work of memory.* London: Verso.

Haug, F. (2000). Memory work: The key to women's anxiety. In S. Radstone (Ed.), *Memory and methodology.* Oxford: Berg.

Ife, J., & Tesoriero, F. (2006). *Community development: Community-based alternatives in an age of globalisation.* Frenchs Forest, NSW: Pearson Education.

Kenway, J. (2009). Beyond conventional curriculum cartography via a global sense of place. In M. Somerville, K. Power & P. de Carteret (Eds.), *Landscapes and learning: Place studies for a global world* (pp. 195–205). Rotterdam: Sense Publishers.

Kretzmann, J. P., & McKnight, J. L. (1993). *Building communities from the inside out : A path toward finding and mobilising a community's assets.* Shokie, IL: ACTA Publications.

Kikumura, A. (1998). Family life histories: A collaborative venture. In R. Perks & A. Thomson (Eds.), *The Oral History Reader* (pp. 140–144). London: Routledge.

Landon, C., Boynton, B., Boynton, G., & Boynton, L. (2008). *Cups with no handles: Memoirs of a grassroots activist.* Melbourne: Hybrid Publishers.

Lippard, L. R. (1997). *The lure of the local: Senses of place in a multicentred society.* New York: The New Press.

Mayne, A. (2009). Strange entanglements: Landscapes and historical imagination. In M. Somerville, K. Power & P. de Carteret (Eds.), *Landscapes and learning: Place studies for a global world* (pp. 175–193). Rotterdam: Sense Publishers.

McLeary, A. W., & Dingle, T. (1998). *Catherine: On Catherine Currie's diary, 1873–1908.* Melbourne: Melbourne University Press.

Michelson, E. (2010). Autobiography and selfhood in the practice of adult learning. *Adult Education Quarterly.* DOI: 10.1177/0741713609358447.

Onyx, J., & Small, J. (2001). Memory-work: the method. *Qualitative Inquiry, 7*(6), 773–786.

Pratt, M. L., (1991). *Professional.* New York: MLA.

Shears, R. (2008). *Swamp: Who murdered Margaret Clement?* Sydney: New Holland Publishers.

Simonsen, K. (2005). Bodies, sensations, space and time: The contribution of Henri Lefebvre. *Geografiska Annaler, 87B*(2005), 1.

Skeggs, B. (1997). *Formations of class and gender: Becoming respectable.* London: Sage.

Somerville, M. (2010). A place pedagogy for 'global contemporaneity'. *Educational Philosophy and Theory, 42*(3), 326–344.

Søndergaard, D. (2002). Poststructural approaches to empirical analysis. *Qualitative Studies in Education, 15*(2), 187–204.

Tonkin, E. (1990). History and the myth of realism. In R. Samuel & P. Thompson (Eds.), *The myths we live by.* New York: Routledge.

Phoenix de Carteret
Monash University

SECTION 3

Teaching Place

We develop our understandings of teaching practice for *Place pedagogy change* in this section. Teaching through the lens of place destabilises fixed positions, not least of these the position of the teacher. We build further on the insight of the previous section that, in practising enabling place pedagogies, teaching and learning can be porous and interchangeable responsibilities. This is a philosophy of teaching that recognises responsibility as *response*-ability, where the planning of pedagogical encounters is directed towards the opening of spaces for experimentation and exploration. Teaching strategies discussed in these chapters include a collective biography in a pre-service teacher education context, the development of resources for teaching about place in English classrooms, and adult community storytelling sites that generate liminal spaces enabling critique and transformation with/in community.

Openness to the other is a feature of these pedagogical sites. This openness to the other, and to the not-yet-known, does not stand in a binary relation to a disciplined attention to the already known, but works together with that disciplinary knowledge in a creative unfolding of knowledges through which the knower also emerges in new ways. Outcomes are not merely short-term in this approach, nor are they locked into predetermined and predictable forms. The outcomes of teaching and of learning have transformative effects that work on subjects over the long term. They enable a response-ability that involves unfixing those elements of life that have become static and have ceased to evolve. They enable a shifting of relations with place and with others in place, including human, non-human and earth others, in ways that are ethically responsible.

The teachers in these places recognise that learning occurs in particular places, and that we have a responsibility to attend closely to the specificities of these places and their effects on the imaginations and desires of ourselves and the learners with whom we work. These teachers recognise that we are *of* places as much as we are *in* them. This requires a pedagogy that is ethically responsive and fundamentally relational. It requires a pedagogy that is emergent and nonlinear and open to possibilities of "world-making" rather than "globe-making".

Although this section shows that teaching and learning cannot be specified entirely in advance, and that learning unfolds towards the not-yet-known, within an enabling place pedagogy teachers work hard to constitute optimum pedagogical conditions. They gather resources, develop materials, and create and nurture networks and relationships, and it is through these connections and creative engagements with place that they invite learners to participate in generating new ways of being in and caring for place. This is an ongoing, iterative and sometimes risky process that rests on an assumption that teaching and learning are always already unpredictable. This pedagogy of ethical uncertainty entails mutual responsibilities to each other and to the non-human and earth others with whom we dwell. It recognises that pedagogical encounters in place and in community might open us and the learners with whom we work to surprise, to wonder and to imagining ourselves towards new horizons and new futures that are not yet known.

BRONWYN DAVIES AND SUSANNE GANNON

COLLECTIVE BIOGRAPHY AS PEDAGOGICAL PRACTICE

Being and becoming in relation to place

In this chapter we go back to the group of students we introduced in Chapter 7. This small group of seven students was enrolled in an alternative Professional Experience unit offered to secondary teacher education students at the University of Western Sydney (UWS). This alternative practicum, Professional Experience Three, or PE3, was designed to give students an experience of learning to be teachers outside the institutional and bureaucratic constraints of school classrooms. In Nancy's terms, PE3 opened up a chance for the students to engage in world–making rather than globe-making (Nancy, 2007). Whereas globalisation, or globe-making, produces over-regulated practices focussed on the production of generic, predictable individuals who are responsive to the forces of government, world-making begins with self-in-relation to the other. World-making requires openness to new directions and possibilities and is not mandated by governmental imperatives. It is emergent from the specificity of particular places in the world and it anticipates the eruption of the new. It has an unpredictable appearance, maintaining a crucial reference to the world as a space of relationality and as a space for the construction and negotiation of meaning. In our place pedagogies strand within PE3 we offered the students the chance to learn about and to put into practice an enabling pedagogy of place with world-making possibilities.

We encouraged students to enrol in our strand and to work together to explore the ways in which they could develop a dynamic relation between the areas they would teach in and the philosophy and practice of enabling place pedagogies. The disciplinary areas they brought to our work together were English, Geography, Art and History. They had all completed a Bachelor of Arts and were enrolled in the Master of Teaching (Secondary) degree. We met with them for two days during the institutional break to teach them about place pedagogy. We discussed the readings on place we had gathered for them[i], we undertook a collective biography with them, and we helped them plan the place pedagogy projects they would each carry out in their communities. It is the teaching of and through collective biography that we will explore in this chapter.

COLLECTIVE BIOGRAPHY AS PEDAGOGICAL PRACTICE

Collective biography is a strategy that works with memory. Memory is not treated here as fixed or real; there is, as Bergson (1998) points out, no drawer in the brain that stores a veridical past. Each time memories are accessed they are re-made, and

M. Somerville, B. Davies, K. Power, S. Gannon and *P. de Carteret,*
Place Pedagogy Change, 129–142.
© *2011 Sense Publishers. All rights reserved.*

lived again in the present. In collective biography work, they are lived again, not only in the mind/body of the one who remembers, but in the minds of the members of the collective biography group who are engaged in listening to each other's memories.

Collective biography can be adapted to diverse contexts, depending on who the participants are and the questions that they wish to explore. We will describe here the philosophy and the practices that have come to characterise collective biography in our teaching and research. We will then go to the specific stories told within the PE3 strand that we taught. Collective biography has always been, for us, both a research and a pedagogical set of practices. Out of each of our collective biography workshops we have written papers on the topics that have been the focus of our memory work. The majority of the participants in our workshops over the last decade have been postgraduate students who have participated in order to learn more about doing research and about writing (see for example Davies & Gannon, 2006, 2009). Ideally, collective biography involves the participants meeting over several consecutive days. Participants should be volunteers, and the topic, although it is likely to have been initiated by the group leader, should also be open to negotiation and refinement to ensure that it is relevant and of interest to all participants. The group begins by talking and reading about the chosen topic.

In this particular place pedagogy workshop the emphasis has shifted more directly toward pedagogy as we sought ways to mobilise collective biography to open up the conceptual spaces and practices of enabling place pedagogies. The first session was spent collaboratively selecting and developing a common topic of interest and selecting the trigger questions for the memory stories in response to the readings on place that we had given participants a month earlier. We settled for exploring our earliest memories of engagement with the outside world—first within our own backyards and then moving beyond the backyard.

In response to the trigger questions participants tell their own remembered stories. Each participant listens carefully to the others' memory stories. They listen in order to come to know how this story is lived in an internal way. They question the storyteller when, as listener, they find they cannot imagine what happened. They listen in order to allow the memory, in its embodied, affective detail, to become imaginable, to be virtually real in their minds and bodies. When each participant, including the group leader, has told one or more memories, each writes her or his memories, paying particular attention to both the affect, that is, the body before language, *and* to the language. The written stories focus on one pivotal moment, attempting to capture what Deleuze and Guattari (1987) would call the *haecceity*, or just-thisness, of that particular moment. In such moments space takes on a not-yet-determined quality, and the boundaries between self and other may dissolve.

> [Haecceities] make no distinction between centre and periphery, inside and outside, subject and object and, therefore, humans and nature. They have a continuous quality…A haecceity is a moment of pure speed and intensity (an individuation)—like when a swimming body becomes-wave and is

momentarily suspended in nothing but an intensity of forces and rhythms. (Halsey, 2007, pp.145–146)

Collective biography stories work toward this sense of multiple open borders, between humans and nature, between one human and another. The writer aims for immediacy and embodied detail. The memories are written without clichés and explanations, and without the moralistic judgements or commentaries that intrude on the pure intensity of the remembered moment. In writing the stories it is suggested that participants be careful not to import expressions that would be foreign to the child subjects in the stories, or that would draw attention to the story-teller in the present. Each writer focuses on finding the words to evoke the remembered moment of being, seeking to capture the thisness of the moment, searching on the deep surfaces of the body for the details that will bring the memory most vividly to life.

In the collective biography workshop with the PE3 students, reflective journals were used for drafting memory stories and for recording other thoughts and fragments of memory both of childhood and of our collaborative discussions about each other's memories. The close work of writing and rewriting, the struggle to find the language to evoke the memory, and the sensibility of each moment of being, can be traced through the multiple drafts and fragments of text in their journals[ii].

After the participants have separated to write one of the stories that they had recalled and told to the group, the group reconvenes and each story is read, in turn, out loud. The participants listen again, openly and with care, attending to the affects carried in the story, and to the words, listening as if to know the story from inside, to register it in the folds of their own listening bodies, as if in order to know for themselves 'the mode of existence that it implies, that it envelops in itself' (Deleuze, 1980, n.p.). When they can't enter the other's story at any point, they make a note of where the words did not open up a space or a mode of being that they could imagine, and the written story is discussed in light of these blank spots. In this flow of talk the listeners offer insights from their own take-up of the story as it resonates in their bodies, asking *is this how it was*? Sometimes the listeners tell some of their own memories as a way of opening up a different entry point to the moment that they cannot find the way into.

The subtle details that were teased out through this collective listening and discussion enabled participants to better know, in their own internalised response to each memory, how it was to be there, in the pure intensity of each remembered moment. This exchange of bodily sensations and intensities creates a double movement in which each storyteller knows their story differently, registering the multiple intensities—their own and others'—that make this moment live. Each listener, in registering those multiple intensities now closely linked and overlapping with their own intensities, their own memories, has become someone other than themselves, a subject whose co-implication in the lives of others has become visible.

In the collective biography with the PE3 students, the precise details of the backyards the students had known in childhood, and the spaces just outside those backyards, were teased out through this talking, writing, reading and responsive listening. Stories were told of the children's containment within backyards, of their secret and special places and of the emergences of new possibilities for being in the world.

In the collective biography workshops, following this reading out loud and open, non-judgemental listening, each story is re-written seeking the words to come closer to the just-thisness of the moment as it has emerged in the discussions. The re-written story is read out loud again to the group. Participants listen again, registering again the just-thisness of being, the haecceity of the moment, in which each is open and vulnerable to the other.

Thought and being emerge in such moments. A shift takes place. The memories are no longer told and heard as just autobiographical (that is, as the assemblage of already known stories that mark one person off from the next person), but as opening up for, and in, each other knowledges of being that previously belonged only to the other as that other's marks of identity.

In working collectively with memories, we open up the possibility of knowing intimately within our own bodies the places and modes of being that previously marked only the specificity of each in their difference from the other.Collective biography aims to invoke a creative mo(ve)ment, a doubled action, provoked through collective storytelling and writing, of dwelling in and on particular *moments* of being, and of simultaneous *movement* toward, or openness to, new possibilities both of seeing and of being in that liminal in-between space. It is an ongoing process, a movement, a coming to know and to be differently from how one knew and was at the beginning. It opens up an experience of world-making. Each subject's specificity in its very particularity, in its sensory detail, becomes the collectively imagined detail through which we know ourselves as human, even as more human as humans in relation to the other, where the other includes the land and the people in it (Cixous, in Cixous & Calle-Gruber, 1997).

WORKING WITH STORIES OF PLACE

Collective biography requires of participants that they read in preparation for the workshop in order to extend the conceptual repertoire that they can bring to the task in hand. The preparatory readings on pedagogy and place presented our students with new concepts for thinking about themselves and others in relation to place. Some of the readings were informed by Deleuze's concept of *univocity*—the co-extensiveness of all beings, of self and other, where other includes human, non-human and earth others. We introduced the students to the concept of (in)scription and how it is useful for understanding how subjects are brought into being as texts written on the deep/surfaces of the body/landscape (Davies, 2000). We introduced a Deleuzian orientation to writing, and the inclination towards art and literature that such an approach invites (Davies, 2008a).

For Deleuze, '[w]riting is a question of becoming, always incomplete, always in the midst of being formed, and goes beyond the matter of any liveable or lived experience' (Deleuze, 1997, p. 1). Writing as a way of coming to know, and writing as a way of keeping knowing open, was implicit in the practice that we incorporated into the PE3 strand, of participants keeping reflective journals on their reading, on the workshop, and on planning and carrying out their own pedagogical practices. Such an attitude to writing suggests that 'the experience/experiment of writing in which the world is not reduced to what [is already known], pushes the writer out into other ways of knowing, into the tangled possibilities of intersecting, colliding and separate lives' (Davies, 2008a, p. 198).

The stories that the students told in response to the trigger questions, which asked for first memories of their backyards and first memories of going outside their backyards, document the children's intense awareness in particular moments of being on the same planes of existence as trees, light, and the people around them.

Being One with the Willow Tree: Univocity

This close work of writing and rewriting, of struggling to find the precise language to evoke the sensibility and affective and embodied detail of each moment of being, is evident in the fragments of text that make up the first memory story that we will work with here. This storyteller[iii] had told us the story of going out into her backyard early one morning when her family was still asleep. The backyard was dominated by a large Weeping Willow tree. She wrote and read us a number of versions of her story as she worked out how she might best represent this sense of being at one with the tree within the imperfect medium of language. In her journal she wrote one version of her story that includes the following fragment:

A soft breeze blew the branches high above my head, shaking the longer branches that trailed along the ground. I watched the branch curl and roll with the subtle movement of the wind. I slowly removed the elastic bands from my hair and combed the plaits through with my fingers until my hair was loose and wild spilling into my lap. Gently I took one of the softly curled branches, it felt cool in my hand. I placed the end of it against my head. I began to plait the rope like branch with two lengths of my hair and when I had finished I could feel the tree branch tighten and tug under the influence of the wind. The breeze subsided and so I plaited more and more of the willow into my hair until I could hear the sound of the wind playing havoc overhead. The tree began to sway as if consenting to a greater force. I could feel the rhythmic movement through my hair and scalp. I could feel the branches rolling and catching in the length of my hair and suddenly I felt the urge to sway and move with the tree. I closed my eyes, lulled by the peaceful rocking motion.

With her comment 'I could feel the urge to sway and move with the tree' and the image of the little girl plaited into the fronds of the willow tree the Deleuzian notion of univocity is materialised, corporealised as the movement of the tree moves her body. The little girl has become, in a sense, part of the tree and the tree has become, reciprocally, part of her. Although of different stuff, or different "intrinsic

BRONWYN DAVIES AND SUSANNE GANNON

modalities", the tree and the girl are together in a space of being where '[b]eing is said in a single and same sense of everything of which it is said, but that of which it is said differs: it is said of difference itself' (Deleuze, in Woodward, 2007, p. 67). This was the sense in which she had talked about that moment of merging with the tree and being subject through the tree, in the ways of a tree, to the effects of wind and weather. However the text did not settle into this version. She continued to write through her memories of being with the willow tree and the final version she proffered for inclusion in the suite of collective biography texts was quite different. In this version she abandons the specificity of plaiting hair and willow together and takes a different stance in relation to her body and its relationship with the tree. In this re-membering, the girl has approached the willow tree because she is looking for the source of birdsong. As she nears the place where the birds' nest is located she experiences a momentary dissolving of the self in a blast of white light:

> *...I pushed my bare toes into the damp grass and lifted my heels and just as my eyes began to focus on something perched in a fork of smooth branches the sun also focussed its energy upon the exact same spot. A white brilliant light filled my entire head. I rubbed my eyes. The strength of the light stayed with me for several moments. I turned away and still blinking from the sudden shock of light I looked down toward the moist ground. Slowly the patches of grass became green again, colour seemed to drain back and I could make out tiny dew droplets clinging to the blades near my toes. I slowly lifted my head trying to focus on the willow tree that graced the very middle of our yard. Most families had a Hills hoist in the middle of their gardens, but not us. No we had a giant willow tree proudly plonked in the middle. For some reason I couldn't quite focus on it. The memory of the bright light would not leave my brain and as I shook my head and blinked I could see the white light had become the willow tree.*

> *I took a step toward it. The willow shone like jewellery in the sunlight. On each of the slender branches that flowed to the ground were tiny droplets of water. Each tiny leaf had captured a moist bud, creating a myriad of luminous ribbons. I gently touched a branch and felt one of the beads roll along my finger and the coolness melt into the palm of my hand. Carefully I parted the branches trying not to disturb the thousands of glistening droplets and sitting hidden I could observe the whole world without being noticed.*

> *The grainy trunk grew from the ground at such an angle that the branches touched the ground and curled gently into the grass. I traced the curls with my fingers...*

In this fragment of her encounter with the tree, the light and tree have merged and the writer is a witness to, and for a moment a participant in, this strange, intense becoming. She says that she sees the tree differently, in more acute and intricate detail, after the light has hit her eyes and blinded her for that moment. It is not clear which version of the story was the first, nor which is the last. She sent us one version by email, and submitted the other version later as part of her reflective journal, and all the details that appear in both of the stories were included in the stories that she told us over those two days. What is evident, however, in both the stories, is what she was struggling to capture in words: the capacity of this child, in this moment, to be still, attentive and at one with the landscape that surrounds her—tree, light, wind, water—with pure intensity and immersion. In each version, her story evokes what Deleuze called univocity. In this view, there is no transcendent knowing, no hierarchy between sentient and non-sentient beings, no hierarchy of mind over matter. Rather, all beings exist on 'one plane of becoming with no point being the ground or the knower', where 'every distinct expression of becoming [is] on par with every other' (Colebrook, 2002, p. 95).

The Making of Cubbies: De- and Re-territorialising Space

One of the intense pleasures of childhood is the transformation of a space into a particular place, a place that is *de- and reterritorialised* so that it becomes one's own small special place, different from what it was before (Deleuze & Parnet, 2002). The intensity of its pleasure lies in its being a deterritorialised space, without a past or a future, but created here, now, for this moment. But reterritorialising a space is to add *striations*, turning it into a recognisable place, a place that is safe in its predictable ordering of experience, and at the same time limiting what is possible. In Deleuzian geo-philosophy, the territorialisation of space is intricately related to the notions of striated and smooth space. Striated spaces are 'rigidly structured and organized' tending to 'produce particular, limited movements and relations between Bodies'; while in contrast, smooth spaces enable movement that is 'less regulated or controlled...where bodies can interact—and transform themselves—in endlessly different ways' (Hickey-Moody & Malins, 2007, p. 11). As they territorialise space, bodies 'create particular habitual relations with the spaces they encounter' in a process that 'is more aesthetic than structural: colors, textures, motifs and tunes, for example, all create a territory' (Hickey-Moody & Malins, 2007, p. 11). Territories provide the necessary stability for launching new lines of flight and of becoming.

In the case of cubbies, we suggest, they are de- and reterritorialised safe places, and at the same time becoming-places. The active making of a new place may generate an intensity of sensation that breaks with habitual ways of seeing and being. Ceppi and Zini (1998, n.p.) observe that '[e]xploring reality is an ongoing condition of early childhood. Young children inhabit the space by continuously constructing places (imaginary and real) within the place in which they are situated'. The process of making a cubby enables the children to put their own creative imprint on the character of the place, which heightens both affect and their sense of belonging. In this story of cubby-building, the children's father is included in the vividness of the present moment that the moment affords:

I am running through the house laughing. My sister is running ahead of me. Our arms are full of sheets that we have just pulled off our beds. Dad is walking behind, yelling for us to slow down. He's carrying the blue and white checked peg bag from the laundry. Lizzie and I run out the front door, down the side of the house, to the backyard and the trampoline. The sun is warm on my face. Dad gets to the trampoline as we are pulling the sheets around. He pegs them to the springs of the trampoline to hold them in place. We crawl inside, the sun is shining through the sheets, and there is a pinkish glow inside our cubby. The grass we sit on is cool. Dad's head is touching the top of the trampoline. Mum brings our lunch to us. We sit eating our lunch, laughing.

The children and their father create a new territory, which is in itself utterly satisfying. They form a new community in the pinkish light under the trampoline. The sensory awareness of their togetherness, of light, of eating lunch, of the father's size, is heightened, and evokes joyful laughter. It is a place that is simultaneously safe and familiar, and a space from which to launch new becomings in which they notice the light and are open to sensation and awareness of their relations with each other. The cubby affords them, simultaneously, smooth and striated space.

Smooth space offers unpredictability and the infinite possibilities of the not-yet-known, inviting lines of flight and discovery, whereas striated space acknowledges that regulated and habitual practices also necessarily impact upon the affordances that any pedagogical space holds. Particular places are striated, but they also hold the possibilities of lines of flight (Davies, 2009). For example, in this story, the children and their father operate within familiar family relations. The father takes up a certain authority, yelling at them to slow down, bringing pegs and constructing the cubby within the confines of an already existing form. But the process of making the cubby, and of being within it, evokes an intense and sensual awareness of being. The smooth space they enter under the trampoline enfolds the children and their father in a new moment of awareness of light and relationality. The pleasures of these new sensations and becomings are evident in their laughter.

Lines of Flight and the Vital Role of Desire

Each of the stories we have discussed so far involves some form of breaking out, a line of flight into the new and unpredictable becoming-other. The girl in the early morning garden has left her bed and her family to experience the unknown and the strange. The children with their father invent a new space to inhabit, at least momentarily, in that afternoon of warm and cool sensations and laughter. Although familiar in some of their contours, these spaces are not excessively limited by habituated, institutionalised, striated modes of being. They include some sense of stability, from which lines of flight can be launched. The third story from this collective biography on place signals the thrills and potential dangers entailed in lines of flight, while it also demonstrates the force that striated spaces and modes of being have in the regulation of childhood.

For Deleuze and Guattari, it is the line of flight that is most productive and powerful as a 'pure movement of change, which breaks out of one form of organization and moves towards another' (Woodward, 2007, pp. 69–70). Lines of flight are multiplicitous and unpredictable. They are not limited by pre-given forms or patterns, but enable life to be enhanced through all sorts of mutations and variations, such that a child might find herself, as in the first story, becoming-tree or becoming-light (Colebrook, 2002, p. 133).

In the third story, the children locate their play on the roadside, near passing cars, aware that the line of flight they are following, breaking out of the striated territory their parents have mapped out, brings with it danger. In this story the children take risks that they find both intensely exciting and also terrifying.

I am sitting in the gutter, with my sister and the boys from down the street. Their driveway is full of squishy cold clay. We are making monsters. This lasts only a short time; boredom has set in. One of us comes up with the idea to put them on the main road. I know that we are not allowed past the letterbox but we are way too excited. The monsters are placed on the road. I sit in the gutter and wait, excitement buzzing through me. Ginny and the others laugh. I stand up and look down the road, no cars, I sit back down. I hear a car, we all wait—the car hits two of the monsters—they are flattened. We laugh with excitement. The other two are half squished—this makes us laugh even more! The car slows down and I have a sudden rush of fear. Then someone calls RUN! And the four of us run down the street—we hide at the park waiting to see if the car turns around.

Lines of flight are instantiations of desire where desire is a force that breaks up the reduction of oneself to a being who can be contained within the striations of institutionalised order. The desire that the children have to place their monsters on the road is a desire that begins collectively and traverses persons. Desire is positive and expansive, opening creative and transformative opportunities. For the children in this story there is intense pleasure in the line of flight, in the smooth space in which the monsters were created and then demolished outside the regulating lines of what the children were allowed, out of what they already knew. They knew they should not go beyond the letterbox and they were both overjoyed at, and terrified by, their line of flight outside the boundaries that sought to keep them safe.

Each of the lines of force elaborated by Deleuze and Guattari holds a negative possibility—none is the perfect line, none creates, on its own, ideal conditions. The negative effect of the striated line is excessive fear, leading to the danger of 'clinging too strongly to rigid structures and entrenched patterns of behaviour' (Woodward, 2007, p. 71). The line of flight is not free of danger either. Even while it is full of positive potential it may be risky. For the children playing at the side of the road there may be evident dangers that warrant some restraint. The question becomes how the life-force of lines of flight can be enabled while also maximising the capacity of the striated lines that keep the children safe. More broadly, in the current risk-averse globalised world, fear of the dangers of the unexpected may work to close down lines of flight, and so preclude their potential for creative, life-giving energy. Enabling place pedagogies necessarily involves risk; responsible pedagogy is willing to take risks in that it opens the learner, and the teacher, to the not-yet-known.

AND SO...

When collective biography is practised as research, the participants conclude the workshop by turning back to the topic in relation to which the stories were generated, and they ask how the stories might contribute to new thought about the topic being addressed. A paper, or series of papers, is then developed, usually in collaboration with all the participants and working with the insights that have emerged through the process of memory-work. This stage of writing may well be the place where further shifts in thought are accomplished. When it is practised as pedagogy, the turn at the end of the workshop is toward the ways in which the insights developed might be incorporated into pedagogical practice. The practices of open listening that are developed through collective biography can contribute to new understandings and relational practices in pedagogical contexts.

This is not unlike the listening that is practised in Reggio Emilia contexts. Rinaldi describes the listening needed for that new form of relationality as a difficult practice, and as one that generates a 'predisposition toward change' (Rinaldi, 2006, p. 114). 'Behind each act of listening there is desire, emotion, and openness to differences, to different values and points of view' (Rinaldi, 2006, p. 114).

Within the collective biography workshops each story comes to reveal one facet of a being; each participant is opened up to a broader knowledge of the multiple differences and relationalities that go to make up the human condition. Each story opens the listener to new insights into the processes of *being* and *becoming* in relation to the world. Participants thus let go of some of their previous over-determined moral judgements and enter the pedagogical space with a curiosity about and awareness of themselves and the other as sensate beings, opening up for themselves, and for the other, new ways of knowing. In letting go of judgement of the other they open up instead to the possibility, not only of valuing the difference of the other, but of loving that difference, that specificity, that possibility of being.

These strategies of listening, of being and becoming differently, are not focussed on the development of a fixed individual identity, but on a twofold movement that includes, first, 'a moment of de-individualization, an escape to some degree from the limits of the individual' and second, 'the constitution of new ways of being in the world, new ways of thinking and feeling, new ways of being a subject' (Roffe, 2007, p. 43). Being and becoming in this sense are generative of individual *and* social change, and they are about participating in a creative evolution of being that is bigger than oneself (Bergson, 1998).

Collective biography thus builds a community in the sense that Ceppi and Zini use that term, through 'the willingness to listen and be open to others...[and through] respect for differences, however they may be expressed...[It comes from and produces a] sense of empathy, a closeness that creates bonds, that enables each group member to recognize the other and to recognize him/herself in the other' (Ceppi & Zini, 1998, n.p.). This does not come about through creating a group committed to sameness, but through making difference a value. Such listening does not judge but opens up in oneself the possibility of knowing in new ways (Davies & Wyatt, 2011).

Listening to affect is integral to being open to difference. It involves openness to intensity, to seeing up close, to seeing in other ways to the habitual, striated ways of seeing. The sensory details invoked in writing and telling the stories are important for enabling listeners to enter the particular affective assemblage that each memory entails for the writer.

> Affect is that which is felt before it is thought; it has a visceral impact on the body before it is given subjective or emotive meaning. Thinking through affect brings the sensory capacity of the body to the fore. When we encounter an image of a bomb victim, smell milk that has soured, or hear music that is out of key, our bodies tense before we can articulate an aversion...Affect is, therefore, very different from emotion: it is an a-subjective bodily response to an encounter. Emotion comes later, as a classifying or stratifying of affect...As a concept, 'affect' enables us to think about how certain assemblages, languages or social institutions impact on bodies in ways that are not conscious. (Hickey-Moody & Malins, 2007, p. 8)

Collective biography stories are not told as individualistic stories that mark out the specificity of one against the generality of the other, but as stories that open up for the participants a multiplicity of facets of being. At the same time, the stories come from the bodily-inscribed memories of each individual participant. The purpose of their telling is not to *reveal* individual identities but to gain insight into the ways in which life in all its multiplicity is generated and lived. The stories are in this sense everyone's stories, and anyone's 'stories-so-far' (Massey, 2005, p. 9), that is, stories that may yet be unfolded in entirely new ways from perspectives not yet known that become available in the space between, the contact zone created by the encounter with the other. That encounter serves to open up the not-yet-known. 'Encounters disrupt, dislodge, disconfirm our usual modes of being, our habitual sense of the way things are or ought to be, including our sense of ourselves' (Clark/Keefe, 2010, p. xiii). It is at once a risky and a responsible business.

The enabling pedagogies of place that we are working towards throughout this book emphasise relationality and the co-implication of one's being in other beings. They promote an ethics of encounter. In this endeavour we break from a version of the self that binds desire in fixed and habitual striations. We find ways to realise the contingent, transient lines of flight where new possibilities and relations become visible. In the intense investigations of embodied memory we aim to make desire visible, to see how it is shaped, how its energy drives the exploration of the new *and* how it is sometimes caught in habitual striations and (re)citations, so shutting off the possibility of something new. Collective biography is a pedagogical strategy that has enabled us as teachers to work in just this way. Through working with the haecceities of embodied memories and with a deep attention to listening to the other, our students have deterritorialised and reterritorialised their own places in the western suburbs of Sydney and developed ways in which they can extend this work into their own teaching.

NOTES

[i] The readings were: Cormack, Green and Reid (2006), Chapters 1 and 2 from Davies (2000), Davies (2008a), Davies (2008b), Gannon (2009), Chapter 4 of Josephs (2005) and Somerville (2004).

[ii] We sought the students' permission to use their journals for the purpose of our research. They were not under any obligation to give them to us and we did not ask for them until after the course assessment was completed. This was important to ensure that the voluntary nature of this work could be maintained without any sense of coercion in relation to course requirements and assessment.

[iii] The storytellers' names are not included in this stage of collective biography writing, since the point of the work is not to mark the individuality of the teller but to open up a collective insight into what it is to be human—and in this case what it is to be human in relation to place.

REFERENCES

Bergson, H. (1998). *Creative Evolution* (Arthur Mitchell, Trans.). Mineola: Dover Publications Inc.

Ceppi, G., & Zini, M. (Eds.) (1998). *Children, spaces, relations. Metaproject for an environment of young children*. Reggio Children. International Center for the Defence and Promotion of the Rights and Potential of all Children: Reggio Emilia.

Clark/Keefe, K. (2010). *Invoking mnemosyne: Art, memory, and the uncertain emergence of a feminist embodied methodology*. Rotterdam: Sense Publishers.

Colebrook, C. (2002). *Gilles Deleuze*. New York: Routledge.

Cormack, P., Green, B., & Reid, J. (2006, April 5–8). River literacies: Discursive constructions of place and environment in children's writing about the Murray-Darling Basin. Paper presented at *Senses of Place* conference, University of Tasmania, Hobart.

Cixous, H., & Calle-Gruber, M. (1997). *Hélène Cixous, rootprints: Memory and life writing* (E. Prenowitz, Trans.). London: Routledge.

Davies, B. (2000). *(In)scribing Body/landscape relations*. Walnut Creek: Alta Mira Press.

Davies, B. (2008a). Life in Kings Cross: A play of voices. In A. Jackson & L. Mazzei (Eds.), *Voice in qualitative inquiry: Challenging conventional, interpretive and critical conceptions in qualitative research* (pp. 197–219). New York: Routledge.

Davies, B. (2008b). *Practicing collective biography. In A. Hyle & J. Kaufman (Eds.), Dissecting the mundane: International perspectives on memory-work* (pp. 58–74). University Press of America.

Davies, B. (2009). *Difference and differenciation. In B. Davies & S. Gannon (Eds.), Pedagogical encounters* (pp. 17–30). New York: Peter Lang.

Davies, B., & Gannon, S. (2006). *Doing collective biography*. Maidenhead: Open University Press.

Davies, B., & Gannon, S. (2009). *Pedagogical encounters*. New York: Peter Lang.

Davies, B., & Wyatt, J. (forthcoming). Ethics. In J. Wyatt, K. Gale, S. Gannon & B. Davies (Eds.), *Deleuze and collaborative writing: An immanent plane of composition*. New York: Peter Lang.

Deleuze, G. (1980, December 12). Cours Vincennes. Retrieved February 10, 2010 from http://www.webdeleuze.com/php/texte.php?cle=190&groupe=Spinoza &langue=2)

Deleuze, G. (1997). Literature and life. In *Essays critical and clinical* (D. W. Smith & M. A. Greco, Trans.) (pp. 1–6). Minneapolis: University of Minnesota Press.

Deleuze, G., & Guattari, F. (1987). *A thousand plateaus: Capitalism and schizophrenia* (B. Massumi, Trans.). London: Athlone.

Deleuze, G., & Parnet, C. (2002). *Dialogues II*. New York: Columbia University Press.

Gannon, S. (2009). Rewriting the road to nowhere: place pedagogies in western Sydney. *Urban Education, 44*(5), 608–624.

Halsey, M. (2007). Molar ecology: What can the (full) body of an eco-tourist do? In A. Hickey-Moody & P. Malins (Eds.), *Deleuzian encounters. Studies in contemporary social issues* (pp. 135–150). New York: Palgrave Macmillan.

Hickey-Moody, A., & Malins, P. (2007). Introduction. In A. Hickey-Moody & P. Malins (Eds.), *Deleuzian encounters. Studies in contemporary social issues* (pp. 1–24). New York: Palgrave Macmillan.

Josephs, C. (2005). *Sacred oral storytelling and transformation.* Doctoral dissertation. University of Western Sydney.

Massey, D. (2005). *For space.* London: Sage.

Nancy, J-L. (2007). *The creation of the world or globalization* (F. Raffoul & D. Pettigrew, Trans.). Albany: State University of New York Press.

Rinaldi, C. (2006). *Dialogue with Reggio Emilia. Listening, researching and learning.* London: Routledge.

Roffe, J. (2007). Politics beyond identity. In A. Hickey-Moody & P. Malins (Eds.), *Deleuzian encounters. Studies in contemporary social issues* (pp. 40–49). New York: Palgrave Macmillan.

Somerville, M. (2004). *Wildflowering: The life and times of Kathleen McArthur.* Brisbane: University of Queensland Press.

Woodward, A. (2007). Deleuze and suicide. In A. Hickey-Moody & P. Malins (Eds.), *Deleuzian encounters. Studies in contemporary social issues* (pp. 62–75). New York: Palgrave Macmillan.

Bronwyn Davies
University of Melbourne
Susanne Gannon
University of Western Sydney

SUSANNE GANNON

REWRITING PLACE IN ENGLISH

I am an English teacher and a teacher educator and my particular passion is for writing. I was born in the south in the damp green landscapes of Gippsland and I now live near the sandstone escarpments of the Blue Mountains in New South Wales. I have lived on the salt stunted soils at the edge of the Mallee in western Victoria and beside cerulean seas in the far north of both sides of the continent. I have travelled to school along fencelines corralling acres of sunflowers that turn their heads one way and then the other at each end of the day, on corkscrew roads over mountain ranges and through rainforests dripping with vines. The first school I worked in as a teacher gathered students from many remote communities, each of whom brought with them their own stories of their places along the coast or far across the desert. I know that each of these places, these landscapes and climates, and the stories that I have shared in them, have had powerful effects on who I am and could be. It seems I have always been reading and writing about the places in which I have lived, imagining how I might write my way in or exploring how other writers have caught the details of each place, and what it does, in language.

During the enabling place pedagogies project that we document in *Place pedagogy change* I realised that my interests in writing, reading and pedagogies of place began long before this project and have threaded through my life and my work as a teacher of English and a teacher educator. In all sorts of projects I have attended to place and its effects in texts, and I have sought to enable my students to begin to write into their places in critical and creative ways. This chapter brings together some of that work on the writing and reading of place in English in secondary schools and, more recently, in tertiary teacher education. The enabling place pedagogies that I illustrate through this chapter are situated at the centre of the English curriculum, and are infused by the particular discipline-influenced orientation to textuality that English classrooms have. My intention is to move beyond the blandness of vague or imprecise notions of place, and to create opportunities for *textualising place* that build students' skills and understandings in English and that also go beyond these as they open students up to investigating themselves in relation to place and to each other in place.

The pedagogies that I have developed and that I describe through this chapter remain to some extent, despite careful planning, inherently unpredictable and non-linear. I've come to understand that it is not entirely possible or desirable to predetermine a narrow set of outcomes. Rather, I want to create opportunities that enable my students to surprise themselves with their ingenuity and capacity to think and write beyond what they believe they already can do. This requires me as

M. Somerville, B. Davies, K. Power, S. Gannon and *P. de Carteret,*
Place Pedagogy Change, 143–156.

a teacher to create a space that oscillates, in a Deleuzian sense, between the smooth space of the new and the striations of the already known. In English, the knowledge that is required to launch lines of flight to new texts and possibilities is an ever-increasing and explicit knowledge of language, and the capacity to put this knowledge to use in increasingly flexible and sophisticated ways.

This work is partially informed by critical literacy approaches to texts (Misson & Morgan, 2006, 2009; Morgan, 1997, 2009) but it moves beyond the limitations of these paradigms. As Misson and Morgan (2009) suggest, much critical literacy work became stuck on a propositional understanding of text, which fixated on purpose and audience and the generic and linguistic features shaped by these, and overlooked more complex and aesthetically sophisticated elements of texts. Like Misson and Morgan, I want a critical literacy that allows poetry in and that acknowledges the pleasures and necessary risks entailed in writing one's way into new imaginings and relations with oneself, others and the world.

READING AND WRITING PLACE IN THE NORTH

I began this approach to place reading and writing when I worked at a small high school in a distinctive community in North Queensland. Every community is of course distinctive in its own ways, but the idiosyncrasies and specificities of place can be overwritten by assumptions about location, advantage and disadvantage. The specificities of our own places that we worked with in the first section of this book show how meticulous this attention to place can be. Each day I drove up and over the range to the little high school that had been built over an old horse paddock outside the town. The curve of the roof of our assembly hall lifted the eye skywards over the green rise of the next hill. Just beyond the edge of the school grounds, hand hewn steps carved into the earth by students and teachers led down to a mountain creek. Patrolling plovers rewrote the perimeters of the sports fields. It was possible to climb through the fence into the forest, as I did once with an English class, to sit on fallen tree trunks and tell stories. Although I didn't live on that road or in that town, and some of the students also travelled in to the school, the school and its environs became a shared place for us all.

With my year 11 English class, I developed a four week unit that began with the collaborative deconstruction of dominant stories of our place. With my students I gathered, mapped and categorised those discourses that were already in circulation about the community. We collected poems, news articles, guidebooks, information texts, short stories, and piles of brochures and other marketing materials that "sold" the town as a tourist destination. We identified particular discourses including: home of "ferals"; entrepreneurial centre; idyllic environmental paradise; culturally rich Aboriginal community; escape from the rat race; artistic creative community; tourist mecca (or nightmare); supportive community oriented small town; hotbed of crime or drug/alcohol abuse; boring place where there is nothing to do for teenagers; dead zone where everything closes at 3pm (when the tourist buses leave); alternative lifestyle centre.

We highlighted the language features through which each of these discourses were manifest in the texts in our collection. We invited local poet, storyteller and author Michael Quinn into our English class to talk about how the rainforest and the town influenced the short story series he was writing. He shared one of his drafts with the class and talked to us about his processes of writing. This marked a shift in the unit towards narrative fiction and the close study of one text—the short story 'Beautiful one day' in *Paradise to Paranoia: New Queensland writing* (Baranay, 1995)—in which we focussed on the generic structure, language features and aesthetic aspects of style and tone of what we called "social realist" short stories. These were stories that were situated in recognisable contemporary contexts. Along with my students and those writers we invited into the class I also wrote texts of place. These were integrated into the teaching and learning. For example, the short story I wrote, set at the open air amphitheatre in the middle of the town, became a text that they used for experimenting with rewriting openings, inserting dialogue, changing voice and contesting tone, style and the credibility of detail of a place that they knew well:

All my memories of going to the amphitheatre are wet ones. On afternoons when the sun was shining, I used to like just lying on my back, looking up and screening out everything but the blue above and the green of the raggedy palms at the edges of my vision. Even on those days, water would slowly seep up and into you through the blades of grass, through your clothes, the ass of your jeans, your skin would get clammy and your bones would chill.

Anyway, that day had no sun. It was bucketing. The ground was total slush, mud everywhere. We didn't really want to go at all but nothing else was happening, as usual. We always got in for free because my mum was on the committee. She was involved in everything, anything that would distract her from us and the hassles at home. Sometimes I'd get behind the bar up the top...

Mantaka or some other local band played first, reggae of course. Not so many people there that day 'cause the morning started so overcast. A few people danced around when the rain first started but even they were cowering up top by the end of the second bracket. There were a few sparks from the mixer at one point and the band had to stop playing while they dried off the connections. Mum was snug and dry in the ticket box at the gate. We were just lurking round the edge of the stage keeping as dry as we could, wondering when they were going to realise it was just too wet and pull the plug completely...

The culminating task for students was to write their own original six hundred word short story for a proposed anthology of writing about this place. Students were to use the town or its vicinity as a specific and detailed location throughout their story and to consider how they might artfully construe the town in particular positive and negative ways through their language. Specific lessons—using the texts I had written alongside the texts we had found—focussed on craft elements of narrative writing. In some of these lessons students rewrote short texts, or compared and evaluated alternative versions of texts. Throughout the unit, reading writing and place were deeply intertwined.

Meanwhile, at the same secondary school, with younger students, place also shaped a unit on poetry where I organised a "poetry field trip" to the busy local tourist markets in the town. During the field trip students completed a number of on the spot writing activities that were intended to gather rich observational material to use back in class in their poetry writing. They filled pages with notes organised around each of the five senses, they conducted close but discreet observations of three different people they encountered at the market, developing imagined detailed characters and biographies for each of them, and they each chose a vantage point inside the markets where they sat for a specified period of time and wrote continuously all the details of that place that they could, including overheard fragments of dialogue and any other passing impressions.

Back in the classroom, the pooled field trip notes became a source of language and ideas for writing that students could take into their own poems. The final assessment task required students to create their own portfolio of original poems in any of the forms we had studied, including haiku, concrete poetry, dramatic monologue, ode and free verse. Rather than the abstractions or clichés that infuse much student writing, the intention of this unit was to better equip them to understand (and to use) the aesthetics of poetic language by attending to specificity, and the concrete and material detail evoked as we attended closely to the possibilities of our place. We practised collaborative writing of poetry and again invited experts into the classroom as we joined an online poetry forum where other writers provided us with careful feedback on our drafts. We sent our market poetry to a regional writing competition, where one of the poems was awarded a prize. All of these activities required close observation of place and of who we each were in our places, and careful work with language.

Throughout the unit we engaged in many different ways with poetic texts as we collected, read, performed, analysed and wrote poems. In understanding place, and the subjectification of people within place, in the section of the poetry unit that was built around the market visit, we incorporated a very specific place-based event into the normal practices of our English classroom. The data we had gathered on our poetry field trip also opened discussions about the ethics and effects of global travel on "the local", the irony of the commodification of culture and of biosphere in ways that might both exacerbate their demise and contribute to their preservation, and the multiple meanings of community.

READING AND WRITING PLACE IN THE CITY

As we have discussed in previous chapters, recent changes of place have been significant for the trajectories of thought and movement for each of the authors of this book. For me, moving to western Sydney provoked a radical and multilayered shift in subjectivity and place. Initially I was alienated by the landscape, by the unfamiliar climate, by a sense of social dislocation in this new site where busy city lives and the vagaries of distance and urban traffic meant that it was difficult to make new connections with people. I worked at the University of "Western Sydney", an amorphous location, a bureaucratic fiction, that is at once a no-place in its vast vague sprawl, and an everyplace in its capacity to swallow and homogenise hundreds of small suburbs across the western and south-western suburbs of Sydney. Many of my colleagues travel west from the inner city and the more desirable suburbs closer to the harbour, or from coastal suburbs north or south of Sydney, or down from the Blue Mountains where I eventually also made myself at home. Yet many of our students and the schools in which they will be teaching are situated within this huge area called "western Sydney".

I began my search for western Sydney, and for ways in to reading and writing place in western Sydney, in the texts that were already available that claimed to represent Sydney. These I thought would help me to identify texts I might use with my own students in critical and creative ways as I helped to prepare them to become English teachers in secondary schools in the region. But the available anthologies and collections also overlooked what was becoming, at least in my working life, "my place". Rodney Hall's anthology *Sydney* (2000) surveys prose from 1788 through to the present, eulogising the inner city and the largely gentrified "inner west", but failing to mention any part of greater western Sydney. The new literary paean to the city, *Sydney,* by Delia Falconer (2010), similarly disregards the broader sweep of the suburbs. Other general collections of Australian texts such as the *Macquarie PEN Anthology of Australian Literature* (Jose, 2009) tend not to make reference to specific places except as peripheral detail in authors' biographies. Place-making in these texts is approached as a huge cultural or even nation-building project. Texts in these sorts of collections are unlikely to include specific reference to the particular locations of any of the schools where my students might end up teaching. I decided to begin to gather texts myself, and to model this practice for my students, to encourage them to create and to use locally specific and situated anthologies. Eventually this led to the production of a resource kit for teachers and schools in western Sydney, and for the teacher education students with whom I worked.

This *Writing Western Sydney* resource kit consists of thirty five unbound double-sided light card sheets inside a paper folder. It includes poetry, prose, drama, photographs and paintings and accompanying analyses of the specific language features of each text, with writing "provocations" based directly on those texts. The pages are not bound or numbered because I designed it to be expanded as more texts are incorporated, and because the double-sided pages can be used in any order or individually. The place-writing pedagogy that I articulated through this kit intertwines reading and writing (of place, self and text) and encourages teachers and students to generate creative writing in response to the close analysis of language.

In focussing on western Sydney, I wanted to directly address a pervasive tendency for the west to be ignored or pathologised rather than addressed in its particularity and diversity. I was also aware of the highly localised "patches" that seem to join up to form "mosaics" of belonging in place in the lives of young people (Comber, Nixon & Reid, 2007). The kit is a sort of textual mosaic of western Sydney that might invite students to find or write their own patches amongst these texts. I also wanted to respond to a context where schools in western Sydney are disproportionately staffed by new teachers. These teachers are developing their skills on many fronts at once and any resource that is useful and anchored to contexts familiar to themselves and their students will be helpful. Thus the kit is as much for my own students, who are about to move into schools to teach, as it is for the Head Teachers of English in secondary schools to which it was distributed across western Sydney in late 2010.

The *Writing Western Sydney* resource kit began with language, as it sourced and reproduced texts, images and excerpts from longer texts and guided teachers and students to focus on what language can do affectively, aesthetically and rhetorically to achieve certain effects. Our campus is located in Penrith, on the far fringe of the western suburbs, and there are several poems with links to Penrith in the kit. Poems are often difficult to source from small press collections or literary journals and are considered by many English teachers to be more difficult than prose texts (Wakeling, 2009). These poetic resources can give new insights into familiar places and develop sophisticated skills with language at the same time. Poems by Penrith poet Jennifer Maiden draw attention to aspects of life in that place that might not be otherwise noticed. Her 'Bound feet' (1990, p. 118) begins as a memoir:

As a girl in Penrith then
I had a Chinese friend.
I have seen her squeezed feet
When they were unbound...

On one side of the card is the text, in this case the full poem 'Bound feet', while on the other side are notes about the author, notes about the text and a section called 'Looking at language' that draws attention to particular features of language in the text. For this poem, students are invited to look at Maiden's use of metaphor and symbolism and how these code the stoicism and helplessness of the immigrant experience into the poem. They examine how the misshapen tiny feet and the limitations of movement that they cause might reflect the difficulties that a migrant encounters in moving through a new country. The writing provocations for this poem suggest that students might write their own poem around a body part that also operates symbolically, or write a memoir from the point of view of a child about an immigrant experience that is marked on the body. These provocations are at once specific and open-ended enough to allow lots of choices for anyone wanting to experiment with language. There are many other ways of enriching the student responses that teachers might generate beyond these initial provocations. For example, they might investigate the particular immigration history of their suburb and write a poem informed by that research. Another poem by Jennifer Maiden gives entry into a familiar suburban image and a suggestion of the constraints of suburban life. Her poem 'Vegetable' (1990, p. 128) begins:

Good country for roses.
Clay.
A rose is a dictator,
needing a hill

well drained
a dry surface

...

The poem takes the reader straight into a suburban front garden, a dry summer and the horticultural habits of a particular species. It also enables teachers and students to consider the elliptical and allusive complexities of Maiden's poetic style. They are provoked to try some of the strategies in the poem as they write their own vegetable poem, based on observation of and research about the habitats and habits of their selection.

Another poem included in the *Writing Western Sydney* resource kit, 'Aubade with dying river' by Anthony Lawrence (1998), introduces teachers and students to a particular poetic form—the aubade—a poem written about lovers separating at dawn. These lovers separate on the banks of the river at Penrith where:

...

The Nepean River throws up
mutated carp
and bass young anglers unpick from lures:
skirting boards
shaped and painted
with whatever's not gone to skin in the shed.

...

The scenes of parting take place in the 'rowing club beer garden' and by 'the dark steel girders of the railway bridge' as another tragedy takes place in the background. In this poem teachers and students attend closely to layout, structure and tone as well as to figurative language and environmental and gendered discourses. Each text, as well as each place, has its own particularities. With this poem students are offered writing provocations that include adapting prose into poetry, writing their own contemporary aubade that celebrates the union of lovers and mourns their impending separation, or writing a text where two lovers have a private disagreement against a dramatic public backdrop where another story is obviously unfolding. From this text students and teachers can learn how details of everyday familiar landscapes can be drawn in and put to work in the world of a poem.

The first section of Peter Boyle's long poem 'Images of the last judgement' (1997), subtitled 'Somewhere near Penrith, the end of a long weekend', is included in the kit. The thoughts of the narrator who is driving back to Sydney drift to the tawdry suburb that now obscures the long history of Indigenous inhabitation:

...

the ghosts of old people wait in a frozen bus shelter.
Concrete and bitumen circle in mazes
round the long dead owners of this land
whose bones the freeway intermingles
with the hacked veins of the gum trees

...

SUSANNE GANNON

Students consider the concept of the 'last judgement' in relation to the violent
dispossession of Aboriginal people, and the brutality of environmental destruction
in the suburbs. The cultural contact zone of this place 'somewhere near Penrith' is
written graphically into the poem. Students are invited to consider their own places
and the histories of colonisation. They generate their own images of last
judgements in their writing as they consider who might be judged and why.

The kit provides precise and specific description of how each text is arranged to
achieve certain effects. It uses an appropriate metalanguage for literary analysis
and demonstrates how literary analysis uses quotations from texts as evidence. The
'Looking at language' section for Lawrence's 'Aubade with dying river' provides
examples of this detailed analysis of language.

> *Layout*: Lawrence uses space carefully here to emphasise pauses and slow
> down the pace of the reading. He does not follow a rigid pattern but instead
> he allows empty spaces on the page to highlight certain phrases and separate
> others more than conventional spacing would allow. For example, important
> phrases like: "Pre-dawn", "The river eased and stank" and "she had" are all
> given a line of their own. His use of space and his line breaks create an
> irregular rhythm for the poem that is closer to everyday spoken conversation.
> He uses italics for the dialogue between the lovers so that it stands out from
> the rest of the poem.

> *Description*: Lawrence makes selective use of figurative language in this
> poem. There are just two similes—the body "like a bar of faulty neon" and
> the spider "like a gnarled hand bogged in blood". He relies more on precise
> and unadorned descriptions, e.g. the names of specific fish: "carp", "bass",
> "nannygai" and "oysters", dried paint having "gone to skin in the shed", or
> the morbid descriptions of the lover: "A bluetongue lizard with a cluster of
> bush ticks riveting its head". Metaphoric uses of verbs can also be found: the
> river is "vomiting" and the ticks look like they are "riveting" the head of the
> lizard. Lawrence is also very sparing with adjectives, using them carefully to
> ensure they have maximum effect: e.g. "mutated carp", "stalled train",
> "faulty neon", "gnarled hand".

> *Theme*: Although an aubade is traditionally a love poem of parting set at
> dawn, Lawrence has approached this theme and form ironically. This is a
> grim "love poem" which leaves one of the lovers sleepless and frightened.
> Like the animals that are seen "giving menace to leaf shadow", as a love
> poem this is quite menacing in its effects.

The *Writing Western Sydney* resource kit gathers together short texts from a range
of literary and aesthetic genres that make some explicit reference to or resonate
with our specific part of the world. It includes excerpts from novels, plays and
short stories, paintings and drawings, and song lyrics. Although the kit provides
elaborate scaffolding and response activities for teachers and students, I expect that
the texts and the activities suggested in it will be used in many different ways. It
provides teachers with some materials that they can adapt or use as models to

support their teaching and their students' learning about language through carefully sequenced and meaningful learning activities. By tying this so closely to place, the *Writing Western Sydney* project underlines how literary analysis can be brought into dialogue with the concerns of critical literacy—how discourses that thread through texts construe certain versions of the world rather than others. In considering, contesting and creating texts, teachers and their students can generate new discourses about their places.

READING AND WRITING PLACE IN TEACHER EDUCATION

Teacher education students were involved throughout the development of the *Writing Western Sydney* kit. A small group of students worked with me to source, shortlist and select the texts. They worked with me to generate close readings of the particular language features of each text. Drafts of the analyses and the writing prompts were trialled and revised by other teacher education students. Another student with a visual arts background did the design and the layout for the final version of the kit. Involving my teacher education students in the selection, analysis and explication of these short texts provided a rehearsal space for them to further develop the close reading skills that they acquired in their first degrees and to imagine how these might be translated for a pedagogical purpose. As the kit is designed to be potentially always under construction, always expanding, my students will be involved in the ongoing development of supplementary resources as we source and work with more texts of western Sydney.

There have been numerous other opportunities for my teacher education students to look critically at place and to open opportunities to engage their own students in schools to work with texts in and of place. In one of their assessment tasks, many of my English method students have created units of work incorporating excursions into different places in the western Sydney area and beyond. These atmospheric locations range from the Glow Worm Tunnel, Mount Tomah Botanical Gardens, the Three Sisters lookout in the Blue Mountains, and a public sculpture garden, to the densely populated sites of Liverpool Plaza, Circular Quay, The Rocks and the Sydney International Airport. Each of these selected sites is used to generate a range of writing activities shaped by the particular features of the location. Each excursion is closely linked to a range of classroom based text and language activities undertaken prior to and following the excursion, that are specifically designed to extend students understandings and mastery of the particular genres of text, or the particular texts, that are the focus of the unit. The first step for the teacher education students is always to visit the site themselves to explore all its potential for stimulating school students' reading and writing, and to consider how it might be able to complement and enrich their learning about language and about the world that begins in the classroom but should not be contained there. As we found with the excursion to our local markets, or the walk into the forest, the places that we live and learn in provide rich embodied and textual possibilities.

My English teacher education students have also textualised their familiar places in new media forms; they have made original short films set in their neighbourhoods. One of the students, for example, used a memory map of his childhood that he constructed one week in a tutorial activity to identify the sites of events that were of personal significance to him at various stages in his childhood. He constructed a ten minute film that was a pastiche of new footage and old still photographs, with a carefully crafted voiceover, to make a multimodal mini "bildungsroman", or coming of age story, intertwining his personal growth with that of the suburban neighbourhood. Another student laid her voice over sweeping sequences of footage, filmed late at night through a car window, that show the empty silent streets of the suburb under streetlights. She provided a wry commentary that unpicks the usual banal representations of her place and draws attention to the otherwise overlooked elements that create a sense of belonging to this place for her.

This year, students who identify as Vietnamese-Australian, Lebanese-Australian and South African-Australian made original films that told their families' immigration stories. Each of these films wove complex here-and-there, now-and-then stories about relationships with place over several generations. Another student created a film that was a love letter to Sydney, as a response to a letter from her mother in Turkey, explaining to her mother why she would not be coming home from this new place that she had come to love. Each of these students worked into a deep and highly individualised examination of themselves in relation to place. Each of them learned new skills through the process that enabled them to work with new and old media in fresh ways. Each of these opportunities to create personal texts about their own places were also invitations to my students to consider, as beginning teachers, how they might also guide their own (school) students to construct individual, group or class based explorations of their places.

In my classes we have also begun to experiment with how other new media platforms might open up possibilities for collaborative textual work around place. During the development of the *Writing Western Sydney* resource kit, the novel *Luck in the Greater West* (McDonald, 2007) and its bleak narrative of raced and gendered teenage violence and thwarted possibilities in western Sydney provoked a small group of my students to set up a closed wiki site, and there to begin drafting a young adult short story that, like McDonald's novel, had an acute sense of place, but that constructed a different sort of representation of the young people of the area. We wanted to resist stereotypes that appear in media and other texts about this area whilst still retaining recognisable details of its landscape and social milieu. The students chose the genre of "teen romance" and the setting of the summer school holidays, and sketched out the characters who would feature in the story. They decided that the story would develop around two pairs of siblings, each older sibling caring for the younger one while their parents worked.

One of the students began the first draft of the text on the wiki site, and when it was underway we invited all students in the class to join the wiki and to add to or change the draft of the story in any way that would help it to meet the purpose we had articulated for the project, that is, to use an aesthetic or literary text form—a short story in the teen romance genre—to create more complex and less stereotypical representations of western Sydney. The wiki story is an ongoing project, but in its present incarnation it begins with two sisters home alone in the school holidays, their parents having left early for work. The story progresses as the sisters make their way to the local swimming pool.

> Once the girls had slipped into their cossies and washed their faces they grabbed their faded beach towels marched out the door. The main road wasn't far from their house, just three short streets away. They were close enough to hear the compression braking of the trucks along the highway at night amongst screeching tyres and honking horns. The Great Western Highway was always a busy road, no matter what time of the day or night it was.

> The girls had to walk about a kilometre and a half to get to the next suburb and then another kilometre to get to the entrance of the pool. They decided to walk along the footpath of the Great Western Highway so the cars and trucks kept them company on their walk.

> "I wanna jump in the deep end to start with. You have to watch me this time Jas, 'cause the last time I did it you had gone to the toilet and then you wanted to leave straight away. Today I think it should be me who says what time we leave 'cause you did last time."

> "Yeah ooooright!!!" Jasmine exclaimed in a distant tone. She was there with Jo but not at the same time. She really couldn't explain it, she was either bored with her life or she was sick of having to always be in Jo's face or the other way around. It wasn't so bad when they were younger and they used to run naked through the sprinkler on a hot summer's day in their backyard, while their white and gold coloured Cocker Spaniel tried to drink the water from the air. Four years difference between them back then was not so bad, but now all she seemed to do was question what she needed to be happy again like that. Jasmine was so deep in thought that she didn't even notice the old red Skyline that pulled up on the side of the Highway, until Jo tugged on her arm for attention.

This collaborative writing project takes up broad generic elements and themes of the young adult fiction the students had been reading elsewhere in their course. And fills these themes out with specific details of the places that some of them grew up in (and where they are also likely to live as adults and to begin their work as English teachers). The degree to which the short story so far might be contesting negative or stereotypical representations of place remains uncertain, however each of the details in the text opens opportunities for conversations about how dominant discourses on gender, culture and class weave through representations of place. The descriptions enable us to consider the grip that these dominant discourses have on our own imaginations and our capacities to observe and recognise details that might construct our own places differently. As Jade and Alicia explored with their art students in Chapter 7, negative and overly simplistic understandings of particular places can seep into our modes of thought and ways of viewing our places, others and ourselves.

The collaborative story also opens the possibility for us to consider the potentially conservative effects of particular genres of text. For example, in this story, do the pleasures that readers anticipate in the (teen) romance genre and the particular narrative tropes of the genre close off possibilities for new ways to tell stories about people and place? The vague dissatisfaction with life expressed by Jasmine—'she really couldn't explain it'—and her exposure to people different from herself out along the highway and at the public swimming pool might begin to suggest that these girls (or girls in general?) are put at risk both because of their developmental stage (with the inexpressible desires that arise at puberty) and because they might be allowed to venture away from the confines of the family home. The developing draft creates opportunities for critique of gendered representations within fiction. The 'old red Skyline' codes pleasure, danger and boys into the story at the same time and we are left at this moment unsure about whether the person in the car is likely to rescue Jasmine or endanger her, or whether both are entwined. We are also instantly drawn to recognise how the geography of this place is instrumental in her exposure. Working collaboratively over and over with a story, endeavouring to work beyond the expected narrative conventions of the genre and beyond the usual expectations about place and people in place will enable my teacher education students to develop critical and creative skills with texts at the same time as they consider the nuances and effects of place in their own lives.

Similar projects can be established in many genres for diverse purposes in English classes, and digital media—through wikis or programs like Google Docs—can create "anytime anyplace" platforms for collaborative drafting and development of writing. The affordances of new technologies and digital platforms for entirely new approaches to composition have barely begun to be appreciated in English classrooms. The collaborations that I described in the previous paragraphs can of course span students and classes in different, distant locations, and there are many examples of collaborative projects between schools and between countries.

CONCLUSION

Throughout this book we are interested in opening spaces for attending to the subjectification of people in place, and in opening up new ways of telling and inhabiting space, and of being in and of landscapes and environments. In my English classes, which privilege text analysis and production, I have tried to create possibilities that legitimise meticulous attention to the specificities of place and that attend closely to language and how it works. I have tried to open spaces and create resources that provoke young people to examine their own relations to place and to begin to contest and re-story these relations. Place work in English is not an addendum, not something extra that people don't have time to do, but something that can be integrated throughout the English curriculum in schools and in teacher education.

The place pedagogies in English that I describe in this chapter respond to the gaps I found when I first went looking for texts I might use in my classes. They reflect my own continuing commitment in my writing and in my teaching to exploring how place and subjectivities in place might be explored in language. They reflect the importance of story in the making of place and relations to place. They are also shaped by my knowledge that the places where I have lived have seeped into my body, my imagination and my sense of myself. The particularities of place differ more than can be captured by broad abstract categories such as "western Sydney", or "north Queensland". Places differ in their detail whether they are separated by half a continent or just a suburb or two, and it is a necessary project for English teachers and their students to begin to unpack the discursive baggage that comes with particular places. This might provide a sort of counterpoint to the generalities of place so vividly captured in the opening of the prose poem 'Australia' by Ania Walwicz (2009, p. 334):

You big ugly. You too empty. You desert with your nothing nothing nothing. You scorched suntanned. Old too quickly. Acres of suburbs watching the telly. You bore me. Freckle silly children. You nothing much...

REFERENCES

Baranay, I. (1995). Beautiful one day. In *Paradise to paranoia: New Queensland writing*. Brisbane: University of Queensland Press.

Boyle, P. (1997). *The blue cloud of crying*. Melbourne: Hale & Iremonger.

Comber, B., Nixon, H., & Reid, J. (Eds.) (2007). *Literacies in place: Teaching environmental communications*. Newtown, Australia: PETA.

Falconer, D. (2010). *Sydney*. Sydney: New South.

Hall, R. (Ed.) (2000). *Sydney*. South Melbourne: Oxford.

Jose, N. (Ed.) (2009). *The Macquarie PEN Anthology of Australian Literature*. Sydney: Allan & Unwin.

Lawrence, A. (1998). *New and selected poems*. Brisbane: University of Queensland Press.

Maiden, J. (1990). *Selected poems of Jennifer Maiden*. Maryborough: Penguin Books.

McDonald, D. (2007). *Luck in the greater west*. Sydney: ABC Books.

Misson, R., & Morgan, W. (2009). The aesthetic and English teaching. In S. Gannon, M. Howie & W. Sawyer (Eds.), *Charged with meaning: Reviewing English* (pp. 45–52). Putney, NSW: Phoenix Education.

Misson, R., & Morgan, W. (2006). *Critical literacy and the aesthetic: Transforming the English classroom*. Urbana, IL: NCTE.

Morgan, W. (1997). *Critical literacy in the classroom: The art of the possible*. London: Routledge.

Morgan, W. (2009). Critical literacy. In S. Gannon, M. Howie & W. Sawyer (Eds.), *Charged with meaning: Reviewing English* (pp. 85–96). Putney, NSW: Phoenix Education.

Wakeling, L. (2009). Facing down the fear. In S. Gannon, M. Howie & W. Sawyer (Eds.), *Charged with meaning: Reviewing English* (pp. 113–122). Putney, NSW: Phoenix Education.

Walwicz, A. (2009). Australia. In J. Kinsella (Ed.), *The Penguin anthology of Australian poetry* (pp. 334–335). Camberwell: Penguin Books.

Susanne Gannon
University of Western Sydney

MARGARET SOMERVILLE

THE PLACE-MAKERS

The day is wild and wilful. A day of barnacles on parade and blue beach flowers with sand scurrying across the beach. Churning sand and salt water. The sand makes its own waves, patterns today.

By the time I return, my footprints are blown away in the wind.

As I crest the dune, I am sand-blasted all over, especially my face, like tiny pinpricks. The easterly wind is so strong that it snatches at my throat and I gasp, unable to shut my mouth. I feel the sticky salt air on my face and when I touch it, it is covered in fine sand.

The endless omnipresent sound of the wind and the ocean as one whole sound which continues in my head and all around me. It is all I can hear. It is not so much loud as everywhere.

I see the patterns that the frothing, swirling waves leave on the wet sand as they retreat back into the ocean. The patterns are so delicate and intricate. I feel very temporary and insignificant as I think how long this has been happening just in this place. (Frankie, Jack Smith Lake, 2007)

All across Gippsland I have met extraordinary community educators who are involved in teaching and learning about place. I identified them from my own learning, recorded in my body/place journal, and from other connections that they generated. I had long conversations with them, some of which continue into the present, and which have left indelible marks of their places on my consciousness. I focus on a small number of these educators in order to analyse in detail their practice of what we are calling an enabling pedagogy of place. This chapter is written from my conversations with them, using their words and stories alongside mine. I ask with them: What is it to come to know and love a place? How is this knowing shared with others so that they too can learn to love and care for places, and for the people and communities who live with/in them? How can we learn to do these relationships between people, communities and places differently for a sustainable future?

Frankie is one of those community educators. She sent me the journal writing quoted above after our long conversation in her office at her workplace in South Gippsland. She didn't know at the time whether she would continue in her paid employment because she was unsure of whether this was the best way forward for what she hoped to do. When I asked her what image comes to mind about this

M. Somerville, B. Davies, K. Power, S. Gannon and P. de Carteret,
Place Pedagogy Change, 157–172.
© 2011 Sense Publishers. All rights reserved.

turbulent time of decision-making she said: 'coming over the dunes at Jack Smith Lake'. I had little idea what this might mean to her but some time later she sent four files, each with a photo and a journal entry about one of her special places. Immediately I could recognise the sensory qualities of the place in her writing about Jack Smith Lake, the turbulent energy of coming up over the dunes and the sense of self-becoming-other in her immersion in salt, sand, wind and sea. We talked about how she came to learn place in this way, and how the trajectory of her work as a place educator had been shaped. Frankie said she moved to South Gippsland to her husband's family home and began a Landcare group as a young mother living on the family farm. Through this voluntary work she was stitched into place and community in a different way that opened up new possibilities for all of the people she worked with. It was not until she studied social ecology by distance education, however, that she was able to articulate this trajectory of place learning through a subject called 'Sense of Place':

I guess that was learning to articulate the journey that I had been on, I was just always in that journey, but with Sense of Place, I felt I could really step back and start to understand what it meant, you know, from a learning perspective. It gave me a whole new perspective on where I lived and how important that was to me, right through my childhood, I suppose. But it just seemed inevitable that I would be here doing what I'm doing.

For Frankie, as with us as educators and authors of this book, a beginning point was an embodied engagement in particular material places, but it was only in the process of its articulation that she could recognise it as learning. Not only that, but it was through this understanding that she could make sense of her practice as a community place educator. After many years Frankie began to question the pedagogy of "doing" in Landcare as too much action, she felt, and too little deep place learning.

I mean, the environment's always been a theme. Learning's always been a theme. But I think if it's about knowing what it is, it's like having to tap into something that's deeper than the obvious, you know? And I think that's what started to frustrate me about Landcare, was that it was all about 'doing', you know. And doing's not enough, it's definitely not enough. That unless you actually create some sort of deeper meaning through tapping into people's aspirations or spirituality or call it what you will, then it will all just remain 'doing' I suppose.

An overemphasis on action is also a characteristic of the approaches to place learning in formal systems of education addressing questions of sustainability. In schools across Victoria there is a proliferation of activities in relation to the slogan 'reduce, re-use, recycle' and an assumption that such activities constitute an educational response to the environmental threat of climate change. In tertiary institutions there is a trend toward thinking that developing green campuses is an appropriate educational response. The practices of the community educators in this study take an entirely different approach, beginning with their own deep place learning. For some of them this has evolved in a continuous process throughout their life, and for others it has been more recently learned. Coming to understand and articulate their processes of learning helps me to understand their pedagogical practices because it is from their deep learning that these practices are formed.

Liz, like Frankie, draws strongly on her earliest experiences of place and identity, describing how they have evolved continuously over time. She described herself as 'the daughter of Freddie Clay and Joycie, I grew up on a market garden out in the eastern suburbs of Melbourne. So we were farming, you know, growing veggies. Veggie family. And with lots of space, lots of lines of veggies, lots of trying to get out of the dishes and walking around down the paddock with my dad'. Her earliest memories of place are sensory memories of the soil:

I think it was feeling things. Like running around with bare feet in ploughed up ground when it was really hot, because it was kind of a little bit sandy down there, good market gardening ground, sandy loam. And feeling the heat on your feet as you put your foot on the sand and then dug your toes into the ploughed ground, you could feel the nice coolness underneath.

Early sensory memories of place connect people to the places of their childhood and recreate a visceral sense of connection to place (Schroder, 2006). For Liz there is a continuity with learning about the importance of soil from her early experiences with her dad that has been a powerful thread in her own identity formation.

Freddie was very much into what he did as a market gardener and his soil was his big thing. I can remember running along after him and he'd be telling me, 'oh this is why the lettuce hasn't grown very well here and this is where the water hasn't reached and this is where the fertiliser bin ran out'. I can remember one particular time when he just sank to the ground, and put his hands in the soil and said, 'look at this, you could eat this stuff'. I didn't really understand what he meant then but later on I did.

Liz added that 'soil is the thing that I think has lots of meaning for me' and spoke about her work as an organic farmer with wide networks of teaching and learning through farmers' markets and government policy makers. Her place learning has evolved from the feel of the soil in Freddie's market garden to thinking about the whole region in her involvement in soil policy and in catchment management[i].

Juneen and Monica share similar experiences of childhood gardens as the origin of place work that has extended to communities and regions. Juneen described growing up on a small island in a self sufficient farming community:

I grew up in a tiny little community, it was actually an island that I grew up on, so community was really important. Mum was probably way before her time, she was into organics and natural, she always had a garden. We milked a couple of cows, made our own cream and butter and Dad always killed a sheep. When we grew up my brother and I used to go rabbiting, so we ate a lot of rabbit, and we'd raise a pig or two, get them cured for Christmas. When you live on an island, you can't travel off it so often.

159

Juneen reproduced this childhood way of living when she moved to the small isolated community of Tidal River[ii] as a young mother. She become involved in community work when her children were young and when they began primary school she made a kitchen garden at the school. Her activities with children in the edible school garden eventually extended into an organic food catering business, a community food garden, and wide-ranging learning support for community groups in other places.

Monica's early memories are of her life in the industrial town of Morwell 'right on the periphery of the open cut; at night I could hear that machinery'. Yet it is her father's garden that made the most impact on her future practice: 'I remember him raising his little tomato seedlings and growing the best corn ever'. Monica moved out of the Valley as a young woman to live in the city but returned some years later to the rich farming land west of Morwell. 'You can take the girl out of the Valley, but you can't take the Valley out of the girl', she said, remembering her origins. She learned about place and community from a group of friends involved in environmental work and later designed and created her own permaculture house and garden. Today Monica is active in the urban landcare group in her community and in educating pre-service teachers about the pedagogical possibilities of school gardens.

Max is also involved in schools, teacher education and community connections to place through his work in the Morwell River Wetlands. I puzzled over his passion and commitment to the Wetlands program until he told me that he comes from a long tradition of beekeepers. 'I have a love of beekeeping so I'm always out in the bush and my beekeeping is a family tradition between parents, grandparents, great grandparents'. Beekeepers learn about places from the cycles of seasons, of weather and of flowering trees, following the honey flow. Kevin, on the other hand, learned mining rehabilitation working for Hazelwood Power and when the Morwell River Wetlands site was planned he became involved in its construction and maintenance. He grew up in the city and says he didn't experience a sense of attachment to place until he moved to Gippsland to work as a civil engineer. He says he likes 'doing things' and understands his environmental work through his vocation as an engineer. 'I mean, I'm an engineer, and building something to achieve an end result, and the measure of that with the wetlands is really what habitat it becomes'. He tells a story about native predators in the wetlands, and generates a whole landscape reading from a dismembered yabby claw lying on the mud:

These little animals scurry, and they stick to the shade or the long grass, and we occasionally see little bush rats, but they're so quick—they scurry in and they've got a little hole somewhere under the roots of a tree, and that's how they stay. Because you watch the swamp areas and that, and [birds of prey have] got the wings out and the head down, and they're just—a bit like if we were snorkelling, and you're concentrating on say, looking at tropical fish or something, and you're just looking down all the time, and as soon as they see something (swishing sound) but they have to be quick, because most things—and you're talking frogs, lizards, crickets, and maybe something small like a bush rat—they're very fast, that's how they survive—very quick.

In the same way that children become frog through their learning in the wetlands, Kevin becomes other-to-himself through his deep engagement. He identifies with the little animals that scurry and the bird of prey, 'wings out, head down', in its hunting. The whole wetland is alive for him and he knows it through his own body. He began the story by saying that the yabby claw 'was a great lesson'—he learns, teachers learn, and children learn, from the intensity of intimate observation of this place repeated over time. It is about knowing a place through its seasons, the cycles of night and day, and its weathers. One day when we were talking about a political threat to the wetlands he said, 'over my dead body', revealing the depth of his identification with the place: if the wetland dies, he dies with it. He has learned this strong sense of bodily identification with the wetlands over time through his labour, his practical knowledge, and his growing attachment and passion. He has been part of the wetlands from its inception so his sense of self, work and meaning are now fully intertwined with the place.

Wayne, an Indigenous community educator, also grew up in the city but learned place from his grandfather as a young child before his family moved from Gippsland.

Grandfather Con Edwards and I would talk as we walked to the local shops, along Haunted Hills Road in Newborough. He would talk to me in our traditional language, and point to things and say the name for it then have me repeat the words. Although I cannot recall the actual words he shared, I believe he was instilling the spirit of language in me at that early age, because when I practice pronouncing the words, I feel a sense of knowing. (Thorpe, 2010, p. 36)[iii]

Wayne learned the feel of the language of place—of birds, trees and plants—in his body to be recalled later when he learned Gunnai language through studying linguistics. He remembers how his parents took him to visit Lake Tyers Mission to learn his culture and his places of belonging from the many Gunnai people who lived there. These early learning experiences gave him a lifelong connection to the language and culture of Gunnai people and he has spent many years studying linguistics, language and archival records, as well as learning from his community Elders, to create his current practice of teaching. He remembers how his grandfather taught him the gumleaf, a signature element in his performance of welcome to country ceremonies:

My grandfather Con Edwards also showed me the skills of whistling the gumleaf; we used the yellow box eucalyptus leaf (Teekin Djirin). This leaf is soft and bends with the lip, which is good for beginners. At first, I could not get the proper sounds, so grandfather chose a leaf for me, one from the round leaf hedge. He showed me how to bend it and at one end hold the leaf tightly squeezed allowing an opening in the middle, and blow through this to make a sound. (Thorpe, 2010, p. 37)

Through this body learning with his grandfather, Wayne recreates the eerie sound of the gumleaf calling up the spirits as he also calls up the people he welcomes to country. As a community educator Wayne has formed a dance company called *Watbalimba,* which translates to mean 'the language of song, story and dance'. In his dance company he teaches Gunnai language and culture through performance in country. He runs cultural camps for men and young people, and participates generally in the revitalisation of Gunnai culture.

> Our Ancestors received the gift of fire and warned about losing it. Fire to the Original people holds the great sacredness needed to connect to our Ancestral dreaming. We have been at a loss for the control of our cultural fire, where we have now become cold and hungry for the flavours of our culture values. The word Watbalimba carries the suggestion to maintain the cultural connection through the language of song, story and dance. Watbalimba uses an affirmation that is of the traditional practice for self-healing by the Gunnai. (Thorpe, 2010, p. 18)

Walking, talking, sounding place with grandfather, sand-blast on face, toes in hot soil, and scurrying-becoming with creatures in the wetlands are the embodied experiences that inform these community educators' learning. These stories represent deep place learning because they are based in a different way of being in, and of knowing, the world, a different paradigm. Their teaching and learning begins with their profound recognition of the intertwining of self and place, a recognition that recalls Levinas' ethics of the other. In such an ethics, one only exists through recognising, and the recognition of, the other. Here I extend this ethics to suggest that for these place-makers one only comes into being in the world through everything that is other-to-oneself. As Frankie said, 'it's a way of looking at yourself in the world, knowing your identity and your place and your history'.

Through deep place learning these community educators take up a vocation in the true sense of the word *vocare,* "a high calling". As one educator put it: 'I can only do it if I have my heart and soul in it'. Through this sense of place-making as vocation they create desirelines of movement in their lives as they negotiate institutional and community parameters and relationships to do this work. None of them are employed full time in the education sector as a "teacher" and yet all of them regard themselves as having a vocation in relation to teaching and learning about place. Their deep place learning, and their sense of themselves as place-makers, are strongly connected to their pedagogical practices.

LANDSCAPES AND PEOPLE

Where you cross over the Morwell River there are several bridges, if you're heading to Melbourne, the first bridge is now where the wetlands overflow— that was a swamp, but it used to dry out in summer and cattle used to graze, and it was owned by Gippsland Water. The second bridge, going towards

Melbourne, is just the river itself and the third bridge is if the river bursts its banks it will flood to the west, and then there's a natural escarpment. It's actually on a monocline in the earth where it's worn down, and the river found its way along that and sort of moved—and there's a ridge through where the power works are, so the river's worked its way between those areas. And so, it was a swamp for a long time and I think it was drained because of problems with mosquitoes and other things, and it was drained for grazing. (Kevin Jones, Morwell River Wetlands website)

The place-makers are shaped by the communities and places where they live and work, as much as they also shape those places. The Latrobe Valley, lying between two mountain ranges, was once a vast swamp. Between fifteen and fifty million years ago waterlogged plants and debris on the valley floor slowly subsided and were decomposed by fungi and bacteria, locking the carbon away in the petrified plant remains. There is a now a seam of brown coal fifty kilometres long and eight to sixteen kilometres wide that stretches from one end to the other, virtually the whole floor of the valley. The coal was once a huge forest of softwood trees and is made up of their fossil woods, leaves, bark, fruit, seeds, spores, pollen grains and resin. Among the trees are Kauri, Celery Top Pine, King Billy Pine, Brown Pine, Sheoak and Banksia; some of them have not grown in Victoria for millions of years. On June 24, 1924, brown coal fired electricity began flowing to Melbourne and the Valley now produces eighty five percent of the state's electricity from burning brown coal.

Latrobe Valley is now regarded as the area comprising the three main towns and the three major power stations. It was once the heartland of the region, a hub of vibrant industrial development. The towns, Traralgon, Morwell and Moe, have a long history of migrant workers and the integration of many different cultural groups from all over Europe. A fourth town, Yallourn, the first built to house State Electricity Commission workers, was dug up for coal. The towns and communities in the Valley were crippled in the early 1990s by the privatisation of the power industry. These towns are still marked by poverty and intergenerational unemployment, but they are also currently experiencing economic growth. People are fearful of the potential impact of a carbon tax and the phasing out of coal-fired power stations, the danger of becoming "double losers". On the other hand, because of the obvious connection between brown coal fired power generation and climate change, there is a robust social movement seeking new directions.

Surrounding the Valley of coal there is an extraordinary richness of natural landscapes with small towns and communities that have grown up amongst them. Aboriginal people of the Gunnai language group once occupied the whole region, divided into five clan areas: Brayukaloong (West), Brabiraloong (North), Krowatungaloong (East), Tatungaloong (South) and Bratowaloong (Fire), four corresponding to the directions of the compass and the fifth, consisting of Yiruk (Wilson's Promontory), the place of the origin of fire (Thorpe, 2010, p. 9). Place and community were learned in songlines that extended across the region as the people moved through its rich landscapes for food and ceremony. The winning of Native Title to areas of Crown Land in October, 2010 will give Gunnai people places to grow their language and cultural learning. This land includes the Yiruk, the fire place, or Wilson's Promontory as we now know it.

The landscape history of Gippsland continues to follow the pattern of eco-social relations of the Gunnai clans. It is probably one of the most altered landscapes in Australia, with forests of the massive mountain ash trees removed to lay bare its rich fertile soils. On the western side of the region closest to the city of Melbourne, the highly fertile agricultural land supports a new movement towards gourmet food production and communities active in learning for sustainability. To the south the areas on the coast are dotted with tiny towns and villages of close-knit communities with longstanding issues of rural poverty and isolation. Those closest to the city have experienced an influx of "sea changers" who have moved there for a less consumer lifestyle and are hungry to form community. To the north there is mountainous alpine country with tiny remote villages and communities that are the remnants of less successful agriculture, and the forestry industry. They tend to be resilient and independent and some of them are transforming because of their locations as to places of snowfield tourism and escape from the city. To the far east, a system of lakes and estuaries, beaches and forests are places for local holidaymakers and small populations who form the backbone of community that keeps them alive.

All of these people and communities are the potential place-makers of the future, living in times and places that require new learning and community transformations. We interviewed community educators from across the region to seek to understand how the pedagogies they practise form a bridge for these communities into the future. Of these, the place-makers in particular work in mobile ways across a range of organisations in both paid and voluntary capacities, seeking out and meeting people where there are possibilities for change. The pedagogies they practise are innovative, emergent and interlinked in exciting ways through networks of exchange. Unconstrained by the curricula of formal schooling and adult education provision they have much to offer formal systems of education in a quest towards a sustainable future.

PLACE-MAKING PEDAGOGIES

Then the fires came along and created another huge impact, one of the worst fires we've ever had. The fires were so intense in some areas that rocks in the middle of rivers exploded with the heat. Now, that has never happened before...Then came the heavy rainfall in June. It was so extreme in some of the areas that the landscape shifted in such a way that it changed the river valley, changed valleys in such a way that hasn't been seen for a thousand years. So, in other words there was landscape change, because some of the valleys have changed—almost like a glacier will change—dramatic change, huge change. Whole hillsides just disappeared. So, we went from drought, to fire, to flood, and now, a second flood. (John Durrant, 2007, interview)

The Gippsland region has been dramatically affected by extreme weather patterns believed to be caused by climate change. We have had fourteen years of drought, the most severe fires and floods in living memory, and constant reminders of our connection to the immanent threat of carbon emissions in the images of our power stations on the television. How do the place-makers respond when they are confronted with massive landscape changes that have never been experienced before? How do they work with others in their place-making pedagogies within a context of climate change?

The world-making of the place-makers has evolved from their own ongoing learning within the places and communities in which they are embedded. While each has a different trajectory and specific aspects to their teaching and learning, it is also possible to discern common patterns, a collective storyline. In each of the following themes that emerged from our conversations I examine examples from the stories of one or two of the educators as representative of the collective storylines.

Learning from the Materiality of Local Places

In analysing the educators' collective stories it became apparent that learning through bodily connection with the materiality of specific local places is an ongoing aspect of their teaching. They invite their learners to be engaged in physical sensory ways with their local places. This means learning with, and from, the physical qualities of these places, as in the place-makers' own embodied learning—hands in soil, sand blast on face, hovering like a bird of prey, walking/talking with grandfather in country. The qualities are the physical elements that make up the place: soil, sand and water, trees and plants, all of the other creatures who live there, including humans, and the ways that humans engage with those qualities. To illustrate this I follow Juneen, in her story about designing a community garden for place learning.

> *To design that garden you have to be in that space on and off a fair bit because you've got to know where the sun is, you've got to know where the shade is, you've got to know where the wind comes from, you've got to know what sort of traffic walks through that plot—do you need fencing, who are your neighbours?*

Choosing a space and designing a community garden is like designing the curriculum for place learning. It means knowing each of the elements—sun and shade, wind and traffic, fencing and neighbours. Each has to be learned and planned for. In thinking about how to teach others who come to her for advice about making a community garden, Juneen considers how these elements must be observed in relation to a particular place:

> *In Foster I stood in that site so many times before I drew it up, and watched the traffic going by. We have somebody in an electric wheelchair and because there's no pathway for him to go on, he has to travel down the*

middle of the road. The very thing I wanted to do was to bring him into the garden. And so, I created a pathway [so] that he could come into the garden and be underneath the tree. And I asked him, 'what do you want out of the garden', and he said, 'all I want to do is get under the shade of the big old tree and watch the birds'.

A person in a wheelchair is in a sense a more-than-human body and the design of the garden needs to create passageways for this more-than-human body. This body then creates the shapes of the learning place, along with the movements of others within that space. Once the pathway into the learning experience is created it is about the desires of this more-than-human body to engage with the other elements, the shade, the big old tree, the birds, which together form the place-making possibilities for this person. Juneen creates these pathways of desire that lead people into engagement with the place, not for her purposes, but for theirs. She understands that she cannot teach these ideas on an intellectual level alone, but that a whole body engagement with the particular place is required to translate it into others' places and communities: 'They're the sorts of things people in other communities need to be aware of, and not just take ideas into their own head without watching, looking at the site and seeing who visits, and all that sort of stuff'. Once others enter the garden space, together they create it as a place of learning.

Everybody wants to have a little chatter, what they're doing in their garden, or dear old John, he loves to tell a story that makes us all laugh, because he's such a character. Then we might just discuss what's happened in the last week or two, whether there's a grant we're going for, or whether somebody's donated something, or done something for us, I like to tell them about that. And then I'll say, well these are the lists of things that need doing and it's up to them whether they choose to do that, or not, they don't have to.

Juneen says that when people visited the garden for Open Gardens Day, 'it wasn't neat and tidy but that's what a vegetable garden's about because things are flowering, and things are going to seed, and things have decided to pop up in the pathway as they do'. There is great joy in the lifefulness of 'things' and it is the bringing together of all of this lifefulness with humans in all of their diversity that is part of this pedagogy. The people with different abilities, she says, have a ball when they come: 'there's lots of things to harvest, it's exciting for them to fill a wheelbarrow with pumpkins and zucchinis and tomatoes'. Juneen designs learning spaces where others are invited to participate in the lifefulness of all the interacting elements of the place and to learn from them. Her pedagogy has a light touch, to bring all the elements together in the best possible way and to offer 'the lists' for people to choose how they want to participate.

Building Community and Collective Place Knowledges

While individual embodied place learning is a fundamental beginning point, all of the place-makers developed pedagogies for community building and collective knowledge making. Place knowledge is held collectively, is ongoing, and is constructed in connection with local places. The nature of this knowledge changes as places change, as they are affected by weather and climate conditions, settlement patterns, and how people choose to interact with them. These changes require community building and collective knowledge-making. Monica described how she returned to Gippsland in her twenties and became involved with a collective of local people who transformed her way of being and knowing her world; 'they had visions and ideas about the world, it's people like that I still hang out with, they've got great ideas and visions for possibility, how things can be'. At each point of her re-engagement was a growing collective of community members who together designed pedagogies of place for their own and others' learning:

Warragul is—like, it's this basin with all this drainage, so there's creeks all over the joint in Warragul, but what happened, six or seven years ago some local people had a vision to make that into a wetland, and it's now called Brooker Park, and what's happened as a consequence is, some lovely walking tracks have been put through there, there's a lovely wetland, fantastic urban forest, really, and it's the only pocket of forest in and around Warragul, because Warragul, as a consequence of the development, has lost a lot of its remnant vegetation.

Even though towns and cities overlay the shapes of natural waterways and their native trees and plants, there are often remnants that form the basis of community action. In Newcastle-upon-Tyne I saw a single line of poetic text in metal on cobblestones to mark the creeks that flowed underground to the River. In Warragul the creek has been restored as a wetland with walking tracks through it for the place learner, like the man in his wheelchair, to enter. The vision has grown to extend the waterway, but also to incorporate groups of people with different investments in land into conversation. The purpose of these conversations in the beauty of the newly recreated place is pedagogical: to generate attachments and connections to place and people.

It's to continue a current sort of tributary of the wetland in Warragul, but it's bigger than that, because we want it to be about people coming to that place and again, in those places we have conversations about stuff, stuff to do with land, and approaches to land use, and who are the particular land users, and they could be developers, they could be black fellas, they could be white fellas, they could be school groups. So, it's kind of a meeting place, or a place for people to be part of.

Monica talks about her own love of and attachment to this place and the pleasure of watching it grow and change, like the growing of the Morwell River Wetlands. The place comes alive with life and meaning, and through this others are invited in to this place learning. These others include the communities of plants and animals that inhabit this place, and the diverse groups of people who are brought together in this contact zone where new meanings can emerge. She speaks about the place as 'a powerful thing for people to have', and about conversations, walking tracks and interpretive signs as some of the ways that people can learn difference, and learn differently. For her, there is also a sense that 'it is time'. Like Monica, the place-makers' pedagogies respond to the relationships within places, to the interactions between people and places, and to the larger flows within which all of these are located.

Working with Indigenous Relationships to Place

For Indigenous people the interconnections between all things in any particular place, and the interconnections between places and between human and ecological systems, were traditionally taught through daily living and through ceremony. These understandings are now communicated in contemporary forms through oral stories, art, and performance. The non-Indigenous place-makers in this study acknowledge, and work with, Indigenous place relationships in their pedagogical practices. They seek responsive ways of interacting with Aboriginal people and their place knowledge, listening to and learning from their stories. Frankie talked about a meeting between their community group and Gunnai Elders:

> *So we've just taken a softly softly approach to meeting with the traditional owners we'd met a couple of times onsite and yeah, out at Warragul Creek and we had a visit up to Ramiyuk as well, just to go into their space, I suppose. Very aware that they were coming into what looks like our space. And just really getting, I guess, the feedback from the traditional owners was, well, the first step really in this journey is to understand more about our cultural heritage.*

In a similar vein John described a meeting between local Indigenous Elders and "elders" of the catchment management authority, where the Indigenous Elders chose the meeting place:

> *And it was the meeting place for Aboriginal tribes, they used to actually come and meet there, so it was a meeting place, a very special place. It's one of those special places for Aboriginal people. Probably, the most special place in this region. So, the Knob Reserve at Stratford. It's on a bluff overlooking the Avon River. And there's grinding stones, ochre stones—and you can just about visualise the way it was. The sad thing is it was also the site of a mass slaughter. So, it's good memories, but it's got sad memories.*

The place the Elders chose is a traditional gathering place with grinding stones and ochres, but it also has important historical significance for Gunnai people as a massacre site. It is a place that is profoundly pedagogical in the relationship between Indigenous and settler Australians. It enables Gunnai people to tell the hidden stories of their past relationship to the places of Latrobe Valley and of the painful experiences of colonisation.

> *So, we sat around and had this long cup of tea first thing. Then, we went for a walk around the site, and we allowed the Elders to talk to us. We did no*

talking and I said to our staff, say very little and ask questions, but, I said, the morning is very much where we want to have the Indigenous people share with us, their story. So, I said, please don't talk, other than just quietly ask questions. I said, it's important for us to get to know them.

In this traditional gathering place it is clear that the Indigenous Elders hold the knowledge and the catchment management elders are there to learn. The place-maker teaches them how to learn—by listening and not talking—in this space of the contact zone where it is so easy to fill the silence with unnecessary words. As Frankie said of their meeting, 'and really, they did just want to tell their stories about where they came from and who their ancestors were and also they made it really clear how much they appreciated white landholders coming to talk to them, to listen to them. They said it had never happened before. It just made us feel very humble'.

Thinking Locally, Regionally and Globally

As each of the place-makers evolves their practices they move to ever greater circles and cycles of connection without losing the materiality of local places. New place teaching and learning connects local, regional and global place knowledges. Liz, for example, begins with her own organic farm and says her organic ethic 'is more than food, it's about health, it's about ecology, it's about fairness and it's about caring for not only animals and your workers, it's also caring about the future and how we want to go'. As an educator she expands from her feet in the soil of her father's market garden to her own organic farming and to pedagogies that invite others to engage in large scale systems thinking.

You can walk on the soil and know how it's going just by how it feels, just by walking on it. It has give, it's got give, it's like walking on a sponge. And then of course it's the plants. You know how your soil is going by looking at the expression of the soil through your plants and if the plants aren't growing very well or if they're being attacked by insects and bugs you know there's something that's not right in the soil. So instead of applying some sort of input to the plant you actually adjust the inputs into the soil, something is going wrong here, so you adjust the soil. You don't deal with the symptom you actually deal with the cause. So that also, that whole thinking systemically, you have to think systemically to farm organically. So it's a really nice way to learn about, not just about the soil and growing things but the interconnection of all things and how we need to think about dealing with this.

Liz puts her desire to teach people about organic farming into practice at the local farmers' market 'where people gather on Saturday mornings and they've got their dogs and their kids and the kids are running around and people are chatting to each other and there's a lot of, a whole lot of conversations that are going on in that market'. Markets are the quintessential event of place where people come together in informal conversations that are for Liz the basis of her pedagogy.

> *In fact at the Rokeby market here, because it's a very social, it's an incredibly social event. There will be ten to twelve people just standing around going yak, yak, yak just catching up. I think that's a really important, potentially has a really important role to play in community building and it's an opportunity for people to, if you were able to culture this, for people to actually use those meetings—very informal things just to throw some things for them out there, for people to think about. I mentioned before that the future is not so straightforward anymore and we've got all these massive changes to have to adapt and tangle with. And a part of making sense of what that means is to talk about it.*

For Liz, as with the others, this is to take a light touch and she says she is going to bring a table and chairs to encourage these important pedagogical conversations. In her more formal practice she uses the same techniques of conversations about the future.

Imagining Futures, Futures Thinking

Finally, one of the strongest and most surprising characteristics of the pedagogies practised by the place-makers was their practice of futures thinking. This consisted of a long-term vision to embrace a future of risk and complexity with imagination. They employed this as a strategy in their own thinking and learning and in the practices they invited others to engage in. Liz said we need to ask how we learn to farm in a changing climate and, even more so, how we learn to live in a changing world. Her response is:

> *...by providing opportunities for people to process their thoughts in a very quick, fast changing world where futures are no longer really clear and we really need to be thinking about multiple futures and how to manage, risk manage, possibilities of dozens of different sorts of futures. How do we get communities to go along with that or to approach things like that? Water, fire, floods, bush. It's all very uncertain. I think it's really important that we find engaging ways to get people to be thinking systemically I guess, thinking about all that complexity.*

For Liz, the pedagogical response is one of engaging people to learn to think of themselves as part of a complex system where everything is interconnected and each action counts: 'food is a really good place to start thinking about how we develop our futures and how we sort of look at what our future, our children's futures are going to look like'. Frankie speaks about the slow emergence of their relationship with Gunnai community: 'it's a bit of a journey, you know, getting to know each other, building the relationship. Just taking the time, I suppose, to build a bit of trust and get to know them'. John describes a process of imagining futures with forty community members to 'unpack a bit of a vision of what each of those catchment eco-systems really means in terms of what they value, what they think of the community values'. Kevin tells a story about the capacity of frogs in Lake Eyre to go into torpor and survive for decades, and the wonder of the frogs returning after rain to the wetlands. Max worries about who will carry on his work after he has gone beekeeping. We tell our teacher education students the stories of the place-makers and take them to the wetlands to learn to be place-makers themselves.

In the chapter's first section, the place-makers, I explored how the subjectivities of these community educators are constituted through deep place learning and a sense of bodily connection to place. Whether this learning began in childhood and continued throughout life, or only began when they were adults, they have come to a different sense of being in the world, and of knowing the world. It is a kind of forgetting the self in order to know self and place differently, a different ontology and epistemology of self-in-place. In the second section I briefly described the landscapes and communities of the region which have evolved in relation to each other. These are the places and communities where these place-makers live and work and within which their practices of teaching and learning are shaped. In the final section I analysed the collective practices of teaching and learning, the enabling place pedagogies of these extraordinary educators. These pedagogies begin with designing place as curriculum and creating desire lines for others to enter into deep place learning through sensory engagement. They necessarily include learning within communities of others, of plants and animals, of peoples and the qualities of places, learning to build community and collective knowledge. For Australians, this also means learning with and from the original inhabitants of this land through listening to the people and their places differently, allowing the new to emerge from the old. The new emerges through thinking in circles and cycles of interconnection between local, regional and global places, always keeping our love and attachments to particular local places alive. By keeping both the intimate and the immense in focus, the place-makers work to shape the future by generating creative conversations of risk, complexity, and imagination.

ACKNOWLEDGEMENTS

I would like to acknowledge the words and stories of the community educators whose conversations were recorded under ethics approval from Monash University. Dr Phoenix de Carteret was employed as a Research Fellow on the project and assisted with the adult and community education aspect.

NOTES

[i] Catchment Management Authorities are statutory authorities under state governments that are responsible for the protection of waterways. They exist in both urban and rural regions and are an important site of community place work.

[ii] Tidal River is the river mouth in Wilson's Promontory National Park on the southern-most tip of Australia, where Juneen still lived when we interviewed her.

MARGARET SOMERVILLE

ⁱⁱⁱ I have worked with Gunnai knowledge holder Wayne Thorpe as supervisor of his Master of Education research about teaching and learning Gunnai cultural knowledge. In keeping with my desire to support Indigenous educators to complete their own research I have used quotes from his thesis rather than recorded interviews with him as I have with the other community educators.

REFERENCES

Jones, K. (n.d.). Morwell river wetlands. Retrieved May 13, 2007 fromhttp://www.wgcma.vic.gov.au/default.asp?action=page&catID=27&pageID =45
Schroder, B. (2006). Native science, intercultural education and place-conscious education: an Ecuadorian example. *Educational Studies, 32*(3), 307–317.
Thorpe, W. (2010). Watbalimba: the language of song, story and dance. Unpublished Master of Education thesis, Monash University, Gippsland.

Margaret Somerville
Monash University

CPSIA information can be obtained at www.ICGtesting.com
Printed in the USA
LVOW07s0857190913

353182LV00001B/12/P